Overcoming Test Anxiety

The Guilford Practical Intervention in the Schools Series

Kenneth W. Merrell, Founding Editor
Sandra M. Chafouleas, Series Editor

www.guilford.com/practical

This series presents the most reader-friendly resources available in key areas of evidence-based practice in school settings. Practitioners will find trustworthy guides on effective behavioral, mental health, and academic interventions, and assessment and measurement approaches. Covering all aspects of planning, implementing, and evaluating high-quality services for students, books in the series are carefully crafted for everyday utility. Features include ready-to-use reproducibles, appealing visual elements, and an oversized format. Recent titles have Web pages where purchasers can download and print the reproducible materials.

Recent Volumes

Clinical Interviews for Children and Adolescents, Third Edition:
Assessment to Intervention
Stephanie H. McConaughy and Sara A. Whitcomb

Executive Function Skills in the Classroom:
Overcoming Barriers, Building Strategies
Laurie Faith, Carol-Anne Bush, and Peg Dawson

The RTI Approach to Evaluating Learning Disabilities, Second Edition
*Joseph F. Kovaleski, Amanda M. VanDerHeyden, Timothy J. Runge,
Perry A. Zirkel, and Edward S. Shapiro*

Effective Bullying Prevention: A Comprehensive Schoolwide Approach
Adam Collins and Jason Harlacher

Social Justice in Schools: A Framework for Equity in Education
Charles A. Barrett

Coaching Students with Executive Skills Challenges, Second Edition
Peg Dawson and Richard Guare

Social, Emotional, and Behavioral Supports in Schools:
Linking Assessment to Tier 2 Intervention
Sara C. McDaniel, Allison L. Bruhn, and Sara Estrapala

Family–School Success for Children with ADHD:
A Guide for Intervention
Thomas J. Power, Jennifer A. Mautone, and Stephen L. Soffer

School Crisis Intervention: An Essential Guide for Practitioners
Scott Poland and Sara Ferguson

Classwide Positive Behavioral Interventions and Supports,
Second Edition: A Guide to Proactive Classroom Management
Brandi Simonsen and Diane Myers

Family–School Collaboration in Multi-Tiered Systems of Support
S. Andrew Garbacz, Devon R. Minch, and Mark D. Weist

Overcoming Test Anxiety:
Tools to Support Students from Early Adolescence to Adulthood
Alex Jordan and Benjamin J. Lovett

Overcoming Test Anxiety

Tools to Support Students from Early Adolescence to Adulthood

ALEX JORDAN
BENJAMIN J. LOVETT

THE GUILFORD PRESS
New York   London

Last digit is print number: 9 8 7 6 5 4 3 2 1

Library of Congress Cataloging-in-Publication Data

Names: Jordan, Alex (Psychologist), author. | Lovett, Benjamin J., author.
Title: Overcoming test anxiety : tools to support students from early
   adolescence to adulthood / Alex Jordan, Benjamin J. Lovett.
Description: New York : The Guilford Press, [2025] | Series: The Guilford
   practical intervention in the schools series | Includes bibliographical
   references and index.
Identifiers: LCCN 2024047455 | ISBN 9781462556779 (paperback) |
   ISBN 9781462556793 (hardcover)
Subjects: LCSH: Test anxiety. | Test anxiety—Prevention. | Anxiety. |
   Anxiety disorders.
Classification: LCC LB3060.6 .J67 2025 | DDC 371.2601/9—dc23/eng/20241107
LC record available at *https://lccn.loc.gov/2024047455*

About the Authors

Alex Jordan, PhD, is a psychologist in private practice in Belmont, Massachusetts, and at McLean Hospital, and is Lecturer in Psychiatry at Harvard Medical School. He treats a wide range of complex psychiatric conditions, with a specialty in anxiety disorders. Dr. Jordan has over 40 publications and has conducted federally funded research. He has taught students ranging from high school to postdoctoral, has provided leadership coaching to C-level Fortune 100 executives, and has been retained as an expert consultant in major civil litigation.

Benjamin J. Lovett, PhD, is Professor of Psychology and Education at Teachers College, Columbia University. Most of his research and clinical/consulting work revolves around testing and assessment, including the nature and management of test anxiety. Dr. Lovett has over 100 publications, including *Testing Accommodations for Students with Disabilities: Research-Based Practice, History of Psychology,* and, most recently, *Practical Psychometrics: A Guide for Test Users*. He works with schools and testing agencies on assessment and disability issues and provides test anxiety treatment.

Preface

Why a book on test anxiety? Despite the prevalence of the problem, there are actually few recent resources for practitioners hoping to understand and treat test anxiety. We wrote this book to create the resource that we had searched for in vain. But test anxiety has also become particularly prominent in the past several years, consistent with more general trends in both anxiety and testing.

Research findings of growing anxiety among young people date back at least to Twenge (2000), who provocatively concluded that "the average American child in the 1980s reported more anxiety than child psychiatric patients in the 1950s" (p. 1007). From our vantage point today, even the 1980s seem calm. Discussions of a "mental health crisis" among youth are common, including recent claims by the U.S. Surgeon General (see Richtel, 2023). Most recently, psychologist Jonathan Haidt (2024) published *The Anxious Generation*, in which he argues that smartphone use among children is a primary cause of unprecedented levels of anxiety. Regardless of the causes, the increase in anxiety is a well-accepted fact among researchers, and tests are one common source of anxiety.

At the same time, controversy has grown over the way that students' learning is assessed. Traditional in-class and in-person tests stand accused of measuring abilities that have been rendered irrelevant by technology (Can't you always look up facts? Can't you use a computer for math problems?) and of perpetuating societal inequities by yielding score disparities across students from different demographic groups. But at the same time, standardized tests are argued by some to be a less biased measure of merit than their alternatives (e.g., Wai, 2024), and technological advancements like artificial intelligence have led some instructors and educational institutions to re-emphasize in-person assessments to prevent students from submitting assignments completed with improper technological assistance

(Lewsen, 2023). In our experience, many students feel caught in the middle, hearing criticism of tests that increases their own natural resentment at being evaluated, while also feeling increased pressure to do well on tests.

This book is our response to these trends. We start, in Part I of the book, by reviewing research on the nature of test anxiety. In Chapters 1 and 2, we discuss its typical symptoms and associated features, its prevalence, its causes, and most importantly its effects. Readers may be surprised by what research shows about the relationship between test anxiety and performance on tests, and the implications of this important work for treatment. In Chapter 3, we consider how to assess test anxiety with rating scales and interview techniques, as well as how test anxiety relates to clinical anxiety disorders, and whether test anxiety ever rises to the level of a disability requiring accommodations. In Chapter 4, we review the research on test anxiety interventions, briefly explaining the different types of treatment strategies and how effective they have been found to be.

Part II of the book presents our integrated, modular treatment for test anxiety. Chapter 5 presents a bird's-eye view of the logistics of the treatment package. In Chapter 6, we present our initial module on psychoeducation, essentially teaching practitioners how to distill the lessons from Chapters 1 and 2 into a student-friendly format. Chapter 7 presents a module on treatment strategies for physiological symptoms of test anxiety, developing students' comfort and confidence in the face of these symptoms. Chapter 8 does the same for cognitive symptoms of anxiety (e.g., worries). Finally, Chapters 9 and 10 cover scientifically proven techniques for studying and taking tests, since as the research literature shows, when test anxiety is associated with poorer test performance, study and test-taking behaviors are the key mechanisms, and those behaviors can be modified.

We hope that readers will come away from the book with a deep understanding of test anxiety and practical tools for its management. Although we have aimed this volume primarily at school psychologists and other clinicians who work with students from about sixth grade through graduate school, we hope that educators, parents, and even some older students may also find its contents helpful.

This book was a labor of love, and the culmination of many years of shared interest in the topic. We came to work on test anxiety from different directions. Alex has been interested in anxiety-related problems since college, when he wrote his senior thesis on obsessive thinking. After training as a researcher, he re-specialized in clinical psychology and developed expertise in assessing and treating anxiety- and trauma-related disorders. In addition, as a leadership coach, he gained extensive experience helping people overcome challenges related to anxiety in high-pressure environments. Now, as a clinician in private practice, he often sees test anxiety in students of all ages. He has been surprised that evidence-supported interventions have not been more widely disseminated in this area.

Ben's interest in test anxiety dates to graduate school, when he started teaching undergraduate classes and was approached by students who attributed their poor test scores to anxiety. He began to include test anxiety measures in his research studies on test-taking skills. Then, as a professor and advisor, he deployed his clinical skills to help students manage their test anxiety. Several years ago, he also began consulting to high-achieving schools, where he started running test anxiety groups for students and training staff on the topic. Much of his research is on testing accommodations for students with disabilities, and as he found that test anxiety was an underlying cause of many accommodation requests, he expanded his test anxiety research as well.

Our collaborative writing projects date back 20 years, and one of our first coauthored publications was actually related to stress and test performance (Jordan & Lovett, 2007). The present volume is our first book together. We're grateful for the opportunity to communicate what we've learned from our clinical experience and our review of the research on test anxiety and its treatment. We welcome feedback from readers.

ACKNOWLEDGMENTS

We would like to thank our editor, Natalie Graham, as well as the series editor, Sandra Chafouleas, for their invaluable guidance and feedback. For their helpful suggestions, conversations, and other contributions at various stages of the book's development process, we also thank Elisabeth Benson, Christine Benton, Sybille Bruun-Moss, Chris Gathman, Kitty Moore, David Rosmarin, Abigail Stark, and Lisa Szczesniak.

Contents

6. Learning About Test Anxiety   78

7. Mastering Bodily Anxiety   93

8. Focusing the Mind   121

List of Handouts

PART I

UNDERSTANDING TEST ANXIETY

CHAPTER 1

The Nature of Test Anxiety

Educational tests have existed for centuries, and so has test anxiety. Research interest in test anxiety has waxed and waned across the years, but concern about test anxiety among the general public appears to have increased in the past 20 years. This trend may be due partly to more openness about mental health issues, particularly in educational settings. For instance, columns about test anxiety are now common in college newspapers (e.g., Boutouis, 2021). The rise in high-stakes tests for K–12 school accountability has also likely played a role. For instance, a large-scale survey of school psychologists found that increased anxiety in students was associated with the introduction of high-stakes tests, and that such tests induced more anxiety than local teacher-made tests did (New York Association of School Psychologists and New York State School Boards Association, 2015). In fact, test anxiety (in children as well as parents) has driven some parents to "opt out" of their children's participation in state exams (Paladino, 2020).

The COVID-19 pandemic initially paused the use of some tests, as schools moved much of their instruction online, and teachers and professors often chose alternative ways of assessing student skills. Likewise, many higher education institutions became "test optional," reviewing applications whether or not students chose to submit admissions test scores (Elias, 2021). However, soon enough, online versions of many tests were developed, and new sources of test anxiety had formed: anxiety over the novelty of taking tests in new ways, anxiety over intrusive approaches to remote test proctoring, and eventually, anxiety over returning to test in person after months of being able to test in the comfort of one's own home (e.g., Caplan-Bricker, 2021; Stevens, 2021). Moreover, adolescents and young adults experienced an increase in generalized anxiety during the pandemic, leading to more extreme reactions to any kind of stressor (Hawes et al., 2021). At this point, most tests have returned, and the test-optional admissions policies that remain seem to have *raised* anxiety among high-achieving students, who still feel pressure to take the tests but are now less sure of how their scores will be used (Selingo, 2022). In short, the pandemic did not decrease test anxiety in any sustained fashion, and the problem continues to be as important as ever.

In this chapter, we introduce the science of test anxiety, including its symptoms, how common it is, and its causes and effects. Myths about test anxiety abound, and the first step in learning how to treat the condition is understanding it thoroughly.

THE COMPONENTS OF TEST ANXIETY

Like most clinical constructs, test anxiety is multidimensional (Zeidner, 1998). It consists of many symptoms that have been grouped into two clusters. We refer to these clusters as the *components* of test anxiety, and almost all test takers will immediately recognize these components. Clinicians should pay special attention to their differentiation, since a comprehensive assessment should cover both components plus problem behaviors associated with test anxiety (see Chapter 3), and distinct therapeutic strategies (detailed in Part II of the present volume) can be used to address each. The descriptions of each test anxiety component (provided below), as well as dysfunctional behaviors associated with test anxiety, derive from empirical studies, scales measuring test anxiety, and our own clinical experiences.

The Physiological Component

The physiological symptoms of test anxiety are similar to those seen in other types of anxiety, panic, and stress-related conditions. Many of these symptoms are consistent with activation of the sympathetic branch of the autonomic nervous system, associated with the stress response. Students with high levels of test anxiety typically report an increase in heart rate and more vigorous heart contractions, felt as palpitations. In addition, various types of gastrointestinal distress are often reported, such as a general unsettled feeling ("butterflies in the stomach"), nausea, vomiting, intestinal cramps, and even a sudden urge to defecate. Muscular tension and rigidity, restlessness, and a jittery feeling are also common. Because physiological arousal makes sleep difficult, students may report poor sleep the night before an exam, or even for several nights leading up to an especially important exam. Less commonly, a student will sleep poorly *after* a test, usually when they are certain that they have not done well. Other physiological symptoms include sweating, a dry mouth or throat, and an urge to urinate. Students report physiological symptoms not only immediately prior to a test but also sometimes in reaction to thinking about an upcoming test or while studying for a test. Physiological symptoms typically continue during a test but subside, at least temporarily, after a test is over.

Laboratory research finds that self-reported symptoms of test anxiety have a basis in objectively measurable physiological arousal. A recent meta-analysis (Roos et al., 2021) reviewed over 30 studies on the topic and concluded that self-reported test anxiety was consistently and significantly related to heart rate, skin conductance (a measure of sweating), blood pressure, and levels of cortisol (an adrenal hormone released in response to stress). It is easy to see how such arousal can be distressing in the context of an exam. However, as we will discuss in greater detail later, autonomic arousal also occurs in the context of positive excitement, not just perceived threat, and students can be taught to reinterpret their symptoms through a different lens. Moreover, arousal symptoms can often be tamed somewhat through relaxation strategies that have long been part of behavior therapy procedures (see Chapter 7).

The Cognitive Component

For many students, the more irksome aspect of test anxiety is cognitive. The most prominent cognitive symptoms of test anxiety involve *worries*—specific propositional thoughts about anticipated negative events. In a classic study, Galassi et al. (1981) recorded the thoughts of students in a large college history course during an actual class exam. The students had earlier all completed a self-report test anxiety scale. Students with high levels of test anxiety reported more negative than positive thoughts while taking their exam, and many experienced the same specific negative thoughts about how they were going to do poorly, their peers were performing better than they were, and their test scores would not show the effort that they put into studying.

Of course, worries often long precede the exam situation itself. Before an exam, many students already expect that the exam will be difficult, that they will do poorly, and that there will be negative and severe consequences of poor performance. Those thoughts continue during the exam, and for some students, the end of the exam fails to bring relief. Instead, after the exam, the students continue to worry about their likely test score and its consequences for their academic progress and for others' opinions of them. The worries may be highly individualized to the student's personal and academic goals. For instance, a high school student may specifically worry about how a low score on a college admissions test will prevent them from gaining admission to a particular desired university. At times, the cognitive symptoms are actually *about* physiological symptoms; as in panic disorders, the student may worry that their rapidly beating heart will lead to fainting or even a heart attack.

To be clear, worries have the potential to be adaptive responses to threats, but as in other clinical anxiety conditions, test anxiety leads to worry responses that are unhelpful in three ways. First, the worries are often irrational, grossly overestimating the chances of negative events. For instance, it is common for test-anxious students with a consistent history of high test performance to nonetheless genuinely believe that each new exam will finally be the one that generates a poor score. Second, the student assumes that their thought is an accurate and informative reflection of reality, rather than merely a cognition that occurred to them. Finally, even when the worries are accurate and rational (e.g., a student might be correct that they got a particular item wrong on a test), the worries have a ruminative quality. Rather than generating a solution that terminates the worry, the student will continue to have a worry thought repeatedly without any resolution.

The cognitive component of test anxiety goes beyond worries. In addition, students report various types of cognitive failures, including memory retrieval problems (being unable to recall information needed for the test), distractibility (extraneous thoughts other than worries), and confusion (e.g., failing to understand test instructions or questions). Students typically describe these experiences as their mind "going blank" during a test, being unable to focus on the test, and not trusting their comprehension of the task directions and items. After the exam, rather than being certain of having performed poorly, some students report having no sense of how they did and find that uncertainty itself to be extremely distressing.

As we discuss in Chapter 2, students typically overstate the direct and causal impact of anxiety on their ability to think, retrieve information from memory, and so forth. But the subjective experience of impaired cognition is what matters here. Thankfully, the maladaptive aspects of worries and perceptions of cognitive failure can be effectively addressed through a combination of psychoeducation, structured writing exercises, mindfulness and acceptance practices, and attention training (see Chapter 8)—as well as strategies for strengthening test preparation and test-taking skills to reduce the experience of cognitive failure itself, as discussed in Chapters 9 and 10.

Problem Behaviors Associated with Test Anxiety

Whereas students are typically all too aware of their physiological and cognitive symptoms, the problem behaviors associated with their test anxiety may be even more important, consisting of the actions that students take and do not take. Like other anxiety-motivated behaviors, actions prompted by test anxiety are maintained through operant conditioning processes. More specifically, the actions yield immediate negative reinforcement through removal or postponement of a threatening aversive stimulus. Students with test anxiety perceive tests as strong aversive stimuli, and therefore, they have a strong motivation to avoid and escape test-related materials and cues. A student may procrastinate studying for a difficult exam, fail to set reminders to study, or use superficial study methods that are less like taking an exam (e.g., rereading material rather than self-quizzing). A college student may select courses and professors that do not have exams, or cancel a scheduled admissions or certification test. A high school student may feign illness to avoid going to school on the day of an exam, plead with a teacher for an alternative way of attaining credit, or make college application decisions based on which colleges require admissions testing.

Just like worries, escape and avoidance behaviors have the potential to be adaptive, but in cases of clinical test anxiety, they usually are not. For instance, procrastinating studying and using superficial study methods will typically lead to *lower* test performance and hence are counterproductive to the student's own goals. Similarly, it is often in a student's long-term best interest to take more rigorous courses or to attend a particular college that requires admissions test scores. More generally, escape and avoidance are only adaptive when a stimulus is a genuine threat to safety; an academic test is not, even if it is sometimes perceived that way.

Other problem behaviors manifest during the test itself. For instance, some students with test anxiety do not read the test directions carefully, do not manage their time well, and do not check their work for mistakes before turning in the exam. Instead of spending the available time working on their exam, these students look around the room at their peers, stare out the window, check and recheck the time, and play with their pencils (cf. Wren & Benson, 2004). These students are apt to score poorly on tests and then attribute their poor performance to anxiety. However, in reality, their ineffective test-taking behaviors were the direct cause of the poor performance. Interestingly, the same is true for students who obsess over individual test items and check and recheck answers before going on,

Physiological Symptoms
- Racing Heart
- Churning Stomach
- Muscle Tension

Cognitive Symptoms
- Worries
- Negative Self-Thoughts
- Confusion

Associated Behaviors
- Procrastination
- Poor Study Methods
- Failing To Check Work

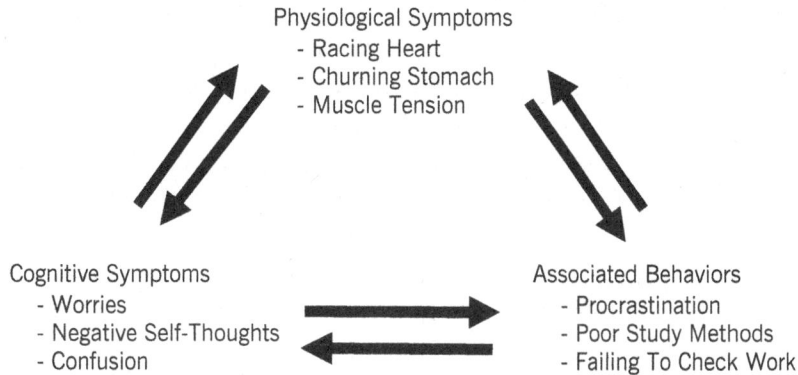

FIGURE 1.1. Bidirectional relationships between test anxiety components and associated behaviors.

rather than allocating their time in an efficient manner. Either way, good test-taking skills are needed. Happily, such skills can be taught, and in Chapters 9 and 10, we discuss how to remediate deficits in study and test-taking skills.

Finally, it is important to acknowledge that some students with high levels of cognitive and physiological symptoms of test anxiety do not show associated problem behaviors. Consider Adam, a top student in the sixth grade who seems to be in a continuous state of worry prior to tests, and who then experiences considerable physiological symptoms during the test itself. He sometimes breaks out in a sweat as the exam starts and feels embarrassed as his sweat leaves his exam paper wet. He nonetheless has excellent study habits and nearly straight-A grades. Like Adam, students who lack the problem behaviors associated with test anxiety tend to be high achievers, often with some degree of perfectionism. They study assiduously, have good test-taking skills, and do well on exams, while still worrying a great deal about their performance and finding that tests induce unpleasant physiological arousal. In such students, treatment can focus preferentially on the cognitive and physiological symptoms of test anxiety, with a minimal focus on studying and test-taking behaviors. This is an advantage of the modular therapy approach detailed in Part II of the book.

The physiological and cognitive symptoms of test anxiety, and the problem behaviors associated with them, all interact with each other, as shown in Figure 1.1. Each component can cause the others, exacerbating test anxiety over time.

TWO REPRESENTATIVE CASE STUDIES

The following two case studies, composites of students we have seen, help to illustrate how test anxiety manifests in different individuals.

Case 1: Samantha

Samantha is a 16-year-old White female living and attending school in a suburb of a large city in the northeastern United States. She has no history of psychiatric diagnoses or psychotherapy and has a general history of positive social adjustment and satisfactory academic functioning. She just started her junior year at a high-achieving public school, where she has typically performed in the average range academically, with most grades in the B range, and a few As in the humanities. Her teachers have emphasized how important junior year performance is for college applications, and she will be taking the PSAT in a month. Her 10th grade PSAT scores were at about the 60th percentile nationally, but this was significantly below average for her school and her group of friends.

Samantha has a long history of feeling at least mild anxiety around tests, mainly worries and feelings of restlessness, but she has performed relatively well on classroom tests, and so for most of her schooling, there was never much concern about the anxiety. However, once she received her 10th grade PSAT scores, her confidence faltered, and her anxiety before and during classroom tests increased markedly. Her test performance did not change appreciably, but she seemed to spend more time talking about her worries regarding upcoming tests. She often slept poorly the night before major tests. Moreover, on exam days in school, she experienced physiological symptoms such as heart palpitations, dry mouth, and nausea. While taking most exams, she found herself distracted by intrusive thoughts about how she was going to fail the exam. Before the final exam in her 10th grade biology class, she ran to the bathroom and vomited due to extreme anxiety.

Samantha's parents had hoped that she would relax over the summer vacation after 10th grade. The break from school was in fact somewhat helpful, but Samantha was already worried about the 11th grade PSAT. Her parents purchased numerous study materials for her and offered to pay for a prep course. Samantha declined to take the prep course and spent very little time actually using the study materials, although she often brought up the PSAT as a stressor that she needed to contend with. Now, with her junior year starting, she is already feeling nervous about upcoming classroom tests, as well as what will be her final chance to score very highly on the PSAT.

Case 2: Christopher

Christopher is a 25-year-old African American male in his second year of training at an osteopathic medical school in a large city in the midwestern United States. He had done well on classroom tests in his K–12 schooling, and although he reports having been a driven student and feeling some pressure to do well, he did not experience typical test anxiety symptoms at that time. He had attended high-need, under-resourced K–12 schools, and in retrospect, he views his high school's standards as having been "really easy." His composite (overall) ACT score was in the 42nd percentile nationally, and when he matriculated to a regional state university, he found the coursework far more challenging than in high school, especially in the courses for his pre-med major. His adjustment to college was difficult, and he had a particularly hard time paying attention in his classes and focusing on studying outside of class. Christopher began to experience significant anxiety studying for exams, taking them, and then anticipating test feedback. During his sophomore year, a family physician diagnosed him with ADHD and prescribed stimulant medication. The medication seemed to help him focus when studying, but he actually did not take it on exam days because it aggravated his physiological symptoms of anxiety.

Christopher graduated college with a 3.1 GPA (with better grades in his last two years, after the stimulant medication was started), and he obtained a full-time job while using his free time to study for the Medical College Admission Test (MCAT). His MCAT scores were middling—around the 50th percentile for all MCAT examinees, and around the 30th percentile for enrolled medical students. Nonetheless, he obtained admission to an osteopathic medical school, where he has found the coursework to be extremely challenging. For him, the cognitive symptoms of test anxiety have been most prominent. He describes himself as worrying "all the time" about tests and their consequences for his medical career, to the point that he finds it difficult to pay attention. In addition, after experiencing several of what he calls "panic attacks," he has stopped taking his stimulant medication, out of concern that the medication might exacerbate any cardiac symptoms of anxiety. He passed almost all of his medical school classes, where exams are heavily weighted, although his grades were often just above the passing cutoff. In two classes, he failed on the first attempt, and he retook the classes and passed. Any students who fail a class are automatically referred to the school's academic support office, where tutoring and more general academic counseling are available, but Christopher never followed up on the referral, and admits that his embarrassment about failing classes likely played a role. He is proud that he managed to pass the classes on his second try without formal support from the school.

Currently, Christopher strongly believes that his professors and the medical school administration think poorly of him, and he expects to be kicked out for poor performance, despite receiving no such feedback, and despite knowing some other students who also needed to retake selected classes. He has avoided looking up the school policies to check the official criteria for academic dismissal, out of worries that he will meet the listed criteria. Similarly, he recently waited a week to open a mailed letter from the medical school, fearing that it was a dismissal notice (it was in fact a fundraising solicitation for the medical school's affiliated hospital). He will need to take the first portion of his licensing exam this year, and the idea of the exam fills him with dread.

Comment on Case Studies

Samantha's and Christopher's cases illustrate both the heterogeneity of the test-anxious population and the features that members of the population have in common. Both Samantha and Christopher appear to have academic skills that are at least average relative to the general population, yet they appear deficient relative to either local norms (for Samatha's high school) or relative to ambitious standards (Christopher's aspiration to become a physician). Samantha did well enough but did not stand out in her high-achieving community, whereas Christopher overcame a less rigorous academic curriculum to work up to ever higher standards, with mixed success. While Samantha has a generally positive academic and social history, and no other clinical concerns, Christopher has a diagnosis of a learning problem (ADHD), and his early good grades may be due to lower standards. Both students have experienced significant cognitive and physiological symptoms of test anxiety. Finally, although problem behaviors associated with test anxiety are less prominent in these descriptions, both students exhibit avoidance in their own ways. Although Samantha is preoccupied with worries about the upcoming PSAT, she has also been avoiding preparing for it, and Christopher is so worried about failing out of medical school that he is not even engaging with any administrative processes that might prevent his worry from becoming true.

HOW COMMON IS TEST ANXIETY?

How common are cases like those of Samantha and Christopher? Because test anxiety is not a recognized disorder in any official psychiatric classification system, it has never been included in large-scale population-level epidemiological studies of disorders. Furthermore, the prevalence of test anxiety is difficult to estimate because there is no single, consensus threshold at which test anxiety becomes clinically significant. However, research studies have repeatedly and consistently found that having some degree of test anxiety is very common:

- In a sample of 335 children in grades 3 through 5, 55% endorsed moderate or high levels of anxiety regarding classroom tests, and 68% endorsed moderate or high levels of anxiety about a state assessment (Segool et al., 2013).
- In a sample of 1,348 ninth and tenth graders, the average student reported experiencing test anxiety symptoms with a frequency between "sometimes" and "often" (Putwain, 2007).
- Of 3,021 community adolescents and young adults, 28.1% reported a fear of taking tests or exams (Knappe et al., 2011). This proportion is likely to be an underestimate since some young adults were not in educational or other settings where they would need to take tests.
- The norms for the Test Anxiety Inventory, a widely used assessment instrument, suggest that between 30% and 52% of college students report experiencing test anxiety "often" or "almost always" (McCarthy & Goffin, 2005).
- Macauley et al. (2018) found that high proportions of 183 healthcare professions graduate students (51% of females, and 37.5% of males) were classified by the Westside Test Anxiety Scale as having at least "moderately high" levels of test anxiety.

In a recent study, Lovett et al. (2024) examined the prevalence of specific test anxiety symptoms in a large sample of almost 3,000 college students at a flagship public university with selective admission standards. The researchers administered a 20-item test anxiety questionnaire, where the items represented many different symptoms. They found that only about 1% of the students failed to endorse any symptoms. Almost every student reported having at least one symptom at least some of the time when taking tests. Moreover, *most* of the students endorsed experiencing each of the following symptoms at least sometimes: feeling uneasy or upset during tests, difficulty concentrating on tests due to preoccupations with course grades, worrying a great deal prior to tests, and being unable to stop worrying about a test after it is over.

From a clinical perspective, the high prevalence of test anxiety suggests that test anxiety is an issue potentially worth addressing in many clients, including those who do not present for therapy for test anxiety *per se*. For instance, students who present to their school psychologist or school counselor with primarily academic concerns often have test anxiety. In addition, test anxiety often accompanies more general mental health issues. Indeed, when a client has other anxiety problems, their chance of having significant test anxiety is even higher (Knappe et al., 2011).

PREDICTORS AND CAUSES OF TEST ANXIETY

Like any other psychological phenomenon, test anxiety has been hypothesized to result from a variety of causes. Different theoretical approaches have accounted for test anxiety in different ways. Sigmund Freud (1900/2010), in his magnum opus *The Interpretation of Dreams*, discussed "examination anxiety" (p. 291). He argued that dreams of failing past exams are the mind's way of preparing for other high-stakes tasks in life. Meanwhile, his colleague Wilhelm Stekel argued that matriculation tests were feared because graduating from school represented an initiation to sexual maturity ("matriculation" and "maturity" reportedly have the same etymological roots; cf. Freud, 1900/2010, p. 292). These explanations are no longer widely believed, and as psychological theory has evolved, so have perspectives on test anxiety. We discuss two types of predictors and potential causes of test anxiety here: internal personality processes and external factors in the environment. Practitioners should be aware of both types of factors—to help identify students at greater risk of having high test anxiety (and a corresponding need for intervention) and to understand associated features that often come up in clinical work with this population.

Personality Processes

Several personality constructs have been consistently related to test anxiety. One, the personality trait of *neuroticism*, has a strong correlation with test anxiety, with a correlation coefficient of about 0.45 (von der Embse et al., 2018). Neuroticism is one of the basic five traits—alongside extraversion, agreeableness, conscientiousness, and openness to experience—that appear to explain the majority of individual differences in personality (McCrae, 2020). Neuroticism is described by Tackett & Lahey (2017) as "a tendency to experience negative affect and emotions, including feelings of sadness, anxiety, and anger" (p. 48), and is strongly related to both physical and mental health outcomes, with higher levels of neuroticism predicting worse health. Individuals with high levels of neuroticism react with more severity to experiences of frustration and loss—such as test failure—and then do not recover as easily. Indeed, one statistical facet of neuroticism is anxiety, and other facets, such as self-consciousness and vulnerability, would also relate to negative reactions to tests (Costa & McCrae, 1995). Basic trait neuroticism may thus fuel test anxiety, since students with higher levels of neuroticism will have more extreme reactions to any stressor, including an academic test.

Another, related personality trait is *perfectionism*. Unsurprisingly, students who experience high levels of test anxiety often have extremely high self-standards. But many scholars believe that perfectionism consists of two distinct dimensions, and these relate differently to test anxiety. *Perfectionistic strivings* involve setting excessively high goals for oneself, whereas *perfectionistic concerns* involve the effect of not meeting those goals on one's sense of self-worth (Osenk et al., 2020). Students with perfectionistic strivings focus on aiming high for themselves, whereas the focus of students with perfectionistic concerns is on worrying about possible mistakes and the consequences of imperfections. In a recent meta-analysis, Burcaş and Creţu (2021) found that perfectionistic concerns relate substantially to test anxiety (the overall correlation coefficient was 0.42), but perfectionistic strivings do not predict test anxiety (the overall correlation coefficient was 0.04). It appears that perfectionistic concerns drive avoidant coping strategies, which in turn cause higher levels of test anxiety (Weiner & Carton, 2012). The research on perfectionism and test anxiety has suggestive implications for intervention. Rather than focusing on reining in highly ambitious personal goals, which are not clearly dangerous, therapists should focus on the avoidant behaviors that appear in students who are preoccupied with concerns about failure.

Clinical anxiety disorders, and text anxiety as well, are associated with another construct known as intolerance of uncertainty (IU; Jacoby, 2020) (e.g., Huntley et al., 2020). Many clients with anxiety disorders—particularly those with prominent worry symptoms—have an excessive need for reassurance that bad things will definitely not happen (and that good things definitely *will* happen). IU manifests in two primary ways: (a) desperately seeking information about the future that is guaranteed to be accurate, and (b) feeling paralyzed and unable to act without such information. Some students with high levels of test anxiety exhibit both of these manifestations. For instance, they may pester teachers repeatedly for more information about what to expect on a test, what options they will have available if they do poorly on the test, and how the class as a whole performed on the test. They may feel unable to begin studying without extreme confidence in exactly what the test items will look like, and may even be unable to progress through the test until they work out their answer to one item repeatedly and feel absolutely certain that they answered it correctly.

A final personality-related construct known to relate to test anxiety is academic self-efficacy—the confidence that a student has in their ability to learn, understand academic material, and perform on academic tasks (e.g., Brandmo et al., 2019). Research has repeatedly found a negative correlation between the two variables, although it is not clear whether self-efficacy directly impacts test anxiety or whether, instead, actual low levels of skill or ability lead to both low self-efficacy and high test anxiety. Regardless of the exact cause–effect relations, as we discuss in detail in Chapters 9 and 10, interventions can build test-taking and study skills, which will boost confidence (test-taking self-efficacy, specifically) as well.

Environmental Factors

Environmental factors influencing test anxiety have proven more difficult to study. Ethical and logistical complications often preclude direct manipulation of these factors, and so most research asks students for their self-reports of perceived levels of environmental variables. Still, certain (reported) environmental factors have been consistently associated with test anxiety. These include pressure from parents and teachers. For instance, Putwain et al. (2010) found that students' reports of parental pressure (i.e., agreeing with statements such as "When it comes to school, my parents expect the impossible"; see Campbell, 1994) were associated with higher levels of worries about tests. The same study found an association between worries about tests and students' perceptions of their teachers' "performance-avoidance goals" (i.e., agreeing with statements such as "My teacher tells us that it is important that we don't look stupid in class"; see Midgley et al., 2000).

Another, related environmental variable is pressure regarding specific tests. In general, test anxiety can be reduced by presenting tests as learning activities or by using tests that are perceived by students as easier (correlation coefficients for these variables and test anxiety are in the range of 0.2 to 0.3; von der Embse et al., 2018). Of course, outside of experimental studies, changing these features of tests is easier said than done—just try convincing high school students that the SAT is a fun game! In addition, presenting tests as ungraded learning activities rather than as evaluative techniques can decrease effort, and describing tests as easier than they are can set up students for failure through lack of appropriate preparation. Even so, it is helpful to know that tests do not uniformly induce anxiety in any particular student. The level of anxiety depends in part on how the test is perceived and presented. Different students take the same test in very different social (family, school, peer, etc.) contexts, and the test can take on many different meanings, with consequences for anxiety.

TEST ANXIETY AND EQUITY OF EDUCATIONAL OPPORTUNITY

The importance of the social context of testing relates to our final topic: the role of test anxiety in threatening equity in academic access. Equity of educational opportunity is an old concept (Burbles et al., 1982) that has taken on more importance in recent years, as disparities in educational outcomes have become an increasingly pressing problem. Educational tests are not merely the means of measuring such disparities; the testing process itself is often thought to be the *cause* of the disparities (Jordan & Lovett, 2007). Since demographic groups do differ in average levels of test anxiety (see von der Embse et al., 2018, for a review), this sets up the possibility of such differences explaining performance gaps. For instance, gender differences in test anxiety are substantial and remarkably reliable, with girls and women exhibiting much higher average test anxiety levels than boys and men. Ethnic group differences in test anxiety are not as well understood, but von der Embse (2018) found data from several studies that yielded a significant difference between Black and White students' average levels, with Black students reporting more anxiety. Finally, students with various disability conditions (e.g., learning disabilities, ADHD, etc.) tend to have higher levels of test anxiety (e.g., Lovett et al., 2024).

Test anxiety has the potential to influence disparities in test performance in two ways. First, it is possible that group differences in test anxiety could lead to test performance gaps in high-stakes settings, even when groups have smaller or null differences in actual skill levels (as measured in low-stakes settings). The high stakes of the operational testing setting could prevent students from showing what they know. This mechanism has been argued to explain differences in SAT performance between boys and girls (Hannon, 2012) and between Hispanic and non-Hispanic students (Hannon, 2019). In this analysis, anxiety induces a type of bias in tests, such that the tests are measuring different constructs in students with low and high levels of anxiety.

As we discuss in Chapter 2, to the degree that test anxiety affects performance at all, the effects appear to be mostly indirect. Specifically, anxiety alters students' methods of test preparation and their behavior during tests, which in turn affects performance (e.g., Jenifer et al., 2023). This provides a second and more likely mechanism by which group differences in anxiety could lead to group differences in test performance. This has been a particularly influential argument in the context of STEM (science, technology, engineering, and mathematics) education, where students form beliefs about their abilities relatively early and can choose to either seek out or avoid more advanced instruction and training in those subject area (Daker et al., 2021). Not coincidentally, these are also subject areas where tests are prominent, and test-anxious students are more likely to prepare poorly for tests or even opt-out of any STEM coursework beyond the minimum that is required.

Regardless of the exact mechanism, test anxiety has substantial implications for equity of educational opportunity, both at the group and individual levels. Students with higher test anxiety are less likely to avail themselves of educational opportunities, simply because taking tests is so aversive. These students avoid testing themselves in preparation for actual tests, even though self-testing is the most effective type of studying. As they grow older and have more choice over their educational path, they avoid taking classes and attending educational institutions in which tests are required.

SUMMARY

Test anxiety is a remarkably common source of distress in students at all levels of education. Consisting of a mix of physiological and cognitive symptoms, test anxiety typically involves unwanted bodily arousal and intrusive worries. These symptoms are usually associated with maladaptive avoidance responses. Almost all students experience test anxiety at least some of the time, but higher levels accompany traits such as perfectionism and intolerance of uncertainty. Higher levels of test anxiety are also present when students feel more external pressures. Moreover, test anxiety is higher on average in female students relative to males, in Black students relative to White students, and in students with other disability conditions. Therefore, though not generally a disorder per se (as we discuss in Chapter 3), test anxiety merits attention from practitioners in schools and clinical settings seeing students of all ages.

CHAPTER 2

Test Anxiety Matters—But Not in the Way Students Think

Many students, especially those with high levels of test anxiety, confidently subscribe to a simple mental model of how test anxiety works: feeling anxious during a test prevents the retrieval of information and execution of skills, thus depressing performance. According to this model, if a student were to feel less anxious during a test, then they would do significantly better on the test. Students holding this mental model are apt to describe themselves as "bad test takers" (Holmes, 2021), as if test-taking skill is distinct from the skills that the tests are designed to measure. These students often report that during the exam, their minds "go blank," and they suddenly cannot do things that they were able to do just before, when studying (Covington & Omelich, 1987). In essence, many students view the effect of anxiety on performance as strong, direct, and causal. This impression goes beyond students, of course; it is popular in many arguments against the use of high-stakes tests. For instance, in a *New York Times* column criticizing the SAT college admissions test, Jennifer Finney Boylan (2014) described the test as "a mind-numbing, stress-inducing ritual of torture" and charged that "it freaks students out so completely that they cannot even think." In a more recent column in the same newspaper, psychologist Adam Grant (2023) was less dramatic, but nonetheless argued that anxiety drains students' cognitive resources, and that if students are "less likely to dread" tests, this will "give them a better chance at putting their best foot forward." Similar claims date back many years; in 1962, testing expert John French noted that "a bitter complaint of some students who take college entrance tests is that the tests are taken under such conditions of pressure that it is impossible for them to show their best work" (p. 553).

Ample research shows that this model of test anxiety's effects, despite being popular, is erroneous. An accurate understanding of the test anxiety–test performance relationship is important for anyone working with students who are bothered by their test anxiety. In fact, it is key information to present to students in treatment. This understanding is at the core of our test anxiety treatment model. In this chapter, we summarize relevant empirical literature on the relationship, and in Chapter 6, we describe how best to present this information to students.

TEST ANXIETY–PERFORMANCE CORRELATIONS

Most research on the test anxiety–performance relationship has examined groups of students who are given both a self-report measure of test anxiety (see Chapter 3 for a full discussion of assessing test anxiety) and an actual cognitive or academic test to complete. The students' test anxiety levels are then correlated with their test scores. The correlation has been quite modest across decades of research studies and across a variety of measurement tools. The average correlation coefficient between test anxiety and test performance is about $r = -0.20$ (see reviews by von der Embse et al., 2018; Zeidner, 2014). The correlation is negative because, on average, higher levels of test anxiety are associated with (slightly) lower test performance. Figure 2.1 shows a correlation of $r = -0.20$ graphically on a typical scatterplot, and a slight negative trend is visible. As test anxiety (on the x-axis) rises, test scores (on the y-axis) tend to decline slightly.

This correlation varies somewhat depending on various factors, two of which are especially relevant for clinicians. First, the type of test anxiety symptoms affects the size of the correlation. Cognitive symptoms, such as worries, have consistently stronger relationships with performance (about $r = -0.30$) than physiological symptoms, such as a rapid heartbeat, do (for physiological symptoms, the average correlation is about $r = -0.10$). Second, student ability level matters. Students with lower general cognitive ability are more likely to show a negative relationship between anxiety and performance, whereas in students with above-average ability, the relationship seems to be insignificant, and may even be positive (e.g., Owens et al., 2014).

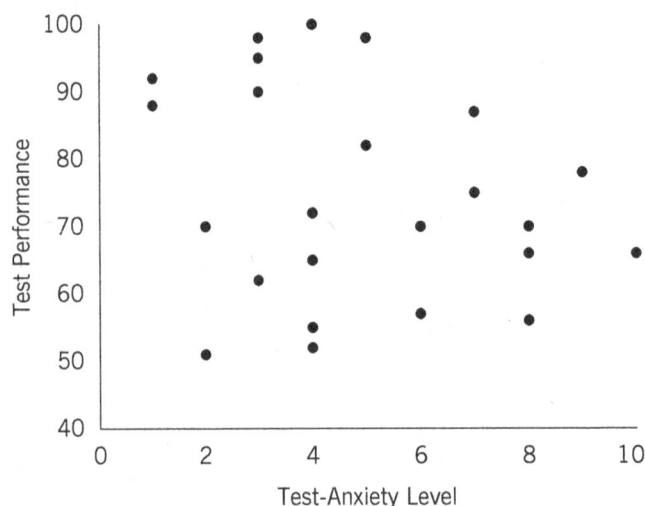

FIGURE 2.1. Scatterplot showing a correlation coefficient of -0.20 between test anxiety and test performance.

Is r = −0.20 Large?

Setting aside for a moment the factors that affect the size of the correlation, let's return to the overall average value of $r = -0.20$. Is that large enough to matter?

There are several ways to interpret correlation coefficients (Funder, 2010). Probably the most common way that researchers interpret these coefficients is by squaring them. A squared correlation coefficient is generally interpreted as showing the proportion of variability in an outcome that can be predicted by a predictor. Applying this logic to our correlation, it suggests that only about 4% (0.20 squared) of the variability in test performance is predictable from test anxiety. Consider what this means—namely, that the vast majority of variability in students' test performance cannot be predicted by students' anxiety levels. Other factors (e.g., test preparation, ability, etc.) are needed to predict most of the variance in students' scores with any accuracy. Students should take this to heart; they cannot use their own anxiety levels during a test to predict with confidence how well they will do. Students with anxiety problems often take their anxiety to be providing useful information about a threat or danger, but research tells us that test anxiety is not useful information.

Another way of interpreting a correlation coefficient is to transform it using the formula $50r + 50$; this will yield the percentage of people in the higher half of the sample on the predictor who are also in the higher half of the sample on the outcome. In our case, the formula gives $50(-0.20) + 50$ or $(-10) + 50$, which is 40. Forty percent of students who are in the top half of their peers in terms of test anxiety levels will also be in the top half in their test scores.[1] Hence, it's common to have above-average test anxiety and to *still perform above-average on tests*. (A quick look back at Figure 2.1 will confirm this.) In fact, many students we treat fall into this category—they have a history of high test performance but are also quite anxious about testing. Remarkably, despite their own experience, even these students tend to assume that anxiety is inconsistent with high test performance. More generally, students are often surprised by the weak relationship between anxiety and performance, and so are teachers and even mental health professionals. But it's useful to consider analogies outside the realm of academic test performance. Many top athletes, musicians, actors, and other people experience severe anxiety about performing in public and nonetheless perform very well (Hickson, 2016).

Is the Relationship Nonlinear?

Generally, the test anxiety–performance correlation coefficient of $r = -0.20$ is interpreted in a simple way: with each increase in anxiety, there is a slight reduction in predicted test score. This assumes that the relationship is linear (see Figure 2.1). However, some psychologists (e.g., Cizek & Burg, 2006) have hypothesized that the relationship may be more likely to take a different form—that of an inverted U-shaped curve (see Figure 2.2). It's theoretically possible that *some* anxiety is better than none at all, but at some point, more anxiety begins to interfere with performance. Having at least a little anxiety could be important to motivate test preparation and engagement, but extreme anxiety could promote withdrawal

---

[1] This interpretation is based on the binomial effect size display (see Rosenthal & Rubin, 1982).

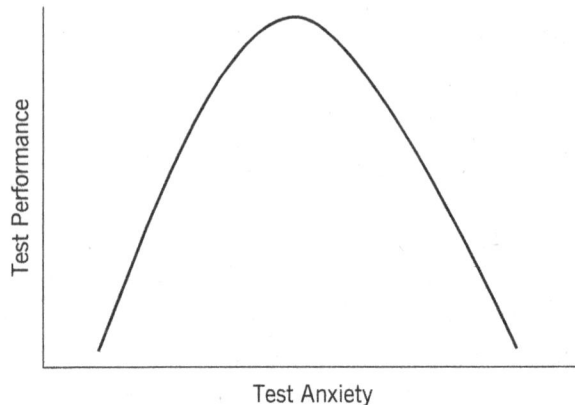

FIGURE 2.2. Schematic showing an inverted-U relationship between test anxiety and test performance.

and performance-impairing panic. After all, sometimes students do better on higher-stakes tests than on lower-stakes tests (e.g., Schlosser et al., 2019), presumably because they take the latter less seriously.

At times, claims of these *curvilinear* effects are tied to a general theory in psychology known as the Yerkes–Dodson law, which proposes that physiological arousal increases task performance up to a point, after which further increases in arousal are associated with decreased performance (American Psychological Association, n.d.). Such a relationship would yield the curve seen in Figure 2.2.

There is an intuitive logic to applying the Yerkes–Dodson law to test anxiety, and at the *extreme* endpoints of the physiological arousal continuum, it seems undeniably correct. Extremely low levels of arousal (stupor, sleep) are certainly incompatible with high task performance, and extremely high levels of arousal (stark panic) may be as well. But the available research suggests that over most of the arousal continuum, the law does not hold (e.g,. Schillinger et al., 2021). This is less surprising when we consider that the Yerkes–Dodson law was never validated across the wide range of situations that it has been assumed to apply to (Corbett, 2015; Teigen, 1994). In fact, few who tout the law know that the original study by Yerkes and Dodson (1908) involved a situation very different from test anxiety and test performance: giving mice electric shocks of varying intensities and examining the effect on rate of motor learning.

Test anxiety psychoeducation has long included the Yerkes–Dodson law (e.g., Damer & Melendres, 2011), and even books for education professionals discuss it as if it were valid (e.g., Cizek & Burg, 2006). It may make students more comfortable to think of some degree of anxiety as being a good thing. However, as we discuss more in Chapter 6, we decline to teach our students a "finding" that has not held up empirically. Instead, we emphasize the weakness of the relationship between test anxiety and test performance, the fact that anxiety during a test does not prevent someone from doing well, and the fact that the (already weak) correlation between anxiety and performance is likely not a cause–effect relationship—a topic that we discuss next.

Correlations and Causes

The modest correlation between test anxiety and test performance means that we cannot predict a student's performance based on their anxiety level. But even if the correlation were much stronger, this would not be evidence that test anxiety *causes* poorer test performance to any degree. As readers likely know, correlation does not necessarily imply causation. In fact, a correlation between test anxiety and test performance could result from any of the following three possibilities:

1. Test anxiety causes lower test performance.
2. Lower test performance causes test anxiety.
3. A third variable (or set of variables) causes both test anxiety and lower test performance.

Figure 2.3 displays these possibilities graphically. To be clear, they are not mutually exclusive. More than one process may be operating, and some causal processes may be stronger than others.

Students tend to assume that their anxiety impairs their performance—that is, possibility #1. Many students argue that in a state of anxiety, they're unable to think, remember things, and solve problems, but that in a less anxious state, they could do all of those things. Below we review the evidence for this claim. But it also seems likely that lower test performance would cause test anxiety (possibility #2). A low test score can easily induce anxiety about the score's consequences, such as failing the class, eliciting negative reactions from

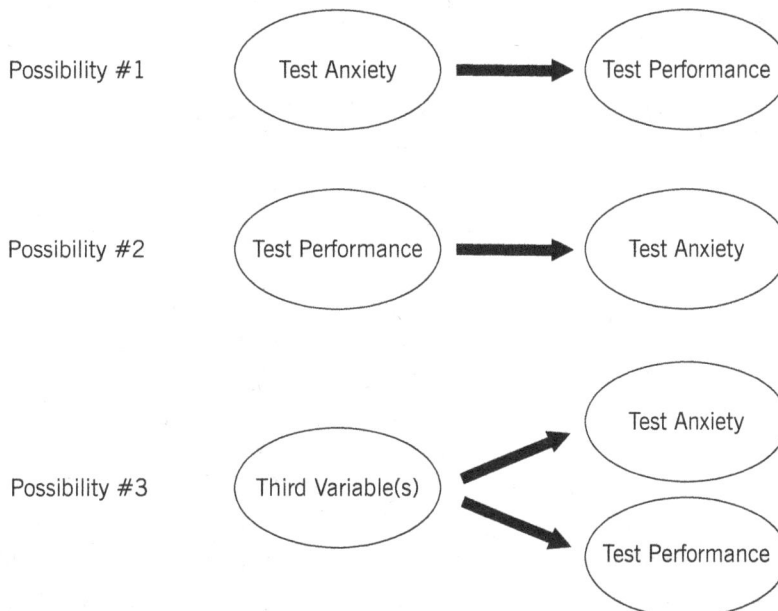

FIGURE 2.3. Possible explanations of the test anxiety–test performance correlation.

parents or teachers, etc. Moreover, a history of low test performance, paired with those kinds of consequences, can lead to anxiety *in anticipation* of the low scores—anxiety that would be present prior to and during the test itself. If the test anxiety–test performance correlation is due, at least in part, to a process in this direction (from low performance to anxiety), performance levels will need to change rather than anxiety per se.

Possibility #3 is also important to keep in mind. There are many factors that can lead to test anxiety while simultaneously lowering test performance. For instance, consider Fatima, a college student who did not have adequate time to prepare for a biology test. She was unexpectedly busy with family activities the weekend before the Monday test. Fatima knows that her lack of preparation is likely to impair her performance, and she is also anxious about a likely low score. Students are more likely to blame their test score on anxiety (something that they cannot control) than poor preparation (something that they can). Even so, anxious students like Fatima will often admit to suboptimal studying; indeed, lack of preparation was the most commonly endorsed source of test anxiety in one sample of college students (Bonaccio & Reeve, 2010). Similarly, consider a student who has low levels of aptitude in a subject area (e.g., low math ability), or at least has lower aptitude levels than a particular setting demands (e.g., average math ability in an advanced calculus class). Such a student will likely not do especially well on a test and will also be anxious about it. But in these two examples, anxiety is not *causing* the lower test performance. Instead, a third variable (poor preparation, or low aptitude) is the cause of both the anxiety and the lower performance. This possibility recasts the correlation between anxiety and performance in an entirely different light. If students who have higher levels of test anxiety are also more likely to have poor test preparation or lower ability levels, we cannot infer that anxiety, and not those other factors, is influencing performance. The simplest correlational studies, then, cannot address the key question of whether test anxiety impairs performance.

CONTROLLED STUDIES OF THE TEST ANXIETY–PERFORMANCE RELATIONSHIP

To distinguish between mere correlation and genuine causation, a controlled study is needed. Third variables need to be controlled for, and the direction of a relationship (A causing B vs. B causing A) needs to be determined as well. In many areas of psychological research, causation is studied with a true experiment, in which participants are randomly assigned to different conditions, and their responses are compared across the conditions. In theory, this approach could be used to study test anxiety. Students could be randomly assigned to low-anxiety or high-anxiety conditions, and their test performance under those conditions could be measured. In practice, this is very difficult to do. For one thing, research ethics boards tend not to permit scientists to deliberately induce distress in their study participants; randomly assigning some students to experience more anxiety would be an example of inducing distress. There are occasions when such research is permitted, but ethics boards weigh the risks of inducing distress against the benefits of the research, and test anxiety work is rarely considered important enough to justify the cost of upsetting participants. There is a second problem, and it's logistical: inducing high levels of anxiety about a test is difficult in laboratory settings. Students tend to feel anxious about tests because their performance on those tests has real implications for their grades, future jobs and education opportunities, and so forth. It's difficult for a researcher to make students anxious about a test in a research study without lying about the consequences of the test, and lying to participants is something else that ethics boards frown on. Therefore, we don't have many true experiments on the effects of test anxiety, and that is unlikely to change any time soon. Instead, intrepid researchers have used a variety of clever study designs to better test causal hypotheses without randomized experiments, and we review the results of these studies below.

Examining Order Effects in Anxiety and Performance

The simplest controlled studies take the typical correlational study of test anxiety and test performance, but add a twist, looking at *when* anxiety comes, in relation to performance. If one thing causes another, the cause has to happen before the effect. For instance, because lightning precedes thunder, it wouldn't make sense to say that thunder causes lightning. In one study, Zeidner (1991) applied this general logic to test anxiety. He looked at Israeli students who were taking a high-stakes college admissions test (one that is coincidentally called the SAT, although it's very different from the test used in the United States). Some of the students completed a test anxiety questionnaire before taking the SAT, as is typical, whereas for other students, the order was reversed. In both groups of students, he examined the correlation between test anxiety levels and SAT scores. When anxiety was measured *before* the SAT, the correlation was extremely weak, $r = -0.11$, but when anxiety was measured *after* the SAT, the correlation was much stronger, $r = -0.40$. These data are more consistent with lower test performance causing anxiety than a cause–effect relationship in the reverse direction. Students likely had some sense of how they had performed, and their knowledge of their likely low performance induced test anxiety.

In a more complex study, Hong (1999) examined many different sets of cognitive and physiological symptoms of test anxiety and their relationships with performance on a final exam in a statistics course. Her finding was essentially the same as Zeidner's (1991); for any set of symptoms, its relationship with performance was stronger when the symptoms were measured after the test than when the same symptoms were measured before the test. Taken together, these two studies suggest that if the anxiety–performance relationship is direct at all, performance has a greater effect on anxiety than the reverse.

"Natural Experiments"

Other controlled studies have been conducted as "natural experiments" in which the same group of students is tested under multiple conditions. In these studies, students are already taking a real-world test that is presumed to induce anxiety, but researchers also give the same students a test that has no significant consequences. One pioneering study of this sort was conducted by John French (1962), who worked at the Educational Testing Service and had access to the SAT administration process. Some sections on the SAT are used solely for research purposes and do not affect official scores. Since students do not know which sections are for research and which are not, their motivation (and anxiety) should be the same across real and "experimental" sections. French looked at performance on these experimental sections, but also examined students' performance on optional, parallel SAT sections taken a few days before or after the real SAT. The optional test sections were *openly* given for research purposes and students were assured that scores from these sections would not go to colleges, to lower anxiety (which was measured as well). If anxiety had a causal impact on performance, students' average performance should be substantially lower on the experimental sections than on the optional sections, particularly in high-anxiety students. However, this did not happen. Instead, the average experimental verbal (reading) section score was only 4 SAT score points lower than the average optional reading section score, and the average experimental mathematical section score was actually 3 SAT score points higher than the average optional mathematical section score. Among more anxious examinees, there was even less evidence of impairment. These data strongly suggest that anxiety did not impair SAT performance.

Covington and Omelich (1987) conducted a similar study with college students taking an introductory psychology course. After taking an actual course test, participating students were readministered exactly the same items in a low-stakes research setting. The investigators reasoned that if anxiety impairs performance by blocking retrieval of information from memory and processing of information (as many students claim), the low-stakes setting should allow students to perform better, particularly for the students who have high levels of anxiety during tests. However, Covington and Omelich found no relationship between level of student anxiety and magnitude of score increase under a lower-stakes setting. As with French's (1962) study, Covington and Omelich did not find evidence of test anxiety having a causal impact on performance.

Studies Controlling for Third Variables

Another research approach is to directly control for possible third variables that are influencing both anxiety and performance. In a recent study, Theobald et al. (2022) did this, gaining access to a unique sample taking a very high-stakes test: over 300 German medical students taking their medical license exam. Students prepared for the exam using an online learning software package, and researchers had access to rich data on the students' study behaviors and performance on practice tests. The researchers added measures of anxiety as well. A correlation of $r = -0.20$ was found between test anxiety and performance on the actual license exam. However, crucially, when the researchers statistically controlled for performance on a mock exam (which would not induce as much anxiety), this correlation went away. Similarly, the correlation went away when just controlling for performance on the online platform's test preparation exercises. Finally, in an investigation of the direction of the anxiety–performance relationship, the researchers found that higher state (momentary) anxiety did *not* predict fewer correct questions answered during test preparation activities on the same day, but fewer correct answers *did* predict more state anxiety on the following day. These findings suggest that test preparation and actual knowledge/skills affect test anxiety, but anxiety does not seem to have causal influence on performance.

Similar conclusions have been reached using a different research approach. Recently, the ACT college admissions testing agency has conducted a research program on the effects of anxiety on ACT scores. Steedle (2018) applied sophisticated multivariate statistical analyses to a large sample of students who took the ACT twice and who were asked additional questions about a variety of factors that could influence performance, including anxiety. He found that the relationship between anxiety and ACT performance was actually attributable to variance in the students' genuine ability levels. It seems that students who are more anxious do worse on the ACT because they actually have lower levels of the skills that the ACT is designed to measure. In a follow-up study, Schiel (2020) also examined a large sample of students who took the ACT twice. As expected, there was a slight gain in performance from the first to the second time, but the size of the gain was virtually the same in students who did versus did not report experiencing "notable stress/anxiety" during the second test. The difference in gain was only about 0.02 standard deviations, a negligible effect. These studies not only undermine the idea that test anxiety exerts a causal effect on performance, they also help to show that test anxiety does not lead to *biased* estimates of students' skills. Many test-anxious students feel that the scores that they get on tests are unfairly low—that in essence, the test is biased against "bad test takers" like them because of their anxiety. Research suggests, instead, that when students who are anxious do worse on tests, deficits in skill levels cause the lower performance, and that may well cause the anxiety as well (see also Musch & Bröder, 1999).

HOW TEST ANXIETY SHAPES STUDENTS' CHOICES

The research reviewed above may leave you wondering if test anxiety has any effects at all. If test anxiety doesn't directly impair test performance, what does it do? In fact, other research suggests that test anxiety has effects, but those effects are on behaviors that are under our voluntary control (at least to some degree). In Chapter 1, we described the often-neglected problem behaviors associated with test anxiety, and those behaviors are the key mediators between test anxiety and test performance. In this section, we cover the effects of test anxiety on studying and test-taking behaviors.

Test Anxiety and Test Preparation

Test preparation starts with students' behaviors during academic instruction, and even at this early stage, test anxiety exerts its effects. Students with higher levels of test anxiety are more likely to be worrying about an upcoming exam rather than paying attention in the class in which the exam will be given. Since engagement with instruction is a key input to performance on a test based on that instruction, these worries are counterproductive and may even lead to a self-fulfilling prophecy of poor performance.

Procrastination is another key effect of test anxiety. Since escape and avoidance are the natural action tendencies when someone is in a state of anxiety (e.g., Plutchik, 2001), it should not be surprising that students with test anxiety have higher levels of procrastination tendencies (Carden et al., 2004; Jia et al., 2021), particularly when test-related procrastination is specifically assessed (Hashemi & Latifian, 2014). Many of the students we treat admit to putting off studying material or preparing for tests due to anxiety, despite knowing that this harms their performance in the long term.

Finally, when test-anxious students *do* prepare for tests, they are likely to study in less effective ways. This has been most thoroughly investigated in the domain of math—a subject known for inducing anxiety. For instance, in one study, Jenifer et al. (2022) studied high school students taking an Advanced Placement (AP) calculus class. The researchers measured the proportion of time that students with low and high levels of math anxiety spent engaging in various specific types of test preparation activities. Less anxious students spent more time solving practice problems than their more anxious peers, whereas the reverse was true for re-reading textbook sections. Jenifer et al. (2022) further found that the differences in study technique choices mediated the relationship between math anxiety and performance on the AP exam. In a similar, follow-up study with college students, Jenifer et al. (2023) also found math anxiety to predict the proportion of time spent solving practice problems. As we discuss in detail in Chapter 9, self-testing (i.e., forcing oneself to retrieve information and explain material without access to readings or notes) is the most effective form of studying. However, because it takes more effort and is more unpleasant for test-anxious students, those students are more likely to prefer alternative, less effective techniques.

Interestingly, when anxious students do practice with actual test-like problems, they may be more likely to choose easier problems. In a clever experiment, Choe et al. (2019) asked people to choose between easier and harder math problems to try to solve, and also offered higher monetary rewards for choosing the harder problems. Participants with higher levels of math anxiety were nonetheless more likely to choose the easier, less remunerative problems. Of course, this is another type of avoidance, one specifically directed at avoiding challenging material. Unfortunately, more challenging tasks are exactly those that best prepare students for tests; optimal studying involves "desirable difficulties"—that is, features that deliberately make the study task more difficult in key ways (e.g., Nelson & Eliasz, 2023).

Test Anxiety and Test-Taking Behaviors

Anxiety doesn't just influence test preparation—at least in some students, it can also change the behaviors that the students engage in during tests. Here, too, test-anxious students may engage in more avoidance and escape responses—attempts to get away and stay away from an aversive testing experience. For example, students may spend time worrying about test items, instructors, their likely performance, and the consequences of that performance, rather than focusing fully on completing the challenging test in front of them. Or they may compulsively check their answers and reread test items, slowing themselves down excessively, possibly as a strategy (unconsciously deployed) to avoid the further anxiety that proceeding forward with the test may cause. Rather than working productively on test items, anxious students may do just about anything else: looking around the room, playing with a pencil, and even staring into space (Wren & Benson, 2004). Early in this chapter, we quoted the *New York Times* columnist Jennifer Finney Boylan, who claimed that anxiety prevents students from thinking during tests. But when she described her own experience of taking the SAT, her avoidance response to the anxiety seemed to matter more. During an uncomfortable section of the test with analogy problems, she turned away from the test:

> I looked up for a second at the back of the head of the girl in front of me. She had done this amazing thing with her hair, sort of like a French braid. I wondered if I could do that with my hair. I daydreamed for a while, thinking about the architecture of braids. When I remembered that I was wasting precious time deep in the heart of the SAT, I swore quietly to myself. French braids weren't going to get me into Wesleyan. (Boylan, 2014)

Anxiety didn't prevent Boylan from thinking; it just made thinking about things other than the test far more attractive.

You can wonder: If such anxiety-associated avoidance behaviors may impair test performance, wouldn't this imply that test anxiety would harm performance, contrary to the research we reviewed above? It's important to bear in mind, again, possibility #3 in Figure 2.3: when a test elicits high anxiety and associated avoidant behaviors, this often reflects insufficient preparation for the test, which is the dominant cause of low performance on the test. If a student simply does not know how to solve a type of algebra problem, their performance may be similar whether they stare off into space, worry anxiously, or work diligently on the problem. Still, we have worked with some anxious students who seem to have developed maladaptive test-taking behaviors as a generalized habit that persists even when they are adequately prepared for a test and even when the test is low-stakes and unlikely to cause a great deal of anxiety. The clinical implication for such students is clear: reducing anxiety per se (as desirable as that goal is) will not have much effect on test performance, unless maladaptive test-taking behaviors are addressed as well. Our treatment for test anxiety includes thorough instruction in best practices for taking tests effectively (see Chapter 10), which helps all students feel more comfortable and confident that they'll be able to fully demonstrate their knowledge and skills on tests, regardless of whether they feel anxious during testing.

SUMMARY

In this chapter, we reviewed the research on the relationship between test anxiety and test performance. Students—and some educators and therapists—tend to assume that anxiety has a direct, negative effect on performance, but the available research consistently shows otherwise. The relationship between anxiety and performance is quite weak to begin with. Moreover, to the degree that it exists at all, the relationship seems to be due to low test performance causing anxiety, or third variables (such as test preparation and student academic skills) causing both anxiety and lower performance.

Test anxiety *does* appear to increase problematic behaviors around test preparation and test taking. When this occurs, the student's anxiety has, in some sense, caused lower test scores, but the mediators of that relationship can be modified directly, through changing student behavior: using the most effective study strategies and learning how to focus on the test rather than spending significant time on other activities during the test.

Imagine, then, that a high school student takes a final exam in a history class under conditions of high anxiety and does poorly, earning a grade of D. The student protests that they knew the material but couldn't recall any of it during the exam due to anxiety. This is a common story, but based on the research reviewed in this chapter, you should be skeptical of it, even if the student honestly believes it. You might now ask: How did the student study for the test? Could they recall the information when the test was over and their anxiety abated? During the test, did they give up or keep trying their best to work on the test? It may seem unkind to be skeptical of the student's explanation of the D grade, but understanding the real nature of the relationship between test anxiety and test performance is the first step in finding a solution for addressing both.

CHAPTER 3

Clinical Assessment

It is relatively easy to gather a group of high school or college students who report having test anxiety. However, each student is likely to have different symptoms and different needs. Test anxiety is one area where thorough assessment is underappreciated. Reviewing questionnaire data, conducting a detailed interview, and developing a treatment plan based on such assessment requires a separate clinical session. In this chapter, we start by identifying different targets for assessment. We then turn to formal, published instruments for assessing test anxiety, which focus mostly on symptoms, and we discuss how to develop scales for measuring test-taking self-efficacy. It is often helpful to administer these instruments prior to an interview. Then, we cover a framework for a semi-structured interview centered on test anxiety-related issues. We conclude by discussing how test anxiety relates to (a) formal anxiety disorder diagnoses and (b) legal disability determination for the purpose of accommodations.

RELEVANT TARGETS OF ASSESSMENT

What is worth assessing when seeing individuals with test anxiety? The obvious place to start is the symptoms themselves. Knowing the approximate level of severity of symptoms differentiates between developmentally typical test anxiety and something that requires an intervention. As we discussed in Chapter 1, symptoms can be broken down into cognitive (e.g., worries) and physiological (e.g., a racing heart) clusters. Associated problem behaviors (e.g., avoidance of studying) are equally important to consider. Different types of therapy strategies are keyed, of course, to different aspects of test anxiety. We will see that standard questionnaires and rating scales focus on cognitive and physiological symptoms, and most do a fairly good job of covering these areas. Problem behaviors are mostly ignored by these instruments, and make for a good interview topic. Interviews should also address the onset and course of the symptoms—both over the student's academic career, and in relation to individual tests—and the environmental factors that seem to trigger them.

A second target of assessment is students' self-efficacy regarding their ability to participate in testing *when experiencing anxiety.* As we discussed in Chapter 2, the effects of test anxiety on performance are generally indirect, and many of the treatment procedures described later in the book focus on helping students to understand that they can perform well—or at least obtain a fair, accurate test score—despite experiencing anxiety. Because self-efficacy is always, by definition, about confidence in one's ability to perform very specific behaviors, we encourage practitioners to develop self-efficacy questions that pertain to individual students, and we share examples of these.

A third topic for assessment involves students' studying and test-taking behaviors. Because these are the variables that seem to mediate the bulk of any effects of test anxiety on performance, it is important to understand how each student prepares for tests and then takes them. At times, as we will see, students' primary problem is not anxiety per se but their approach to learning and taking tests. In fact, sometimes it is the student's study strategies that are causing or maintaining the anxiety.

Fourth, and relatedly, a student's history of performance on tests should be assessed, along with different variables (mostly not anxiety) that are likely to be affecting that performance. Proceeding chronologically but efficiently through a student's educational history yields more effective, tailored treatment strategies, and often sets the stage for the psychoeducation that starts early in the treatment. A student who never had difficulties with test performance until this year, when tenth-grade honors math overwhelmed him, requires a different response than a student who has significant learning problems identified in second grade and still has areas of academic skills that are far below average. A student who virtually always does very well on tests, and nonetheless experiences severe anxiety, requires still different treatment, and this performance history provides evidence for an important psychoeducation message about the lack of relationship between anxiety and performance.

Finally, a comprehensive assessment should inquire into more general features of each case. For instance: Does the student have any other clinical conditions? Mental health and learning/cognitive disorders are obviously important, but certain physical conditions are also relevant if these would preclude participation in intensive interoceptive exposure exercises. Table 3.1 provides an outline of all of the targets of assessment discussed here.

PUBLISHED RATING SCALES

Why use a quantitative rating scale at all? Certainly, its items may not capture the student's full experience of test anxiety, and many rating scales only examine a subset of possible symptoms. Still, quantitative ratings are helpful for determining how severe a student's symptoms are and whether intervention has been effective. In the same way that behavioral therapists often ask patients to rate different situations on a 0–100 scale of Subjective Units of Distress (SUDs; Spiegler & Guevremont, 2003) to gauge changes in anxiety severity over time, assigning a number to a student's test anxiety level can be useful for tracking improvement or worsening of symptoms. In addition, in school-based settings, rating scales are an efficient way to screen all students and determine which students may be appropriate for test anxiety intervention. Here, we present several options of published rating scales to con-

TABLE 3.1. Target Constructs of Test-Anxiety Assessment

I. Test-Anxiety Components
    A. Cognitive symptoms—Worries, negative self-thoughts, etc.
    B. Physiological symptoms—Stomach churning, sweating, fast pulse, etc.
    C. Associated problem behaviors—Avoiding studying, obsessive checking of answers to test items, etc.
II. Test-Taking Self-Efficacy—Students' confidence in their ability to engage in specific test-related behaviors (e.g., composing an essay) under conditions of anxiety
III. Typical Studying and Test-Taking Behaviors
    A. Approach to studying for tests
        1. How long in advance of tests does studying begin?
        2. Cramming for a single study session vs. spacing out briefer study sessions
        3. Exactly what studying methods are used, and how active are they?
    B. Approach to test taking
        1. The temporal sequence of events (e.g., skimming the whole test before starting on the first item)
        2. Any time-management strategies (e.g., skipping over items that the student does not know the answer to, returning if there is time)
        3. Approach to checking work before turning in the test
IV. Test Performance History
    A. Overall grades throughout the student's educational history
    B. Specific scores on high-stakes tests, and note if classroom test performance differs from overall grades
V. Clinical Psychological/Medical History
    A. Any prior diagnoses of psychological disorders, particularly anxiety disorders, mood disorders, learning disabilities, and ADHD
    B. Any prior diagnoses of relevant medical disorders, particularly neurologic, cardiac, and pulmonary disorders
    C. Prior psychotherapy/counseling treatment experience, and if present, note the perceived efficacy of prior treatment

sider. In Table 3.2, we present a quick guide to the advantages and disadvantages of each one. In addition, we use psychometric terms (e.g., T-score, internal consistency reliability) in our discussions of the measures. Readers can find in Appendix 3.1 a primer on understanding psychometric features of assessment tools.

Test Anxiety Inventory

The Test Anxiety Inventory (TAI) was developed by Charles D. Spielberger (1980) for adolescents and young adults, with a particular focus on high school and college students. The TAI consists of 20 items, each of which describes an experience related to test anxiety. For each item, students rate on a four-point scale how often they experience whatever the item describes: almost never (1), sometimes (2), often (3), or almost always (4). Eight of the 20 items relate to cognitive symptoms, such as "Thinking about my grade in a course interferes with my work on tests." The sum of responses to these items forms a composite called the "Worry" subscale ("TAI/W"). Another eight items relate to physiological symptoms and general experiences of nervousness, such as "I feel my heart beating very fast during important tests." The sum of responses to these items constitutes an "Emotionality" sub-

TABLE 3.2. Choosing a Published Test-Anxiety Scale

Scale	Advantages	Disadvantages
Test Anxiety Inventory (TAI; Spielberger, 1980)	• Norms for college and high school students • Good reliability and validity evidence • Separate scores for cognitive and physiological symptoms	• Norms are dated and only available in a gender-specific form
FRIEDBEN Test Anxiety Scale (FTA; Friedman & Bendas-Jacob, 1997)	• Good reliability and validity evidence • Has a unique subscale for measuring "social derogation" • Open-access (free)	• No normative data • Slightly awkward item wording due to translation
Westside Test Anxiety Scale (WTAS; Driscoll, 2007)	• Very brief (10 items) • Some reliability and validity evidence • Open-access (free)	• No normative data • Few psychometric details in official materials • No coverage of physiological symptoms
Multidimensional Test Anxiety Scale (MTAS; Putwain, von der Embse, et al., 2021)	• Excellent psychometric qualities • Norms available • Open-access (free)	• Available norms are gender-specific • Deliberate exclusion of behaviors associated with test anxiety

scale ("TAI/E"). The remaining four items count toward the overall composite score but not toward either the Worry or the Emotionality subscale. One of those four items actually asks respondents how often they feel *confident and relaxed* during tests, and that item is reverse scored, as it points in the opposite direction from the other 19 items.

The TAI manual has full, separate norms (percentiles for each raw score) for male and female students in each of the following groups: four-year college students, four-year college freshmen, two-year college students, and high school students. In addition, partial norms (means and standard deviations) are provided for navy recruits.

The TAI was originally developed in the late 1970s, and neither its items nor its norms have been officially updated since then. However, more recent studies with large samples show remarkably similar data, in terms of average scores (Lovett et al., 2023; Szafranski et al., 2012). The scores also boast good reliability and validity evidence (Spielberger, 1980). In different samples, the overall composite score typically has an internal consistency (Cronbach's alpha) reliability coefficient of above 0.90, and the two subscale scores have alphas of above 0.80. Test–retest reliability has been estimated at about 0.80 for test–retest intervals of a month or less, but somewhat lower (about 0.60) across a six-month test–retest interval in high school students. Validity evidence includes significant positive correlations with measures of general anxiety and other relevant personality traits, and negative correlations with test/academic performance.

For brief assessment of overall test anxiety symptoms, Taylor and Deane (2002) developed a short form of the TAI consisting of just five items. They found that the total score from those five items was quite reliable (alpha = 0.87) and valid (in terms of correlations with state anxiety measured right before an exam).

The full list of TAI items can be found in Taylor and Deane (2002), and the manual with norms and other information can be purchased ($50 at the time of this writing) from *www. mindgarden.com.*

We find the TAI, despite its age, to be a dependable workhorse, and not so long that it taxes students' attention (unless it is part of a much longer battery). We have found the separate Worry and Emotionality scores useful to discuss during treatment. One downside of the measure is that it only has separate norms for male and female students. Not only is this problematic for the growing number of students who have a gender identity beyond one of those binary choices, but even for non-gender-minority students, the TAI scores always describe their symptom levels only relative to same-gender peers. It is understandable that, given the significant gender differences in test anxiety, it may be helpful to use gender-based norms at times, but *only* having such norms is also a limitation (cf. Lovett, 2023).

FRIEDBEN Test Anxiety Scale

Friedman and Bendas-Jacob (1997) developed the FRIEDBEN Test Anxiety Scale (FTA) to address criticisms of earlier measures such as the TAI, specifically criticisms that the earlier measures did not include items relating to self-esteem or social comparison issues in test anxiety. These researchers asked high school students what thoughts, feelings, and behaviors would be typical of students with and without significant test anxiety, and used these answers (513 statements) to generate an initial item list. The final FTA has 23 items, each rated on a six-point Likert scale, from 1 ("Does not characterize me at all") to 6 ("Characterizes me most perfectly"). Each of the 23 items is on one of three subscales: (a) Social Derogation (threats to self-esteem and self-efficacy in social or academic domains), (b) Cognitive Obstruction ("hindrance in cognitive performance"), and (c) Tenseness ("physical and emotional arousal"). Each subscale generates a score and then an overall score is calculated as well.

The FTA has good psychometric properties and has been used in many research studies. Friedman and Bendas-Jacob (1997) found that Cronbach's alpha was 0.91 for the total score, and the subscale internal consistency reliability coefficients were 0.86, 0.85, and 0.81, respectively. Validity evidence came in the form of factor analysis results validating the three-factor structure, as well as strong correlations with the TAI (0.84 for boys, 0.82 for girls) and with a one-item *peer* rating of test anxiety. The FTA was designed specifically for high school students, and all of the psychometric data came from high school samples.

One advantage of the FTA is that its Social Derogation subscale addresses specific worries related to perceptions of oneself by teachers, parents, and peers. A sample item from this subscale is "If I fail a test, I am afraid my teachers will believe I am hopelessly dumb." Inspecting a student's item-level responses can raise issues that can be discussed in therapy sessions. The Cognitive Obstruction subscale also goes beyond TAI constructs to focus specifically on what students perceive themselves as unable to do during a test (i.e., areas of low self-efficacy). Another advantage of the FTA is that it is open-access and need not be purchased; it is listed in full in Friedman and Bendas-Jacob's (1997) article.

A disadvantage of the FTA is that it was apparently designed and administered in Hebrew, and then translated into English for the purposes of publishing the article on its development.[2] The language of some items may therefore appear a bit awkward, although the translation is certainly competent, and a brief form of the English version of the FTA has been validated in an English-speaking sample (von der Embse et al., 2013). Another, more significant disadvantage of the FTA is that there are no norms for it. Friedman and Bendas-Jacob's (1997) article does not provide means or standard deviations for the scores of the students in the development samples. Therefore, while it is possible to compare students to each other on the FTA, and it is possible to observe changes in test anxiety over time (e.g., before and after intervention) in the same student, a single measurement cannot be interpreted as indicating whether a particular student's level of test anxiety is above average. Of course, a school-based practitioner could still use the FTA as a screener and choose the students with the highest scores for more detailed assessment and potential intervention. Moreover, the scores for individual items can be interpreted directly as showing, for instance, that a student found an item about their "heart pounding strongly" during an important test to be a perfect description of their experience.

Westside Test Anxiety Scale

Many clinicians like to use Driscoll's (2007) Westside Test Anxiety Scale (WTAS), an open-source, 10-item scale. Although the scale is brief, the content of its items ranges widely, covering the periods before, during, and after tests. The focus of the content is on worry and cognitive interference: experiences of difficulty concentrating, worrying about performance, and only remembering the answers to questions after an exam is over. A sample item is "During important exams, I think that I am doing awful or that I may fail." Driscoll explicitly did not include items concerning physiological arousal. Each item is rated on a five-point scale ranging from 1 ("not at all or never true") to 5 ("extremely or always true").

The WTAS generates a single composite score, which is the simple average (mean) of the 10 item responses. Driscoll (2007) offered guidelines for interpreting the composite score as follows:

1.0–1.9	Comfortably low test anxiety
2.0–2.5	Normal or average test anxiety
2.5–2.9	High normal test anxiety
3.0–3.4	Moderately high (some items rated 4 = high)
3.5–3.9	High test anxiety (half or more of the items rated 4 = high)
4.0–5.0	Extremely high anxiety (items rated 4 = high and 5 = extreme)

However, although one range is described as "normal" or "average," Driscoll's (2007) paper never provides an actual average score for any sample. Nevertheless, there is some logic to the interpretation, in that (for instance) endorsing 10 statements about test anxiety as each being "extremely" or "always" true of oneself does seem to literally suggest "extremely high" levels of test anxiety.

---

[2] The Friedman and Bendas-Jacob (1997) article is not entirely clear on this point, but the researchers were working in Israel and mentioned needing to use Hebrew versions of other measures.

Driscoll (2007) did not report any reliability data, but Talwar et al. (2019) reported an internal consistency reliability coefficient of 0.88 for a sample of Malaysian college students. Driscoll's (2007) principal method for validating the WTAS was atypical; he reported that in samples of students who participated in test anxiety intervention programs, the students' degree of increase in academic test scores (pre vs. post intervention) correlated significantly with the reduction in their WTAS scores.

The WTAS's popularity likely derives from its brevity and its open access (free) nature. Even the paper where the items appear was deposited in an open access resource library that is now online, and readers are explicitly granted free access for personal or institutional usage. These are certainly advantages of the measure. One substantial disadvantage is the lack of coverage of physiological symptoms. Driscoll (2007) argued that he had deliberately left out this domain because it has been found to be less related to functional impairment (i.e., actual performance consequences). While this is strictly true, physiological symptoms can still cause considerable distress and are an appropriate focus of treatment, and hence, WTAS users should make sure to supplement the measure with other questionnaire or interview questions regarding physiological symptoms. A second disadvantage of the WTAS is the lack of norms for the measure.

Multidimensional Test Anxiety Scale

Recently, Putwain, von der Embse, et al. (2021) presented a new scale, the Multidimensional Test Anxiety Scale (MTAS). As its name suggests, it has several dimensions (four, in fact), which we list below with a sample item from each:

1. Worry (W): "Before a test/exam, I am worried I will fail."
2. Cognitive Interference (CI): "I forget facts I have learnt during tests/exams."
3. Tension (T): "Just before I take a test/exam, I feel panicky."
4. Physiological Indicators (PI): "My hand shakes while I am taking a test/exam."

Each dimension is measured with four items, for a total of 16 items. Students respond to each item on a five-point scale, where 1 means "strongly disagree" and 5 means "strongly agree." Putwain et al. (2021) noted that the Worry and Cognitive Interference dimensions are both essentially "cognitive" in nature, whereas the Tension and Physiological Indicators dimensions are both "affective/physiological." To choose these dimensions, the researchers made a remarkably thorough analysis of all of the existing theoretical models and scales for test anxiety. Putwain et al. (2021) reported considering adding items about behavioral signs of test anxiety (e.g., playing with one's pencil during a test) but noted that these behaviors are not specific to anxiety, and hence decided against including them. Similarly, they argued against measuring tendencies toward avoidance of evaluative situations because this could be viewed as a personality *antecedent* to test anxiety and not part of test anxiety itself.

Putwain et al. (2021) reported good internal consistency reliability of MTAS scores; McDonald's omega was 0.91 for the total scale score and between 0.80 and 0.87 for each of the four dimension scores. Test–retest reliability was relatively impressive for a four-month test–retest interval: 0.80 for the total scale score and between 0.65 and 0.82 for the dimension scores. Concurrent validity was established against the TAI, with MTAS-TAI correlations being quite strong, especially for subscores that are more conceptually related (e.g., the MTAS Worry score and the TAI Worry score). Factor analytic evidence supports the scale's validity as well. Finally, the cognitive dimensions of the MTAS were consistently found to predict lower scores on major exams.

The MTAS has been published in full, along with norms. Putwain et al.'s (2021) article contains the items, and the electronic supplemental material for the article has norms with percentile ranks and z-scores for male and female students aged 11 to 18. These are significant advantages. The lack of coverage of certain features of test anxiety, while deliberate, may be considered a disadvantage.

Other Rating Scales

We have focused our review on several published instruments that have relatively broad coverage of different test anxiety symptoms and that were designed for the age range—adolescents and young adults—for which our intervention program is designed. Here, we briefly note a few other scales that may be of use to clinicians:

1. The Children's Test Anxiety Scale (CTAS; Wren & Benson, 2004) was developed on a somewhat younger sample (children in grades 3 through 6) and has 25 items covering three dimensions. The "Thoughts" subscale covers worries, but also other types of negative thoughts, and some are quite specific (e.g., "I think that I should have studied more"). The "Autonomic Reactions" subscale covers familiar physiological symptoms. The final dimension, "Off-Task Behaviors," is not addressed well by other test anxiety scales, and consists of several behaviors that an anxious student may engage in during a test (e.g., checking the time, looking at other people). Wren and Benson's (2004) article lists all items, but there are no detailed norms.

2. The Cognitive Test Anxiety Scale (Cassady & Johnson, 2002), which has been widely used in research studies, was developed to focus on "the tendency to engage in task-irrelevant thinking during test-taking and preparation periods, the tendency to draw comparisons to others during test-taking and preparation periods, and the likelihood to have either intruding thoughts during exams and study sessions or relevant cues escape the learner's attention during testing" (Cassady & Johnson, 2002, p. 277). Therefore, the authors did not include any items measuring physiological symptoms. The resulting scale has 27 items that only yield a single, total score. Cassady and Johnson's (2002) article lists all items in an appendix, but there are no norms.

3. The Adult Manifest Anxiety Scale (AMAS; Reynolds et al., 2003) is worth noting because its college version (the AMAS-C) has a subscale devoted to test anxiety. Clinicians who are assessing a college student can administer this measure and get a separate score for test anxiety. The scale's norms allow for T-scores that indicate whether a student's test anxiety level is above average. The AMAS-C has a total of 49 items, 15 of which concern test anxiety. Most of those 15 items are fairly general

in referring to test anxiety without differentiating symptom types, but a few items mention specific cognitive or physiological symptoms. The AMAS is available for purchase from *www.mindmuzik.com*.

RATINGS OF SELF-EFFICACY

As we discuss throughout this book, effective management of test anxiety begins with students' understanding that they can still participate, and even do well on tests, when they are anxious. In some cases, therapy may not substantially reduce anxiety per se, but it will raise the student's confidence that they can perform in the face of anxiety. This confidence is a type of *self-efficacy*. As Bandura (1982) noted, our perception of our own efficacy affects the effort that we put forth and the emotions that we feel in response to challenging situations. Thus, self-efficacy should be measured separately from symptoms. Self-efficacy can be assessed in an interview (see below), but a rating scale can be constructed as well. Because self-efficacy is specific to a particular set of behaviors, Bandura (2006) warned against "one size fits all" efficacy scales and suggested that researchers instead create domain-specific scales regarding the particular behaviors that they are studying. The same logic holds true for clinicians assessing self-efficacy in applied practice.

Bandura (2006) offered further advice for creating self-efficacy scales:

- Items should inquire about respondents' belief that they *can* do something, rather than their *intentions* to do something.
- Writing items requires detailed knowledge of the domain of behavior under study. (The implication for test anxiety is that the items should be tailored to the types of tests that particular students take.)
- Items should represent a range of difficulty levels. (You will want to assess students' belief in their ability to perform easy tasks as well as hard ones.)

Finally, Bandura suggested that the instructions for self-efficacy scales ask respondents to rate their *confidence* that they can do various activities at the present moment, using a scale from 0 ("cannot do at all") to 100 ("highly certain can do").

Given this expert advice, we have developed and used a wide variety of self-efficacy items. For example, we have asked students about their confidence that they can perform these highly specific behaviors:

- Solving math problems even though your heart is racing.
- Finishing the essay questions on your history test.
- Staying focused on answering the exam questions instead of thinking too much about the amount of time you have left.
- Showing what you know on a test and getting an accurate score.
- Testing yourself with flash cards the day before an exam, until you are able to get the information consistently correct.

When we deliver test anxiety treatment in a group format, it is typically done with a small group of students who are in similar settings or dealing with relatively similar test demands. In this case, we may make items that are a bit more general or else make a longer list of specific items based on information we learn from the group during the first session, which focuses on students' goals for treatment.

One final point: when assessing self-efficacy we do *not* include items asking about students' confidence in their ability to not have anxiety symptoms. Self-efficacy is ultimately about voluntary behaviors over which we can acquire control, and central to our therapy approach is that students may not always be able to control anxiety itself, but can learn to control what they do in the face of anxiety. Similarly, we do not include items about particular test performance outcomes (e.g., getting an A on a math test) because this too may not be fully under the student's control.

THE SEMISTRUCTURED INTERVIEW

Beyond the formal instruments reviewed above, an interview can capture additional details regarding symptoms and self-efficacy. We typically open the interview by determining the principal complaint, or the primary reason for seeking help. This information indicates where to focus to give the student the greatest chance of reaching their goals. It can also give us a sense of whether a student has realistic expectations for therapy; for instance, "I need to raise my SAT score by 200 points" is not a goal that test anxiety therapy is designed to accomplish, at least not in the most efficient way!

We then assess symptoms and self-efficacy. If the student has already completed the types of formal measures mentioned above, this can be done in a condensed manner, with a focus on the areas of concern that were already endorsed. Otherwise, start by asking about different symptom areas and self-efficacy (see Table 3.3 for a guide). Either way, we try to react to reports of symptoms and low self-efficacy in a sympathetic but matter-of-fact way that communicates that we have seen many similar cases and that test anxiety is a common problem. When students show a bit of good-natured humor when reporting what they take to be extreme symptoms, we try to reinforce that, while also conveying compassion for their experiences.

After reviewing symptoms and self-efficacy, we inquire about studying and test-taking behaviors. "How do you usually study for tests?" is sometimes too general and vague to elicit a clear answer, and so we follow up with "It might depend on the class that you're studying for." Sometimes we need to probe for more detailed responses: Do you study alone or with other people? Do you reread textbooks or other assigned readings, or use test prep manuals? Do you reread your class notes? Do you ever recopy class notes? Do you highlight or underline text from assigned readings when you're studying for a test? Do you use flash cards or anything like that? Many students, particularly younger ones, will give one-word answers (yes or no) to such questions, but respond well to a subsequent "Could you tell me more about that? What does that look like? What exactly do you do?" The goal in asking these questions is to determine how a student tends to prepare for the tests that they are most anxious about performance on.

TABLE 3.3. Sample Interview Prompts about Test-Anxiety Symptoms and Self-Efficacy

1. When you're taking a test, what is your body doing? Does your body feel anxious? How can you tell?
2. When do those things usually start? After the test starts? Or earlier in the day? Maybe even earlier, when you're studying? What is it like?
3. What about after the test is over with? Does your body calm down?
4. Do you get worried before taking a test? What are those worries like? What kinds of thoughts are you having?
5. Do those worries continue during the test itself? Are you ever thinking about those worries instead of working on the test items? Do any other kinds of thoughts tend to happen during the test?
6. After the test is over, what happens? Do the worries and negative thoughts stop, or do they continue? Are they different thoughts or worries at that point?
7. In the lead-up to the test, do you ever find yourself avoiding studying? Distracting yourself from thinking about the test? What does that look like?
8. During the test, do you ever skip items, stop working on them, or not check your work because you just don't want to think about that material?
9. How confident are you that you can remember information that you need for your tests when you're anxious? What has your experience been like there?
10. How confident are you that you can solve problems on math tests when you're anxious? What tends to happen on math tests when you're anxious?

Relatedly, we ask about the student's test-taking process. Here, we try to determine if the student is a strategic, thoughtful test taker who uses executive skills to plan, organize, and then execute an approach to taking tests. Some students will be puzzled by the questions, "How do you take tests? What is your strategy?" That puzzlement is itself an important piece of information about the student. Other students will describe strategies: looking through an entire classroom test as soon as it is received, or flagging items that are harder so as not to waste time on them before completing the rest of the exam. Occasionally, students will describe *bad* strategies that can then be addressed in therapy (e.g., *not* reviewing answers because of a belief that a test taker should always go with their first instinct).

The final core part of test anxiety assessment involves the student's actual performance history. For a typical high school or college student, asking about GPA and grades in classes as well as scores on individual tests is helpful. Where appropriate, ask to see records. High school students can easily bring (or send) in report cards, and college students often just pull up their transcript on their phone; in only 30 seconds, we can learn a lot from reviewing it. In many cases, students can access their specific test scores in learning management software (e.g., Blackboard, Canvas, Moodle, etc.) that they have access to at all times. Look out for students who describe their test performance as impaired, when in fact the performance is quite good. Such students may really be describing how hard they believe they are working, how much distress they feel about tests or school, and so forth. Again, this is useful information, but it should not be confused with evidence of actual poor performance, and it points toward a different balance of treatment strategies.

As we mentioned above, a more general history and psychological screening can be helpful, and we tend to leave this for the end of individual intake interviews. At this point, we ask about prior formal diagnoses of psychiatric problems such as anxiety or mood disorders, as well as neurodevelopmental disorders (such as learning disabilities and ADHD) that are associated with higher levels of test anxiety. We ask about the student's history of special education or accommodation supports, particularly in recent years. And if we see evidence of severe distress in someone who has not seen a mental health professional in recent years, we sometimes conduct our own screening of relevant disorders, asking one or two screening questions each about several common disorders: generalized anxiety disorder, social anxiety disorder, panic disorder, major depressive disorder, and obsessive–compulsive disorder. (Practitioners who are working in learning support settings in schools or who lack general training in psychological assessment would generally not conduct that screening.)

TEST ANXIETY AND CLINICAL ANXIETY DISORDERS

As we discussed in Chapter 1, test anxiety symptoms can be severe, and the extreme distress that some students feel leads many people to think of test anxiety as a disorder. However, test anxiety is not mentioned in the current version of the *Diagnostic and Statistical Manual of Mental Disorders* (the DSM-5; American Psychiatric Association, 2013), nor is it listed as a disorder in the *International Statistical Classification of Diseases and Related Health Problems* (formerly the *International Classification of Diseases*, the ICD). Can test anxiety nonetheless be diagnosed clinically? The short answer is "no." Test anxiety is not a recognized disorder *per se*, and most test-anxious students will not meet the full criteria for any official anxiety disorders. However, as we discuss below, there will be cases where some kind of diagnosis is justified. Before comparing test anxiety to specific clinical disorders, we consider why it is not listed as its own disorder.

When the DSM-IV (American Psychiatric Association, 1994) was being developed, the working group studying anxiety disorders considered test anxiety for inclusion as a recognized type of social anxiety disorder. The group concluded that the criteria would be too subjective, and the diagnostic category too capacious, capturing an estimated 40% of the population (see Bögels et al., 2010). When experts convened to develop the DSM-5, one group considered including test anxiety as a type of specific phobia, but concluded, after a review of the empirical literature, that there was insufficient research supporting test anxiety as a clinical syndrome at all (LeBeau et al., 2010). At present, test anxiety is not even mentioned in diagnostic manuals. But is this appropriate? Neither subjectivity nor high prevalence are necessarily barriers toward defining a clinical syndrome. All symptoms that are internal experiences (such as emotions) are, in a sense, subjective, and specific symptoms of some other disorders also occur in high proportions of the population (see, e.g., Lewandowski et al., 2008). One team of researchers (Herzer et al., 2014) sought to identify a threshold at which test anxiety would go from typical, "nonclinical" levels to a "clinical manifestation." These researchers used an expanded version of the TAI (see above) and found a minimum threshold score that almost all of a clinically referred group of test-anxious college students would meet, while also excluding all members of a non-clinical comparison group. It was certainly interesting that such a score could be found, but the result seems to beg the question of whether the clinically referred group actually had a disorder. In any case, this was a single study with a small sample of participants, and there is currently no consensus cutoff at which point test anxiety symptoms become "clinical." Because test anxiety is not in any psychiatric classification system, there is no number or intensity of symptoms that a clinician can reference to justify a "diagnosis" of test anxiety.

Ultimately, the decision to classify a group of symptoms as a disorder reflects, in part, the personal values of the classifiers (Wakefield, 1992), and it seems that test anxiety has generally been viewed as a less serious educational problem rather than a clinical disorder. Nonetheless, clinicians have sometimes sought to use existing diagnostic categories to cover test anxiety. Below we discuss the relationship between test anxiety and the more common anxiety-related disorders.

Test Anxiety and Generalized Anxiety Disorder

The hallmark of generalized anxiety disorder (GAD; F41.1[3]) is excessive, uncontrollable worry. As we saw in Chapter 1, worries are a typical, core area of test anxiety, but the obvious difference between test anxiety and GAD is that in the latter, worries are not about a single activity such as test taking, or even a single area of life such as academic functioning. Of course, students who have GAD will often have test anxiety (Manassis, 2012)—indeed, it would be unusual for them not to! Nonetheless, sophisticated analyses of relationships between different anxiety symptoms show test anxiety to be statistically distinct from GAD symptoms (Putwain, Stockinger, et al., 2021), and test anxiety would not itself constitute GAD, even if the test anxiety is severe.

Test Anxiety and Panic Disorder

A better fit might seem to exist between test anxiety and panic disorder (F41.0). After all, physiological symptoms of test anxiety are common, and it is not unusual for students to report having "panic attacks" before or during tests. However, there are two problems with equating test anxiety and panic disorder. First, panic disorder does require panic attacks, and despite the language that students sometimes use, their episodes of anxiety generally do not constitute true panic attacks. Technically, a panic attack requires *several* simultaneous symptoms from a list of mostly physiological experiences (e.g., sweating, feelings of choking), and the symptoms are so severe that people having a true panic attack often believe themselves to be in serious danger of dying (fear of dying is actually one of the other symptoms on the list). Panic attacks are also noticeably discrete episodes; even if they occur against an already-present state of anxiety, they involve "an abrupt surge of fear or intense discomfort" that peaks fairly quickly (American Psychiatric Association, 2013, p. 214).

The second problem with diagnosing test-anxious students with panic disorder is that panic disorder does not merely require panic attacks. The attacks must also be *unexpected*, in the sense that there is no obvious anxiety-provoking stimulus (such as a test) present. People with panic disorder will have at least some of their panic attacks at what seem to be random times—for instance, during what are supposed to be relaxing leisure activities. To meet diagnostic criteria, they must also develop a fear of having the panic attacks, leading

---

[3] Consistent with the DSM-5-TR (American Psychiatric Association, 2022), we only report ICD codes.

to either persistent concern about attacks or else problematic behavioral changes designed to prevent future attacks. In our experience, test-anxious students rarely meet the criteria for panic disorder.

Test Anxiety and Social Anxiety Disorder

Social anxiety disorder (F40.10) is another superficially attractive diagnosis to apply to test-anxious students. Certainly, the core of social anxiety disorder is a fear of evaluation by others, and tests are tools of evaluation. The DSM-IV (American Psychiatric Association, 1994) had mentioned that patients with social anxiety disorder often fear test taking, but did not include test anxiety as a subtype of the disorder, or claim that test anxiety would be sufficient to meet criteria for the disorder. Upon closer inspection, test anxiety and social anxiety disorder have two notable differences. First, in social anxiety disorder, the individual must fear that others will see their anxiety, and most academic situations do not lead to easily *observable* symptoms of anxiety. The exceptions are tests that involve public performances: oral tests (especially in front of peers), working out math problems on a chalkboard, and so forth. Unsurprisingly, then, the available research has found that anxiety for oral tests is distinct from anxiety for written tests (Sparfeldt et al., 2013), and symptoms of social anxiety only correlate with anxiety for oral tests (Laurin-Barantke et al., 2016).

Another difference between test anxiety and a typical case of social anxiety disorder is that the latter usually involves more than just a single situation such as test taking. Even though the criteria for the disorder permit diagnosis in single-situation cases, children and adolescents with social anxiety disorder usually have severe trouble with many types of everyday peer interactions, well outside the academic or testing realms (Ryan & Warner, 2012). Students who meet criteria for social anxiety disorder often have a baseline of anxiety throughout the school day, but tests do not reliably further increase anxiety in these students; other situations—sometimes, surprising ones such as eating in public in the lunchroom—actually seem to generate more anxiety.

Test Anxiety and Specific Phobia

Since other anxiety disorders involve symptoms that are too general or pervasive to capture most cases of test anxiety, the specific phobia diagnosis (the situational type; F40.248) seems like a better alternative. We have, in fact, seen cases of test anxiety that meet the full criteria for a specific phobia. In such cases, almost all tests lead to intense anxiety, even when the tests do not have significant consequences for the student (e.g., school accountability tests, quizzes that have minimal effects on the student's grade, and even practice tests). These students also typically try very hard to avoid or escape testing situations. As with most genuine specific phobias, this is more common in younger students who lack the cognitive maturity to differentiate between tests that are higher and lower stakes, and lack the self-regulatory skill to view test taking as instrumental for achieving long-term goals. Nevertheless, these are genuine cases of a specific phobia of tests.

More often, test anxiety does not meet the criteria for specific phobia. Most test-anxious students feel varying levels of anxiety depending on the subject area, teacher, test type, and other factors such as stakes/consequences, feeling relatively little anxiety at times. These students can still benefit considerably from intervention, but they do not have a clinical disorder.

Test Anxiety and Obsessive–Compulsive Disorder

Finally, although obsessive–compulsive disorder (OCD; F42) is no longer classified as an anxiety disorder in the DSM-5, it typically involves anxiety in reaction to obsessions (unwanted mental content) and/or as a driver of compulsions (repetitive behaviors that the individual feels compelled to perform). A possible connection between OCD and test anxiety had been noted by a group of experts preparing recommendations for DSM-5 (Bögels et al., 2010), and we have seen test anxiety present as a part of cases of OCD. Often, OCD involves an organized system of related obsessions and compulsions, and in the cases that we have seen, the most common symptoms reported are obsessive thoughts of having made mistakes on the test, and corresponding compulsions to check one's work. The symptoms tend to increase in proportion to the chance for errors. For instance, indicating answers to test questions on a Scantron ("bubble") sheet introduces more possibility for errors, and leads to an even stronger urge to compulsively check and recheck one's answers. In cases of genuine OCD, the compulsive behaviors only provide modest and transient reassurance, if any, and so the individual repeats them over and over again in the vain hope of finally obtaining some lasting relief. On tests, this presents as the student reporting "running out of time," since there will never be enough time to infinitely recheck work. However, "running out of time" is often a misleading description of the situation, because the student's productive work finished long ago, and additional time would be unlikely to uncover correctable errors and yield higher test performance.

Although it is helpful to understand how test anxiety presents in cases of OCD, test anxiety is very unlikely to meet the definition of OCD on its own. Students who have OCD generally exhibit checking compulsions outside of test situations as well, or at least have intrusive thoughts or images of negative outcomes. These students present with a fairly general tendency to engage in ritualistic behaviors designed to reduce worries about a variety of potential negative outcomes. Therefore, test anxiety is not generally a form of OCD.

Implications for Diagnostic Documentation

Practitioners working in educational settings generally do not need to be as concerned with formal diagnosis before providing treatment, whereas those in clinical settings may need to document that the criteria for a recognized disorder are met. This is particularly likely when students are using health insurance to pay for treatment.

If a student does meet the full criteria for a recognized disorder reviewed above, usually through having symptoms that go beyond test anxiety, it is easy enough to diagnose that disorder, and document that test anxiety is one manifestation of the disorder. If this is not the case, clinicians may want to consider other labels:

- Other Specified Anxiety Disorder (F41.8). This label is reserved for any problem "in which symptoms characteristic of an anxiety disorder that cause clinically significant distress or impairment…predominate but do not meet the full criteria for any of the disorders in the anxiety disorders diagnostic class" (American Psychiatric Association, 2013, p. 233). Whether the student's test anxiety symptoms are actually "characteristic of an anxiety disorder" is a judgment left to the clinician, and this is difficult to either justify or dispute. However, if this code is used, the clinician should specify "test anxiety" and provide a description of the symptoms. Officially, the clinician is also expected to explain why "the presentation does not meet the criteria for any specific anxiety disorder."

- Unspecified Anxiety Disorder (F41.9). This label is used similarly to Other Specified Anxiety Disorder, except that for whatever reason, the clinician does not wish to provide further description or explanation of the student's presentation.
- Adjustment Disorder With Anxiety (F43.22) or with Mixed Anxiety and Depressed Mood (F43.23). Often, test anxiety presents in a new situation, such as when a student moves to a new level of education, otherwise switches schools, or needs to prepare for a major exam for a high-stakes purpose (e.g., admissions, employment, or certification). In these cases, *if* the student's symptoms rise to the general level of an adjustment disorder—unreasonable distress or significant impairment in reaction to an identifiable stressor—these diagnoses should be considered.
- Academic or Educational Program (Z55.9). This code is technically not for a disorder but for an "other condition that may be a focus of clinical attention." It would include school- or exam-related difficulties that do not rise to the level of a disorder. Note that if this is the *only* label applied, health insurance may not reimburse for care.

TEST ANXIETY AS A DISABILITY CONDITION

In recent years, an increasing number of students have sought testing accommodations, such as extra time or a private testing room, on the basis of test anxiety (e.g., Daniel, 2020). Therefore, we discuss the legal framework for disability status and the clinical advantages and disadvantages of accommodations.[4]

The disability discrimination laws in the United States are similar to those of many other countries. In the U.S., there are two primary such laws (Yell, 2019). Students at public K-12 schools, some private K-12 schools, and almost all colleges (public or private) are protected by Section 504 of the Rehabilitation Act. Technically, Section 504 applies to all entities that receive funding from the federal government. The Americans with Disabilities Act (ADA) applies to these entities as well as all others, including all private schools and all testing agencies (the companies that administer standardized tests for admissions, certification, and licensure). In educational settings, these laws can lead to an accommodation plan (a 504 plan, where relevant). On standardized tests, there is no "plan" per se, but applicants can be approved to receive accommodations, and this is documented in writing, typically through a formal letter or e-mail from a testing agency.

---

[4] Nothing in this book should be construed as professional legal advice, and readers are referred to a licensed attorney for such advice.

Is Test Anxiety a Disability?

Both Section 504 and ADA use the same definition of disability: a physical or mental impairment causing a substantial limitation in one or more major life activities (Yell, 2019). The "substantial limitation" is assessed relative to the average person in the general population. The "major life activities" include learning, thinking, concentrating, and reading, and no exhaustive list is provided in the law. This definition of disability raises the question: does test anxiety constitute a disability under the law? Lovett and Nelson (2017) provided a recent analysis of this issue, and here we update and expand that analysis.

An "impairment" generally refers to a recognized disorder or a dysfunction of a body system. As we discussed above, test anxiety is not, by itself, a recognized disorder, and we would not describe it as a dysfunction of a body system either. However, if the test anxiety comes as part of a recognized disorder (e.g., GAD), this threshold would be met. Even then, does the disorder cause a substantial limitation in a major life activity? Courts have disagreed about whether "test taking" is itself a major life activity, and as we discussed in Chapter 2, test anxiety does not generally impair test taking in a direct manner. Whether it substantially limits another activity such as concentrating or reading is a judgment that must be made for each individual student. The judgment should be made based on objective evidence rather than subjective self-reporting. Objective evidence might include data from diagnostic performance testing, real world records of test performance under different conditions, and clinician observations of mental status.

Are Accommodations Appropriate?

Testing accommodations alter the way that a test is administered without changing the content of the test (Lovett & Lewandowski, 2015). Accommodations can alter the timing or scheduling of a test (e.g., providing additional time or breaks), the setting in which the test is administered (e.g., providing a private room), the way in which the test is presented (e.g., reading test items aloud to the student), or the way in which the student is permitted to respond to test items (e.g., providing a laptop computer rather than requiring handwritten answers).

Disability discrimination laws such as Section 504 and ADA ensure that students with disabilities have *access* to tests, and access can be described as the ability to participate in tests and obtain an accurate score. Testing accommodations originated in cases where it was clear that a student needed some kind of adjustment for access—for instance, a blind student needing an audio version of a U.S. History test. In the case of anxiety, this is far less clear. Students who have anxiety often seek accommodations that nondisabled students also report wanting (Lewandowski et al., 2014). Moreover, as we discussed above, anxiety tends to be accompanied by low self-efficacy. Anxious individuals think they cannot do things that they in fact *can* do, and hence, when anxious students report what they feel they *need* to access a test, they may be honest but inaccurate in their self-assessment. Test anxiety can cause discomfort and even distress during tests, but this does not mean that the student will not be able to access tests. As we discussed in Chapter 2, and as we emphasize throughout our treatment program, students can be anxious during a test and still do well, and the vast majority of the students in our treatment program have at least sometimes obtained good test scores while anxious. Since comfort is—while desirable—not strictly needed for access, accommodations are usually not truly *needed* either.

Worse still, accommodations can actually backfire in their effects, interfering with evidence-based treatment and reinforcing students' low self-efficacy. In a recent review article, Kagan et al. (2017) were quite direct about the dangers of accommodating anxiety:

> It is clear that, despite the widespread societal belief that accommodations are desirable, this is not always the case for youth with OCD and anxiety. Unlike a wheelchair ramp provided for individuals with physical handicaps, unconditional accommodations in the context of anxiety deny the child the opportunity to encounter the feared situation. Rather than promoting increased independence and functioning, such accommodations prevent youth from improving their functioning. (p. 92)

Not all accommodations for anxiety are bad, but when done to reduce anxiety, it is easy for well-intentioned accommodations to enable avoidance—a process that tends to *increase* anxiety in the long term. Unfortunately, in a recent study of the school-based supports of students with anxiety disorders, Phillips et al. (2022) found that of the top five recommended supports, three had significant potential to promote avoidance: (a) reducing the amount of required work for the student, (b) allowing students to complete tests or other work in a separate room, and (c) providing additional time on tests or other work.

Two other top-recommended supports identified by Phillips et al. (2022) did not promote avoidance: clarifying instructions and providing reminders. Clarifying instructions and providing reminders are certainly accommodations that can be provided on tests, though it is telling that these accommodations are far less common than extended time and separate room accommodations (see, e.g., Government Accountability Office, 2022). A third accommodation that we recommend in some cases is breaks during tests, specifically to give the student time to use anxiety-management strategies that they are learning as part of counseling or psychotherapy. Even this accommodation is one that we try to recommend as temporary, with the goal of transitioning the student to take tests in the same manner as their peers.

As readers can likely infer from this discussion, we recommend strong caution before claiming that test anxiety (even as part of a recognized disorder) meets the threshold for a disability condition under Section 504 or ADA. Moreover, even in the rare case that it does, practitioners should apply the same caution toward recommending accommodations. If a student is doing well on tests without accommodations, then the student is accessing the tests, even if they are experiencing significant (and treatable) discomfort. Even in cases where test performance is lower, it is crucial that practitioners ensure any recommended accommodations do not promote avoidance. Enabling avoidance runs counter to the treatment philosophy and procedures that we discuss in the rest of the book, and can only reduce the efficacy of this treatment.

A Psychometrics Primer

Published assessment tools, such as cognitive tests and structured questionnaires, typically yield numerical scores, like an IQ score of 110. Test anxiety measures are no exception. Items on a test anxiety scale may ask a student to rate the frequency with which they experience a symptom (e.g., a racing heart) on a 1–5 spectrum, with "1" meaning "never" and "5" meaning "almost always." If a student obtains a score of 30 on a self-report scale of test anxiety symptoms, is that high or low? Moreover, is that a trustworthy score—can it be relied on? *Psychometrics* is the science behind such assessment tools, and here we provide a very brief primer on psychometric features (for more details, see Lovett, 2023).

INTERPRETING TEST SCORES

Generally, test anxiety scales are constructed so that higher scores indicate more severe symptoms. On some measures, only *raw scores* are available; these are often computed by simply adding up a student's numerical response to each of the items. By looking at the response options, you may be able to determine if a student's raw score suggests high or low test anxiety levels. However, raw scores cannot be used to determine if a particular student has higher or lower test anxiety than what is typical. In contrast, *norm-referenced scores* allow such an interpretation. There are a few common types of norm-referenced scores found on test anxiety measures:

- *Percentile ranks* (also known as *percentiles*) indicate the proportion of the population that the student's score exceeds. A score at the 88th percentile would indicate test anxiety levels higher than 88% of people in the population. The average person is, by definition, at the 50th percentile.

- *T-scores* also define 50 to be the average, but almost everyone has a *T*-score between 20 and 80. Scores between 40 and 60 would constitute a rough average range, and students with *T*-scores over 65 or 70 have clinically significant levels of a problem.
- Finally, *z-scores* define 0 as the average score, so negative *z*-scores (scores below 0) indicate below-average scores, and positive *z*-scores indicate above-average scores. Here, scores between −1 and 1 are roughly the average range, and scores above 1.5 or 2 would suggest clinically elevated levels of a problem.

RELIABILITY OF SCORES

Reliability is the degree to which a test score is dependable, stable, and consistent. One type of reliability is *internal consistency*—the degree to which all of the items on a scale are measuring the same trait. Getting a single, total score from a test anxiety scale suggests that all of the items are measuring the same thing (test anxiety), and internal consistency is the degree to which someone tends to give similar responses to all of the items on the scale. If a scale with 10 items asks about 10 different symptoms of anxiety, and people who report having one symptom are more likely to report having all of the other symptoms too, the scale will have greater internal consistency.

Another type of reliability is *test–retest reliability* or *stability*. Because test anxiety is thought of as a stable trait, students who obtain high scores on a test anxiety scale should generally continue to obtain high scores if asked to complete the same scale again, several weeks or months later. Test–retest reliability is the degree to which students' scores obtained at one point in time predict their scores obtained at a later point in time as well.

Reliability is typically quantified using a *reliability coefficient* that varies between 0 (no reliability) and 1 (perfect reliability). As you can see, higher coefficients are generally better. There are several statistics used for internal consistency, including Cronbach's alpha, coefficient omega, and the "split-half" coefficient. They are calculated in slightly different ways, but they have roughly the same meaning. Internal consistency values of 0.80 or above are generally desirable.

Test–retest reliability is usually interpreted through a *correlation coefficient* (*r*); although this statistic can vary between −1 and 1, test–retest reliability coefficients are almost always positive (between 0 and 1). Here, 0 would indicate no relationship at all between students' scores at two points in time (a student's score at the first point in time does not allow you to predict their score at the second time point at all), whereas a correlation coefficient of 1 would suggest a perfect relationship (e.g., the student with the highest score at time point 1 must also have the highest score at time point 2). For test–retest reliability, coefficients of 0.70 are generally desirable, particularly over shorter intervals of time (e.g., two time points that are a week apart).

One final point: many test anxiety scales yield more than one score. For instance, a comprehensive test anxiety symptom scale may have separate *subscales* for physiological and for cognitive symptoms, each with its own score. Each score has a separate reliability value; some scores from a scale may be less reliable than others. Generally, you should focus your interpretation on the most reliable scores.

VALIDITY IN SCORE INTERPRETATION

Imagine that you are told that a "test anxiety scale" has reliability coefficients of 0.90 and above, but when you look at the items on the scale, they are all about the student's level of extraversion rather than their symptoms of test anxiety. This scale would be reliable, but it does not appear to be *valid*. A valid scale, by definition, measures what it claims to measure.

There are several types of evidence that are used to judge the validity of scales. First, *content validity* evidence shows whether the content of the scale items corresponds to the generally accepted understanding of the trait that the scale is designed to measure. For a test anxiety scale, experts in test anxiety might be asked to rate the relevance of each item, to determine the scale's content validity, or the test developers might start by reviewing the research literature on test anxiety to make a complete list of all reported symptoms to ensure that their scale isn't leaving any entire areas of symptoms out.

Another type of validity evidence is based on statistical relationships between a new scale and already accepted scales of similar traits. Scores on a new test anxiety scale should show high correlations with other measures of test anxiety, and there should usually also be a significant correlation with established measures of similar traits such as math anxiety or general anxiety. Scale developers will use the correlation coefficient mentioned earlier to determine this.

A final common type of validity evidence comes from a sophisticated statistical procedure called *factor analysis*. Factor analysis can examine the relationships between all of the items on a test and identify which items show stronger and weaker relationships with each other. We would expect that, for instance, different physiological symptoms of test anxiety (e.g., a racing heart and a churning stomach) would show a stronger relationship with each other than a physiological symptom and a cognitive symptom would show with each other. Factor analysis can show this with quantitative precision and can help to justify the use of subscale scores (such as separate scores for physiological and cognitive symptoms).

CHAPTER 4

Intervention Research

Research on interventions for test anxiety has been underway for over half a century. Two systematic reviews (Soares & Woods, 2020; von der Embse et al., 2013) and four meta-analyses (Ergene, 2003; Hembree, 1988; Huntley et al., 2019; Robson et al., 2023) have appraised this literature. The main conclusion shared by the authors of these papers is that a variety of psychotherapeutic treatments, similar to those used for other anxiety problems, have proven helpful for reducing test anxiety in students at the elementary school, middle school, high school, and university levels. Moreover, group interventions appear to work at least as well as individually administered treatments, with some evidence suggesting that a combination of the two modalities may be most effective (Ergene, 2003). Research on the treatment of test anxiety through means other than psychotherapeutic techniques (e.g., pharmacology; Brewer, 1971) has been scant and is beyond our scope.

In this chapter, we will delineate the main types of intervention that have been tried and the level of empirical support for each type. Where possible, we will draw on meta-analytic findings to provide estimates of the magnitude of benefit, on average, for each kind of treatment (see Appendix 4.1: Effect Sizes). We will also describe specific examples of treatment studies to illustrate different intervention approaches. Finally, while noting limitations of the existing research, we will draw out implications for designing an evidence-based, modular, comprehensive test-anxiety treatment program.

Although the test-anxiety treatment literature has focused mostly on the effects of interventions on reducing test anxiety, we will also note effects on test performance or more general academic performance such as grades where applicable. Many students hope that test-anxiety treatment will help to boost their academic performance, and there is some evidence suggesting this as a possible outcome. We have emphasized in prior chapters that feeling nervous (i.e., physiological arousal) does not by itself exert major effects on test performance, but test-anxiety treatment may nonetheless improve students' performance to the extent that it may reduce distraction from worries (including worries about the impairing effects of anxiety), or it may cause students to adopt better study habits or more effective test-taking behaviors. Indeed, many well-supported test-anxiety treatment packages include direct instruction in study skills and/or test-taking skills, with the rationale that one good way to help students feel more at ease with testing is to boost their actual competence at preparing for and taking tests.

TREATMENT TYPES

Reappraising Test Anxiety

By necessity, most test-anxiety interventions have included at least some education about test anxiety. For example, basic information about the physiology of anxiety is helpful when communicating the rationale for a relaxation-based treatment. But some recent interventions have chosen to specifically target the way that students *think* about test anxiety. In one study, 93 students in remedial math classes at a community college were randomly assigned to either a control condition or the treatment, in which they read brief summaries of scientific articles about how their test anxiety was healthy rather than threatening (Jamieson et al., 2016). They learned about how various aspects of the stress response, such as an increased heart rate, can be useful for dealing with environmental demands (e.g., by increasing blood flow to the brain). Students in the treatment condition showed greater decreases in test anxiety compared to the control participants, with a medium effect size. Students in the treatment condition also showed improved math exam performance compared to control students, again with a medium effect size. This improvement was mediated by increases in students' perceptions of their ability to cope with stressful testing. Although the researchers did not investigate the mechanism of improved test performance in any finer grained detail than this, it's possible that when students perceived themselves as more capable even when anxious, they in turn demonstrated better test-taking behaviors, such as persisting longer in their efforts. Alternatively, they may have been less distracted by worries about their anxiety harming their performance and were thus able to focus more effectively on the exam.

In a study using an even more minimal intervention, 431 introductory psychology students at a selective private university were randomly assigned to a treatment or a control condition (Brady et al., 2018). The night before their first exam in the course, students in the treatment condition received an email that included a paragraph stating that research has revealed that anxious arousal during tests is normal, does not impair performance, and is not a cause for concern. For first-year students (but not older students), receiving this intervention led to reduced worrying during the exam (as measured by a questionnaire after the exam) and improved performance on the exam compared to control students, both with small-to-medium effect sizes. The authors posited that first-year students may have especially benefited from this kind of intervention because their newness to college exams may have made them more worried about the test, may have caused them to pay more attention to the email, or may have meant that their thoughts and behaviors around exams were more malleable.

Supplementing this specific research on stress reappraisal interventions for test anxiety is a high-quality set of large, double-blind, randomized controlled trials looking at anxiety symptoms more generally (Yeager et al., 2022). In this research, adolescents and university students completed an online training module that taught them that physiological signs of stress can be adaptive in performance situations and that engaging with challenging tasks can increase one's abilities. Afterward, compared to control students, these students reported decreased anxiety symptoms and greater well-being, showed lower physiological markers of chronic stress, and improved their academic performance. Other experimental research has indicated that reappraising anxiety as functional (e.g., telling yourself that you're "excited" when feeling performance anxiety) can improve performance in other domains where people worry about stress impairing them, such as public speaking and karaoke singing, in addition to academic testing (Brooks, 2014).

Exposure Therapy

The cornerstone of behavioral approaches to anxiety treatment involves deliberate *exposure* to anxiety-provoking situations or stimuli. For a century now (e.g., Jones, 1924), psychologists have used various techniques to carefully plan exposure experiences. While the specific techniques vary, they all involve facing one's fears directly in a sustained way, thereby developing a new association between the feared stimuli and a sense of safety, and perhaps a greater tolerance for anxious feelings when they do arise (Abramowitz et al., 2019). Behavioral interventions such as exposure therapy and relaxation procedures (see "Relaxing the Body" below) have been studied more extensively for test-anxiety treatment than any other techniques (Huntley et al., 2019), and there is robust research support for their efficacy, with meta-analyses indicating medium-to-large effect sizes on average (Ergene, 2003; Hembree, 1988; Huntley et al., 2019).

The most studied exposure-based treatment for test anxiety has been systematic desensitization. In systematic desensitization, students construct an *anxiety hierarchy*—a list of situations that are ordered sequentially from those that would cause only mild anxiety to those that would cause the most intense anxiety. Often, each situation is rated on a 1–10 or 1–100 scale in terms of how much distress it would cause (the Subjective Units of Distress Scale, or SUDS). In the case of test anxiety, a typical hierarchy (modified from Garlington & Cotler, 1968) might include the following situations:

- a teacher announcing the date of an upcoming test
- studying for a test
- being in bed the night before a test
- walking to class to take a test
- waiting for the test to be passed out to students in the class
- seeing a test question you don't know the answer to
- a pop quiz being announced in class

After constructing the hierarchy, students learn to self-induce deep calmness through a muscle relaxation procedure (see "Relaxing the Body" below). Then, they learn to visualize the situations from the hierarchy in their minds, basically learning to vividly simulate encounters with external stimuli in their imaginations (*imaginal exposure*). Finally, students systematically, sequentially visualize the fearful stimuli that are the targets of the anxiety treatment while simultaneously keeping themselves in a relaxed physiological state that isn't compatible with anxiety. Test-anxiety treatments using this method have tended to select for students very high in test anxiety and have been quite resource-intensive, typically involving 6–12 weekly or twice-weekly individual therapy sessions of at least 30 minutes duration. The majority of the sessions are spent doing imaginal exposure, working up the student's personal hierarchy of fearful situations related to test anxiety. Systematic desensitization has proven useful for reducing test anxiety in a wide variety of populations, such as American and Malaysian university students and Nigerian high school students (Egbochuku & Obodo, 2005; Garlington & Cotler, 1968; Rajiah & Saravanan, 2014).

Other exposure-based treatments for test anxiety have involved procedures that do not include any relaxation component, and these appear to be equally effective to systematic desensitization. For example, in one study, test-anxiety scores dropped just as much in undergraduate students assigned to an *implosive therapy* treatment as they did in students assigned to systematic desensitization (Smith & Nye, 1973). In the former condition, students skipped learning muscle relaxation and instead of gradually working up a hierarchy of feared situations, they immediately began with visualizing those cues that elicited the most extreme test anxiety for them.

Relaxing the Body

As described above, meta-analyses have indicated that behavioral treatments, including relaxation and exposure-based interventions, effectively reduce test anxiety, with medium-to-large effect sizes on average (Ergene, 2003; Hembree, 1988; Huntley et al., 2019). In the one meta-analysis that provided separate effect size estimates for relaxation and exposure treatments (with systematic desensitization representing the latter exclusively), the two types of behavioral intervention appeared comparably powerful for mitigating test anxiety (Hembree, 1988). Whereas exposure treatments involve repeatedly facing feared stimuli, including, in some cases, one's own fear response, relaxation treatments involve practicing tactics for calming the body, without any direct encounters with the feared stimuli (either visualized or in vivo) as part of the intervention.

Relaxation treatments for test anxiety have often included training in calm breathing and muscle relaxation. For example, in one study, 177 third-grade public school students were assigned to either a control condition or a relaxation condition (Larson et al., 2010). Those in the treatment condition practiced diaphragmatic breathing with visualization ("elevator breathing") for about 5 minutes, and a muscle relaxation sequence for about 8–10 minutes, in twice-weekly sessions for five weeks, and their scores on a self-report test-anxiety measure decreased significantly by the end of this training.

Some relaxation interventions have included biofeedback technology, with which students can observe real-time, objective data on their physiology (e.g., heart rate, muscle tension, body temperature) as they learn to modulate their relaxation versus stress responses. In one such study, 136 tenth-grade students were assigned to either a control condition or a treatment condition in which they trained twice a week for one semester using a biofeedback device (Bradley et al., 2010). Specifically, students received real-time feedback on their heart-rate variability while practicing an emotion regulation technique that involved activating positive emotions such as compassion. The intervention appeared to reduce Test Anxiety Inventory scores in students who had high test anxiety at baseline.

As with all test-anxiety treatment approaches, not every study has been uniformly supportive of relaxation training. For instance, in a study of 105 eleventh-grade students in the United Kingdom, participants were assigned to a relaxation treatment, a cognitive-behavioral therapy (CBT) treatment (see "Challenging Anxious Thinking" below), a combined treatment of both relaxation and CBT, or a control condition (Gregor, 2005). The treatments were delivered over five 45-minute sessions by a teacher and a psychologist. Even with this intensive approach, there was not a significant reduction on a self-report test-anxiety measure in any condition, although a teacher rating form indicated the greatest reduction in anxiety in students who completed the relaxation intervention. Of course, the relatively small number of students in each treatment condition makes it hard to infer much from statistically nonsignificant results, a point we will return to later in this chapter, when discussing limitations of the research literature in general.

Challenging Anxious Thinking

Interventions aimed at helping students challenge and change their anxious thoughts have typically been labeled as a type of CBT. Meta-analyses have indicated that CBT treatments may be about as effective for reducing test anxiety as behavioral treatments such as exposure therapy or relaxation training, with medium-to-large effect sizes on average (Ergene, 2003; Hembree, 1988; Huntley et al., 2019). However, this finding must be qualified in two important ways. First, there is a smaller body of evidence regarding CBT, compared to behavioral techniques, for treating test anxiety, and there is especially a paucity of evidence about how long any benefits from CBT for test anxiety may last (Huntley et al., 2019). Second, when providing effect size estimates for CBT interventions, meta-analyses have combined traditional thought-challenging approaches with treatments that instead focus on training of attention (see "Mindfulness Training" below). Therefore, as with the pooling of relaxation and exposure-based therapies under the single rubric of "behavioral" interventions in the test-anxiety treatment meta-analytic literature, it is challenging to determine the relative efficacy of challenging anxious thoughts versus training one's attention.

Some studies have used the classic cognitive therapy approach of teaching students to put their negative thoughts on trial, so to speak, by looking at the evidence supporting them versus the evidence supporting more positive, less anxious thoughts. Aaron Beck (1976) pioneered this technique, often known as *cognitive restructuring*. The CBT treatment in Gregor's (2005) study described above used this approach. In this traditional thought-challenging paradigm, students learn to question and discount catastrophic thoughts such as "I'm definitely going to fail this exam, since I couldn't answer all of the practice problems correctly" by considering, for example, past instances when they passed an exam despite imperfect preparation. They learn to replace such distorted anxious thoughts with more accurate ones. In our experience, many students with test anxiety do indeed seem to forget the many instances in which they have done well on tests, or otherwise exhibit patently irrational beliefs regarding tests, providing an intuitive foundation for this approach to therapy.

A limited amount of recent research has taken an approach to challenging anxious thinking that is less strictly adherent to the cognitive therapy tradition. In one study, 71 German university students who self-identified as struggling with test anxiety or procrastination problems were assigned to either a control or an "inquiry-based stress reduction" condition (Krispenz et al., 2019). This treatment involved a three-hour procedure in which students answered questions that caused them to reflect on the emotional and behavioral costs and benefits of beliefs they harbor, which may incline them toward greater academic stress (e.g., belief in low self-efficacy). Students considered, for example, whether their beliefs brought peace or stress into their life, how they react when they have the thought, and how they treat other people or themselves when they have the thought. Thus, rather than focusing strictly on whether their anxiety-producing thoughts were an accurate, true reflection of reality, students were asked to take a pragmatic lens to their beliefs, looking at their practical functions and learning to step back from unhelpful thoughts. This aspect of the treatment, which reduced students' Test Anxiety Inventory scores and increased their self-efficacy, places it somewhere between a classic cognitive therapy intervention and a more third-wave behavioral therapy approach such as acceptance and commitment therapy (see discussion of Zettle, 2003, below).

Mindfulness Training

The term *mindfulness* has been used in many ways, both in popular culture and in the treatment literature. Here we focus on test-anxiety interventions including exercises that bring nonjudgmental attention to the present moment, exercises designed to cultivate the capacity for focused concentration, and exercises intended to develop an accepting rather than antagonistic relationship with anxiety and other uncomfortable feelings and thoughts. As reviewed above, meta-analyses that have lumped together certain mindfulness tactics (e.g., attention training) with more traditional CBT have indicated that these treatments work to reduce test anxiety, with medium-to-large effect sizes on average (Hembree, 1988; Huntley et al., 2019).

Recent research has examined the efficacy of mindfulness-related contemporary psychotherapies such as metacognitive therapy (MCT; Wells, 2009) and acceptance and commitment therapy (ACT; Hayes et al., 2011) for treating test anxiety. In one study, 40 fourth-grade Iranian students were assigned to either a control or a MCT condition (Sattary-Najaf-Abady & Heidary, 2015). Students in the treatment condition received nine sessions of MCT and showed decreased test anxiety at the end of the treatment. MCT includes elements of detached mindfulness practice (observing negative thoughts nonreactively, just letting them go), attention training practice (learning to stay outwardly focused), and practices aimed at helping students relate differently to cognitive processes such as worrying (recognizing that they can choose to delay such processes and stay with the present task instead).

In another study, 24 university students with substantial math anxiety received individual ACT or systematic desensitization treatment over six weekly one-hour sessions (Zettle, 2003). Students in the ACT condition showed reductions in Test Anxiety Inventory scores (and in a more specific measure of math anxiety) just as large as those of students who completed systematic desensitization, a test-anxiety treatment method with a strong track record of efficacy, as reviewed above. These improvements were maintained through a two-month follow-up. In the ACT intervention, students practiced mindfully observing their thoughts and feelings without judgment or attempts to control them, learned about the futility of aggressive attempts to eliminate unwanted thoughts and feelings, and learned to center their efforts on achieving goals consistent with their values, even when doing so might require a willingness to feel quite anxious.

Some researchers have investigated less conventional mindfulness-type interventions for test anxiety. For example, in one study, 193 Canadian eighth-graders from high-achieving public schools did an art task for 15 minutes before taking a spelling test, the results of which would supposedly be shared with the students' parents (Carsley & Heath, 2018). The students were assigned either to color mandalas for the 15 minutes—which the authors characterized as a mindfulness exercise, involving focused absorption in the present—or to freely draw and color as they wished. In this and in a similar study involving fourth-to-sixth grade students as participants (Carsley et al., 2015), students showed similar reductions in test anxiety after completing either art task. This indicates that any distracting activity might help reduce students' anticipatory anxiety prior to the spelling test, underlining the impact of attentional processes on the experience of test anxiety and suggesting that interventions aimed at helping students deploy their attention strategically (e.g., the attention training in MCT) may be helpful for test anxiety.

Building Study and Test-Taking Skills

Based on the understanding that test anxiety may sometimes be rooted in students' inadequate preparation for exams and subpar strategies for actually taking tests—that is, the idea that students would feel more confident if they knew how to master academic material and how to best show that mastery on exams—some researchers have delivered interventions focused on teaching students best practices for studying and test taking. Meta-analytic support for these skills-building interventions has been equivocal, with little evidence that they decrease test anxiety when delivered on their own, but very large effect sizes when these have been delivered in combination with proven behavioral or cognitive-behavioral test-anxiety interventions (Ergene, 2003; Hembree, 1988; Huntley et al., 2019). This indicates that adding study and test-taking skills instruction to other test-anxiety treatments increases the efficacy of those other treatments for reducing test anxiety. However, Huntley et al. (2019) noted that most interventions of this kind in the test-anxiety literature have not been described in any detail and probably are not rooted in the current best science in educational and cognitive psychological research, in terms of what is known about how best to improve academic performance. This suggests there is probably room for study and test-taking skills interventions to be even more impactful than has been documented in the test-anxiety treatment literature so far.

Test-taking strategy interventions have sometimes been aimed at students who are struggling with academic performance, more than those whose primary complaint is test anxiety. For example, one study focused on two groups of adolescents from a lower performing public high school (Carter et al., 2005). The 38 students, with an average age of 16, were not on track to meet state testing requirements to graduate high school; most had learning disability diagnoses, and some were intellectually disabled. Each group of students received six 90-minute lessons on taking tests effectively (e.g., checking one's work, keeping track of time, completing easier questions first). Test Anxiety Inventory scores decreased, and performance on a standardized math exam increased, for only one of the groups following the intervention—emblematic of the generally mixed evidence for the efficacy of test-taking interventions by themselves.

Despite the equivocal meta-analytic evidence, treatments aimed at increasing test-taking skills have sometimes performed favorably when compared to other test-anxiety treatments. For instance, in one study, 50 university students with high levels of test anxiety were assigned to one of three treatment conditions or a control condition (Kirkland & Hollandsworth, 1980). Two of the treatments were aimed directly at reducing test anxiety, through muscle relaxation or meditation, while the third treatment involved learning effective test-taking strategies, such as skimming the whole test upfront and allocating time wisely and putting more effort into sections that are worth more. All of the interventions were delivered over five 90-minute training sessions. Students who learned test-taking skills outperformed all other students on a stressful test after the intervention, and they experienced fewer distracting, anxious thoughts while taking the test.

The strongest evidence for the potential of training in study and test-taking skills as a test-anxiety intervention comes from research in which academic deficits have been directly remediated. For instance, one study examined 21 German students of varying grade levels, who had dyslexia but otherwise normal intellectual abilities (Faber, 2010). The students received 80 hours of academic instruction on spelling. Afterward, they showed a very large reduction in test anxiety, according to a specialized scale focused on spelling anxiety in particular, alongside extremely large concomitant improvements in their performance on spelling tests. Supportive evidence also comes from research on treating math anxiety, a construct that correlates with test anxiety. In one study, 224 Italian fourth-graders with math anxiety were assigned to one of two treatment conditions or a control condition (Passolunghi et al., 2019). The interventions were delivered over eight weekly 60-minute training sessions. One of the interventions aimed directly at reducing math anxiety through relaxation, mindfulness, and cognitive therapy techniques. The other focused instead on develop students' calculation abilities and their use of wise strategies in solving math problems. Both interventions decreased math anxiety substantially, but only the students who were trained in math skills also showed improved performance on math tests.

Idiosyncratic Techniques

Several test-anxiety treatments featured in research studies are difficult to categorize into the aforementioned intervention types. Some studies have used unique techniques to try to increase students' self-efficacy or their belief that they can do what it takes to succeed—a mechanism that has also been targeted by the interventions described above that have encouraged reappraisals of test anxiety as normal and functional. For example, in one study of 240 Indian high school students, some students were assigned to a "guided mastery" condition in which they practiced solving difficult anagrams while receiving feedback and encouragement from a counselor (Lal Zinta, 2008). Test anxiety was unaffected by this intervention. In a study of 219 German high school students, students in the treatment condition, which was meant to prime greater academic self-efficacy, were asked to imagine a technically and scientifically proficient person and then to list that person's abilities and adjectives that would describe them (Lang & Lang, 2010). Finally, these students were asked to describe how the highly competent person would feel prior to doing a challenging task. In this and a similar follow-up study of 232 German high school students (also in Lang & Lang, 2010), the priming intervention decreased the relationship between students' cognitive test anxiety and their performance on intelligence test batteries. That is, compared to students in the control condition, the test performance of students who completed the priming intervention was less affected by the level of worrying they experienced about testing. There was some evidence that this effect was due in part to their engaging more fully with the test.

Other research has explored the potential for regularly writing about positive emotions to decrease test anxiety. In a study of 75 Chinese high school students with high test anxiety, the students assigned to the treatment condition wrote for 20 minutes every day, for 30 days, about positive emotions they felt that day (Shen et al., 2018). Students wrote about things like meals they enjoyed, time spent learning among peers, and physical exercise that was gratifying. The students who completed this writing, compared to those in a control condition who wrote about their daily activities in general over the same period, showed a large decrease in self-reported test anxiety. The author proposed that this effect may have been due to students' learning to turn their attention to positive events and interpretations in general, which may have carried over to testing situations. Thus, the results from this unique study could be interpreted as supporting the utility of attention training interventions more broadly.

Some studies have tested the potential utility of very minimal interventions. For instance, 29 American fifth-grade students were randomly assigned to complete a physical education class period (or not) immediately before standardized math and reading tests (Thompson et al., 2016). There was no significant effect on test anxiety (although, as with so many studies on the topic, the sample size was too small to be confident about the absence of a benefit). In another study, 117 Greek sixth-grade students completed a test in a high-stress situation (e.g., a countdown timer was visible, and a gift card could be won for high performance; Mavilidi et al., 2014). In the experimental condition, students had one minute at the start of the test to preview all the questions on it, whereas other students could only see one problem at a time. This ability to look ahead to the test as a whole did not decrease students' test anxiety.

A small body of research has suggested that conditions that would normally be considered a "control" in test anxiety intervention research may actually, in some cases, exert an active and desirable effect. For example, when 173 Swiss university students were assigned to either take twice daily, for three weeks, a placebo pill (which they knew was a placebo!), or even simply to *imagine* taking a placebo pill for the same period, they showed reductions in test anxiety compared to students who did neither of these, suggesting that in some cases, simply feeling as if you are doing something to address your test anxiety may actually help with that anxiety (Buergler et al., 2023). In a study of 180 German university students with high test anxiety, participants were randomized to one of three conditions, all involving five weekly group sessions lasting three hours each (Reiss et al., 2017). Two of the conditions involved active test-anxiety treatments led by a psychologist. The interventions included exposure therapy, relaxation, study skills, cognitive therapy, and reimagining past experiences with test anxiety in a more positive way. In the third, control condition, students discussed their experiences with test anxiety, but in a self-led way. This self-help treatment reduced test anxiety just as much as the two therapist-led treatments did, with improvements lasting for at least six months afterward. This result, in our view, illustrates the power of mere learning about test anxiety (e.g., its commonness among peers) to attenuate the phenomenon.

Combined Treatments

Many test-anxiety treatment studies have deployed interventions that include several components, such as certain treatment conditions from Passolunghi et al.'s (2019), Gregor's (2005), and Reiss et al.'s (2017) studies, which, as described above, entailed combinations of exposure therapy, relaxation, mindfulness, and cognitive therapy techniques. Here we will summarize other examples of treatments incorporating multiple types of intervention in a single package.

In a study of 255 Israeli ninth-grade students from two urban schools (one Arab, one Jewish), participants were assigned either to receive eight weekly one-hour treatment sessions or to be in a control condition (Yahav & Cohen, 2008). Psychologists administered the treatment in a group format. It included psychoeducation about the multifaced nature of stress, practice in challenging one's thinking about everyday stressors, and muscle relaxation and other calming techniques. The relaxation component was accompanied by biofeedback for the last four sessions. Compared to students in the control condition, students receiving this intervention package showed significant decreases in their Test Anxiety Inventory scores.

In a study aimed primarily at reducing social anxiety, rather than test anxiety in particular, 240 Dutch high school students with substantial social and/or test anxiety were randomized to a cognitive-bias modification (CBM) treatment, a CBT treatment, or a control group (Sportel et al., 2013). The CBM treatment, delivered in 20 computer-mediated sessions over 10 weeks, was a focused intervention, involving hundreds of trials in which students were guided to interpret ambiguous scenarios in more positive ways, and to direct attention toward positive rather than threatening stimuli. The CBT intervention, on the other hand, involved several components. In 10 weekly 90-minute group sessions led by a psychologist, students in the CBT condition learned about anxiety, trained their attention, challenged their anxious thoughts, and practiced exposure to anxiety-provoking situations. Test anxiety decreased following the CBT (moderate effect size) but not the CBM treatment, and this benefit lasted for at least 12 months afterward (see also de Hullu et al., 2017).

In another study that used a computerized intervention, 56 United Kingdom high school students completed six weekly treatment sessions of 40 minutes each (Putwain & Pescod, 2018). The intervention included components of psychoeducation about anxiety, challenging negative self-talk and encouraging positive self-talk, practicing relaxation techniques, learning studying and test-taking skills, and setting goals. All treatment sessions included quizzes to reinforce students' learning. After completing the treatment—which was given immediately to some students, and after a delay to other students—participants showed moderate to large reductions in test anxiety.

In a study of 30 ninth graders at a predominantly Black high school in New Orleans, about a year after Hurricane Katrina battered the region, a multi-component test-anxiety intervention was delivered to students either immediately or after a delay (Weems et al., 2009). The treatment consisted of five weekly lessons and covered psychoeducation about anxiety, relaxation practice and systematic desensitization, exposure using a mock test, and various tools intended to increase self-efficacy (e.g., self-praise, drawing oneself as calm and successful, writing a story about success). Students showed large average reductions in test anxiety after completing the treatment, and GPAs also increased more for these students, compared to peers who did not undergo test-anxiety treatment, in the academic quarters following the treatment. The same group of researchers administered a similar intervention to 259 students from the same school system, ranging from grades 3 to 12, who scored high on test anxiety or who were recommended by their schools for treatment (Weems et al., 2015). For younger students in this sample, there was greater emphasis on drawing and other picture-based content, and less emphasis on verbal discussion and reading texts. Once again, test anxiety decreased following treatment, with moderate to large effects. These improvements were maintained at follow-up two years later.

A study of 115 Singaporean fourth-grade students examined the efficacy of a multi-component CBT treatment versus a control condition (Yeo et al., 2016). The CBT intervention was administered in a group format by a psychology graduate student. It included psychoeducation about anxiety, relaxed breathing, relaxation through self-talk and recollection of calming memories, systematic desensitization, and instruction in study skills, with homework assigned after each session. Compared to control students, those receiving the intervention showed medium-sized reductions in test anxiety two months following the treatment completion.

A final study we wish to highlight did not include any quantitative measurement of outcomes but featured a creative set of interventions. In a study of 241 fourth graders at lower-performing New York public schools, students from two schools completed a test-anxiety treatment program, while students from one school served as a control group (Lobman, 2014). The treatment involved 10 weekly one-hour sessions. The three principal emphases of the program were normalizing and destigmatizing test anxiety; building a friendlier, more flexible relationship with anxiety; and developing skills for taking tests effectively and modulating one's emotional response while doing so. Compared to many test-anxiety interventions in the literature, this treatment program included rich interpersonal aspects, alongside conventional components such as relaxed breathing. Students were encouraged to share openly with each other about their test anxiety, and they practiced acting out, playfully, what their test anxiety versus a state of calm would look like from the outside. They participated in a "stress doctor" play in which the program directors taught students that test anxiety is normal and healthy. They produced a collective set of statements—representing the "class voice"—that they could remember when they needed to "talk back" to their test anxiety, and they practiced regarding test taking like playing a game. Qualitative interviews with teachers and students indicated that students found the treatment program helpful and drew upon its content when taking tests afterward.

LIMITATIONS OF THE RESEARCH LITERATURE

It is unclear whether the efficacy of various test-anxiety interventions may be moderated by student age. Research on test-anxiety treatment has skewed heavily toward college students, probably largely because of the convenience of sampling from this population for university faculty. In a meta-analysis of studies ranging from 1973 to 1998, only 12 treatment groups involved students between kindergarten and 12th grade, whereas there were over six times as many groups (76 total) of university students meeting criteria for inclusion (Ergene, 2003). Two systematic reviews of research on treating test anxiety in K–12 students located only 21 additional studies published between 2000 and 2018 (Soares & Woods, 2020; von der Embse et al., 2013).

Only one major meta-analysis of test-anxiety treatment research (Huntley et al., 2019) has followed modern standards in the overall protocol for its review of studies and in its analytic strategies (see, e.g., Higgins & Green, 2011). This meta-analysis focused exclusively on randomized controlled trials using university students. The authors argued that the evidence for any test-anxiety intervention's efficacy was "low quality" at best, according to conventional contemporary standards for assessing clinical trial evidence. For example, one major problem in the test-anxiety treatment literature, even in recent years, has been incomplete and inadequate reporting of methods, data, and results of statistical analyses. A second problem has been limited follow-up. Only one-third of the 44 studies analyzed by Huntley et al. (2019) included any kind of follow-up data beyond the completion of the intervention, and only three of these included a follow-up beyond six months. A third problem has been substantial heterogeneity between studies, such as in the severity of test anxiety in the student samples. A fourth problem has been samples that are too small to confidently assess the presence and magnitude of any benefit from interventions. The authors note that to have a solid chance of detecting even a fairly large effect from a test-anxiety treatment (i.e., in technical terms, to achieve 80% power with an α of .05 to detect an effect size of 0.70 [Cohen's d]), a minimum of 34 students should be in each treatment condition. In the 152 treatment groups included in their meta-analysis, only 5% met this threshold for a minimally adequate sample size, with the average treatment condition having fewer than half this many participants in it.

Robson et al. (2023) found only eight randomized controlled trials meeting their inclusion criteria for treatment studies on primary school students, and they echoed Huntley et al.'s (2019) concerns about poor reporting standards. With limited information available about most studies' methods and results, it is challenging to assess rigorously which test-anxiety interventions work best, and to replicate treatment techniques. The authors noted that researchers should preregister their studies moving forward, to allay concerns about selective reporting of data and idiosyncratic choices of analysis that may be systematically biased to yield researchers' preferred conclusions (e.g., that an intervention they designed is efficacious).

As we have reviewed, many test-anxiety treatment studies have included combinations of intervention types. This is another limitation in the research literature. In the absence of high-quality component analysis studies, it is difficult to determine which intervention components contributed most to any multiple-component treatment's efficacy. Moreover, the existing research sheds little light on individual-difference moderators of treatment response. For instance, it is possible that students who are bothered most by the uncomfortable physiological aspects of their test anxiety would benefit most from exposure- and relaxation-based treatments, whereas students who are most bothered by worries about how their anxiety will affect their test performance would benefit most from reappraisal- and mindfulness-based interventions.

Furthermore, the distinctions between classes of test-anxiety intervention are far from airtight. For example, several putatively distinct test-anxiety treatments might exert their effects partly through mindfulness-type mechanisms, even when the authors do not highlight this pathway: reappraising test anxiety as harmless and possibly adaptive probably engenders a more accepting, mindful attitude toward one's emotional arousal; conventional exposure therapy likewise builds willingness to encounter anxiety; relaxation techniques such as paced breathing share a lot in common with many mindfulness exercises; and some CBT interventions may cause students to develop a more distanced, pragmatic, nonreactive relationship to their thoughts.

SUMMARY

Existing research has clearly demonstrated that a variety of evidence-supported interventions for anxiety disorders in general can also help alleviate students' test anxiety. The volume of support for this conclusion is especially strong for older students. The test-anxiety research base is not robust enough, however, to draw fine-grained conclusions about the superiority of any particular treatment technique. A kitchen-sink approach, as used in studies of multiple-component treatments, may therefore make the most sense, to ensure that all bases are covered. Because the same treatment strategies that work for other anxiety problems appear to work well when tailored to test anxiety in particular, drawing from state-of-the-science contemporary psychotherapeutic treatments for anxiety disorders (e.g., Barlow et al., 2017; Hayes et al., 2011; Roemer & Orsillo, 2020) also seems wise when assembling a comprehensive test-anxiety treatment, even if some aspects of these therapies have not been exhaustively tested for test anxiety per se.

A complete test-anxiety treatment would include education about test anxiety, exposure practice, relaxation techniques, strategies for managing worries and keeping attention trained outward, and instruction in the best habits for studying and taking tests. It would thus target the physiological and cognitive symptoms of test anxiety, as well as associated problem behaviors. In the absence of high-quality research on moderators of treatment response, a commonsensical modular approach also seems reasonable to adopt. By this we mean that treaters may selectively emphasize components of treatment that appear to meet a particular student's needs most effectively, when time and other resources may be limited.

Effect Sizes

To estimate the extent of impact of an intervention, an *effect size* statistic is typically used. An effect size indicates the magnitude of the difference between different groups (e.g., one receiving a test anxiety treatment, the other not receiving treatment) on a variable of interest (e.g., test anxiety). The best known effect size statistic is Cohen's *d*, also known as the standardized mean difference.

Cohen's *d* tells us how far apart the means of two groups are in standard deviation units—that is, how many standard deviations away the means of the score distributions are. (A standard deviation, in turn, is an index of the variability within each group.) Consider a measure of test anxiety given to two groups of students, one a control group that didn't receive any treatment and the other a treatment group that received an intervention designed to decrease test anxiety. The score distributions of both groups have standard deviations of 10, but the control group's mean score is 65 and the treatment group's mean score is 60. The two group means are 5 points apart, and each group's standard deviation is 10, so *d* is 0.5 (5 divided by 10). The group means are half a standard deviation apart. For making sense of effect sizes in everyday language, Cohen (1988) offered a rule of thumb: a *d* of 0.2 would generally represent a small difference, a *d* of 0.5 would be a medium-sized difference, and a *d* of 0.8 would be a large difference. We use Cohen's (1988) convention for labeling small, medium, and large effect sizes throughout this chapter. To convey a practical sense of what these effect sizes mean in treatment research, it is useful to note that, using Cohen's rule of thumb, cholesterol-lowering statins have a small effect on major cardiovascular events, antipsychotic medicines have a medium effect on schizophrenia symptoms, and Ritalin has a large effect on attention deficit hyperactivity disorder symptoms (Leucht et al., 2015).

It is useful to express group differences in standard deviation units because this tells us the degree to which the two groups overlap. To see this, first consider the group difference situation shown below:

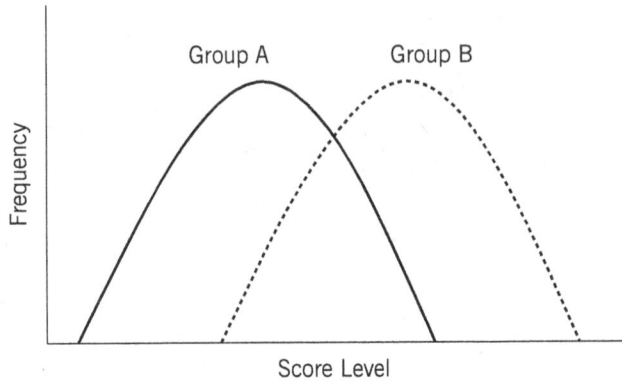

Groups A and B have means that are clearly different; Group B has a substantially higher mean. However, the two groups each have a lot of variability—that is, the standard deviations for the groups are fairly high—and so the two score distributions have a lot of overlap. Contrast this situation with the one below:

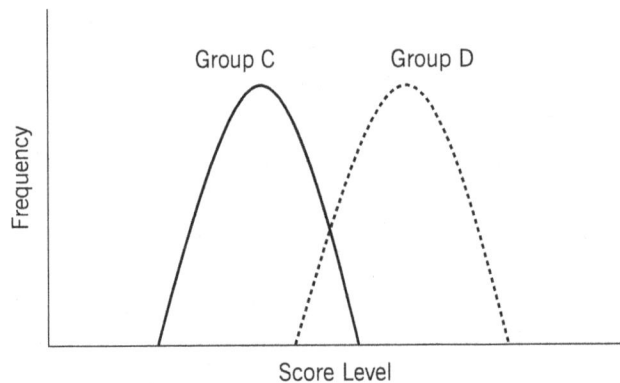

The mean difference between groups C and D is the same as the mean difference between groups A and B, but groups C and D have much lower standard deviations, and so the two distributions have much less overlap. The effect size d would be much higher for the Group C-Group D difference than for the Group A-Group B difference, and this should make sense; two groups are more differentiated from each other when their standard deviations are lower.

PART II

TREATING TEST ANXIETY

CHAPTER 5

Treatment Overview

We have developed a comprehensive treatment for test anxiety by drawing upon what's known about its nature (see Chapter 1) and how it relates to academic performance (see Chapter 2), as well as the body of research on interventions for test anxiety and anxiety problems more generally (see Chapter 4). Our treatment aims to free students from anxiety-based avoidance to unlock their academic potential. The treatment also helps students to feel more comfortable and to better enjoy school and their lives outside school.

In this chapter, we present an overview of our treatment. The treatment is not a strict protocol but instead involves a menu of components that can be flexibly applied, tailored to the student's profile and needs (see Chapter 3), the treatment setting and format, and the therapist's preferences. Here, we describe the rationale underpinning our treatment, the five modules that make up the treatment, how treatment can be delivered individually or in groups, how treatment can be delivered briefly or more extensively, measuring change during treatment, and incorporating treatment into multi-tiered systems of support.

RATIONALE FOR TREATMENT

With some clinical issues, judiciously avoiding or escaping triggers of distress or problematic behavioral urges can be wise. For example, for a person with a cocaine use disorder, it would make sense to reduce the likelihood of cravings by not keeping any cocaine at home and not spending time at a party where people will be using the drug. Similarly, for a person working on anger management, it may be important to learn to walk away from especially upsetting situations to take a time-out before doing anything impulsive and potentially regrettable.

Test anxiety, however, is an issue for which avoidance and escape behaviors tend to create problems rather than provide solutions. Students' fears that test anxiety will harm their performance, and their wishes to rid themselves of uncomfortable physiological and cognitive symptoms of test anxiety, can lead them to constrict or otherwise alter their behavioral routines in ways that harm their learning and academic achievement, not to mention their overall life quality. For example, an underprepared student might avoid practicing math problems before an exam because doing so may stir up their anxieties about attempting similarly difficult work on the upcoming timed test in class. To quash worries about that same upcoming exam, another student might instead adopt a strategy of overpreparation, to the point that their life becomes imbalanced, dominated by rigid academic work routines, and their time use may get out of alignment with their overall values and aspirations.

Our treatment therefore explicitly targets dysfunctional aspects of students' relationship with their test anxiety and with situational triggers of that test anxiety. The treatment helps students normalize, disaggregate, and reappraise their test anxiety as perfectly compatible with high academic functioning, so that they are freed up to do what is best for their learning, rather than being driven to avoid or escape from anxious distress. We help students develop a friendlier, more compassionate relationship with their test anxiety. Students learn to observe their experiences of test anxiety without excessive entanglement and judgment, thereby growing more flexible in enacting adaptive academic behaviors, even when the behaviors might cause anxiety. Students who complete our treatment also report reductions in their experiences of test anxiety (even while decreasing their efforts to avoid it!), a welcome change that makes their lives in and out of school more comfortable and pleasant.

Promoting a Virtuous Cycle

A crucial insight underlying our test anxiety treatment is the bidirectional relationship between (1) the magnitude of students' aversion to experiencing test anxiety and (2) ineffective studying and test-taking routines. Unwillingness to experience test anxiety tends to incline students toward inefficient, ineffective studying and test-taking strategies that impair their ability to achieve their potential. Underperformance then undermines confidence and exacerbates test anxiety and, further, students' fears of their test anxiety. On the other hand, when students learn skills to better tolerate and even mitigate experiences of test anxiety, their willingness to use the most effective test preparation methods increases. When our treatment program helps students learn about and practice highly efficient, effective ways to study and take tests, their academic confidence grows and their test anxiety naturally diminishes. In this way, a positive feedback loop takes hold.

ALIGNING TREATER ATTITUDE WITH TREATMENT CONTENT

A central message of our treatment is that test anxiety is a normal experience, even if an uncomfortable one, and that a flexible, well-lived life will entail frequent encounters with anxiety. We aim to develop in students a more open attitude toward their anxiety, a willingness to embrace it when it makes sense to. We try to counter the idea that anxiety is embarrassing or shameful or that it signifies impending failure and should be feared and shut down. In academic settings, in particular, anxiety is a normal part of learning new things and stretching outside one's comfort zone into areas one hasn't yet mastered (e.g., doing problem sets and taking practice tests in a hard class).

We therefore recommend that throughout the treatment, treaters model a humble and accepting attitude toward their own anxiety (see Hayes et al., 2011, and Roemer & Orsillo, 2020, for related recommendations for psychotherapy more generally, beyond test anxiety). A great opportunity to do so is whenever you (the treater) notice yourself experiencing some anxiety or insecurity about performance during the treatment. For example, suppose that you fumble an explanation of a concept and have to start over. You might seize the moment to say something like, "Well, that didn't make as much sense as I'd hoped! I notice some anxiety coming up for me, and a temptation to rush ahead to another topic to get rid of that anxiety—that's what happens when we get anxious, we want to escape it!—but I know that what we're focusing on right now is important, so let me try to explain that again." When students ask questions and you aren't sure of the answers, this is another opportunity to demonstrate humility, and an acceptance of imperfection, by simply stating that you don't know and that you'll be eager to learn more about whatever the student raised. When you're leading students through experiential exercises such as hyperventilating to induce physiological anxiety, it helps students find their own willingness if you participate fully yourself—which would mean, in case of hyperventilation, breathing as hard as you can and disclosing afterward the various uncomfortable sensations or thoughts the exercise might have brought up for you. We also encourage self-disclosure of personal experiences with test anxiety or related forms of performance anxiety, such as around public speaking, throughout the treatment, whenever it's relevant.

In addition to modeling acceptance and openness toward one's own anxiety, it helps to consistently show compassion toward students' experiences of anxiety. After all, we hope to help students develop greater self-compassion, which has been linked to reduced reliance on avoidance-oriented coping (Chishima et al., 2018). The more that students' anxiety can be validated and normalized, the less they tend to get caught up with it and derailed by it.

We recommend modeling an accepting, nonjudgmental attitude toward anxiety itself, even apart from one's own or students' experiences of it. One of the most effective ways to do this is to avoid labeling anxiety as a "negative" emotion, and to refrain from labeling emotions in general as positive or negative. Instead, anxiety can be acknowledged as "uncomfortable" or "intense" (Ehrenreich et al., 2018). All emotions can be useful and functional, and none are inherently bad or meriting of categorical avoidance, even if they might cause discomfort.

Overall, consistent with the theme of anxiety's universality and normality, we suggest a more egalitarian than authoritarian style when delivering our test anxiety treatment, regardless of whether you're engaged in nondirective exploration (e.g., discussing students' beliefs about test anxiety in Module 1) or a directive component of treatment in which the therapist is highly active (e.g., communicating test-taking tactics in Module 5). While the therapist may be the expert on general-purpose behavioral and cognitive principles, the student is the expert on their unique experiences, and it is important for the treater to demonstrate consistent curiosity.

THE FIVE TREATMENT MODULES

Module 1: Learning About Test Anxiety (Chapter 6)

In this treatment module, we engage students in an exploration of the physiological and cognitive symptoms of test anxiety, as well as associated problem behaviors. Recognizing that test anxiety is not monolithic but instead a collection of varied components is a helpful first step for empowering students to approach their test anxiety with curiosity rather than fear. Next, students reflect on how test anxiety relates to test performance. Many students think that feeling anxious during testing ruins performance, perhaps because they have indeed tended to do poorly on exams during which they were very nervous. Learning that test anxiety does not have any substantial, direct bearing on test performance is often a surprise for students (perhaps their nervousness and poor performance in the past co-occurred because of inadequate preparation!). Understanding this central fact about test anxiety—that it is normal and not, by itself, harmful—can help to immediately reduce students' reactivity to their physiological and cognitive test anxiety symptoms, and thus can improve their behavioral flexibility. By way of analogy, this part of the test anxiety treatment is like the psychoeducation component in the treatment of panic disorder, in which patients learn about the mundane causes of the physical symptoms constituting a panic attack, as well as the fact that panic attacks are physiologically benign. They then become less fearful when these same panic symptoms show up in the future, and they behave less avoidantly.

Module 2: Mastering Bodily Anxiety (Chapter 7)

This treatment module helps students gain mastery over the nervousness they feel in their bodies when experiencing test anxiety. Students complete a series of physical exercises that directly induce bodily feelings associated with anxiety (e.g., shortness of breath, dizziness). By repeatedly, purposely bringing on such symptoms, in an innocuous setting with no real threats present (academic or otherwise), students gradually learn to regard their physiological anxiety with more openness and less aversion. Students also practice techniques (slowed breathing, muscle relaxation) that can sometimes calm bodily anxiety. Students are reminded that controlling anxiety is not the overarching goal of the treatment, but our approach is practical, and learning strategies for modulating anxiety can make life more pleasant for students and can actually facilitate greater engagement in valued academic behaviors. Our experience is that students can appropriately use techniques such as slowed breathing without deepening their commitment to an unrealistic agenda of controlling all their inner experiences, and without strengthening inaccurate beliefs about the harmfulness of test anxiety. In this treatment module, students also practice doing more things in their everyday lives that they might normally avoid due to the physical nervousness that doing these things might bring on. Behavioral flexibility is also increased through the completion of various mentally and physically challenging tasks after purposely inducing physiological anxiety.

Module 3: Focusing the Mind (Chapter 8)

As with Module 2, the third test anxiety treatment module involves a lot of experiential learning, compared to the more didactic first treatment module. Students are introduced to a series of exercises that help them get less tangled up with their anxious thoughts. As in Module 2, the primary goal is to help students become less reactive to their anxiety—in this case, the cognitive rather than physiological component—and ultimately to free up their bandwidth to focus on doing what really matters for them. Students practice a writing exercise that helps them build distance from their own worries and to extract what's practically useful from the worries, while learning to postpone and ultimately forgo excessive processing of worries that may ultimately just be a way of avoiding constructive action in the world. Students also practice simply watching their own thinking unfold, with openness and curiosity, which helps them develop a nonjudgmental attitude toward their own minds and helps them recognize that anxiety-charged thoughts do not constitute an emergency— they can be tolerated, and they will naturally rise and fall, even if one does not *do* anything to try to get rid of the anxiety. As in Module 2, however, the agenda is not exclusively reducing reactivity to anxiety, and students are also equipped with practical tools for disempowering unhelpful thoughts and training their attention to more useful content. Students try out tools that can drain specific thoughts of their emotional resonance (e.g., repeating a thought aloud until it sounds silly or meaningless), and they are introduced to formal and informal exercises that can build up their attentional control—their capacity to focus on studying, for example, without getting sidetracked by their worries or by other distractors in the environment.

Module 4: Studying for Success (Chapter 9)

Treatment Modules 2 and 3 focus on inoculating students to test anxiety and enhancing their willingness to face (and capacity to manage more comfortably) whatever physiological and cognitive anxiety may arise in academic situations. In contrast, Module 4 goes beyond improving students' relationship with their anxiety and aims to directly enhance students' studying skills. When students adopt more efficient and effective methods for mastering academic material, they enter testing situations with more confidence and perform better, which also has the happy effect of mitigating their test anxiety in the future. In this treatment module, students learn that the most effective ways to study involve trying to retrieve knowledge and practice skills without referring to any notes or other materials—for example, taking a practice test, or trying to teach someone else what one has learned. These kinds of study techniques naturally can evoke a lot of anxiety, especially when they expose areas in which students' knowledge or skills are still rusty—but this is one of their advantages, compared to more comfortable but passive study tactics such as rereading textbooks, which can make students feel they know the material better than they really do. Equipped with more tolerance for anxiety (from earlier treatment modules), students learn to use more effective means of studying. They also learn how to time and space out their studying to maximize learning. Additionally, they learn best practices for reducing distraction and procrastination when studying (e.g., getting sucked into their smartphones). Finally, students are introduced to tools for improving their sleep; a better-rested student is typically much better able to study and learn.

Module 5: Doing Your Best on Tests (Chapter 10)

Students with high test anxiety are especially likely to think that they are "bad test takers," which is to say, that they are less able to demonstrate their knowledge and abilities on exams than other students are. Treatment Module 5 focuses straightforwardly on teaching students the most effective techniques for ensuring that they do as well as possible on tests, given their level of preparation and their intellectual capabilities. Students learn best practices for taking any sort of test, as well as a set of tactics that are specifically tailored to multiple-choice tests. The module includes a sample test that demonstrates to students how these tactics can help them identify correct answers even when they have only limited knowledge of a subject area. After completing Module 5, students are typically more confident about taking tests and more motivated to prepare for them, knowing they have the skills to do as well as any other student who enters the exam with a similar mastery of relevant content.

TAILORING MODULAR TREATMENT TO THE STUDENT

In Chapter 3, we provided guidance for assessing students' test anxiety and other characteristics pertinent to treatment, such as their test-taking self-efficacy, their test performance history, and any history of prior treatment for psychological disorders. Information gleaned from this assessment can be used to tailor the modular treatment to particular students. Modifying the treatment is most straightforward when the treater is working with an individual student one-to-one, but our recommendations apply equally to group treatment, to the degree that the group may be at least somewhat homogeneous on one or more relevant dimension.

Test Anxiety Symptoms

The prominence of different sorts of test anxiety symptoms obviously has implications for shaping treatment. Students who are more bothered by physiological symptoms may benefit from a greater emphasis on Module 2, whereas a greater proportion of time spent on Module 3 may make sense for those students who report a preponderance of cognitive symptoms. Emphasizing Modules 2 and 3 also makes sense for students who are especially concerned about feeling more comfortable and reducing preoccupation with the subjective experience of test anxiety symptoms. When students' biggest concern is improving their academic performance, or when problem behaviors associated with test anxiety are prominent, a proportionally larger emphasis on Modules 4 and 5 is appropriate, with the focus on studying and test-taking skills.

Test-Taking Self-Efficacy

Many students who are interested in help for their test anxiety are low in test-taking self-efficacy. That is, they are not confident that they can complete test-related behaviors successfully when anxious. With these students, the psychoeducation in Module 1 is especially crucial. With students who really doubt that they personally can perform academically when anxious, we recommend actively soliciting their objections when presenting arguments in Module 1 about how test anxiety doesn't directly impair test performance. It's important to demonstrate humility and validate the counterintuitiveness of this finding and to thoroughly engage with students' concerns and questions. For students low in test-taking self-efficacy, some of the last exercises in Modules 2 and 3 also have special relevance. Specifically, these students benefit from practicing test taking and other challenging activities after having purposely induced anxiety in themselves (Module 2), and also from practicing paying attention to one thing, such as reading test instructions, while purposely having competing "noise" in the environment, analogous to naturally occurring worries that might arise during a test (Module 3). Through such practices, students can improve their confidence about their ability to perform even when they experience physiological and cognitive anxiety. Of course, Modules 4 and 5 help to shore up the confidence of such students that they know how to study and take tests effectively in general, regardless of their anxiety levels.

Test Performance History

A student's test performance history actually intersects with the issue of test-taking self-efficacy. If a student consistently earns high grades—or has at least sometimes done very well on tests, especially high-stakes tests that would be expected to induce anxiety—this can prove useful when providing psychoeducation in Module 1 about how test anxiety does not cause poor test performance. Having students reflect on times they have done well when anxious is often far more persuasive to them than any impersonal description of experimental research study results, and is a great way to build test-taking self-efficacy. Discovering that a student has a history of very high grades also suggests that their test-taking skills (Module 5) are probably already adequate. However, one should not assume that such a student is using the most effective study skills (Module 4). Many high-performing students with test anxiety use less efficient (but also less anxiety-provoking) study techniques and therefore spend many more hours to achieve mastery of academic material than would be necessary if they used the most evidence-based methods of studying.

History of Prior Treatment for Psychological Disorders

If a student has a history of treatment for psychological disorders or distress, it's helpful to take inventory of exactly what they recall about the content of the treatment. Several of the interventions in Modules 2 and 3 of our treatment (e.g., interoceptive exposures, worry journaling, attention training) are included in some evidence-supported treatments for a variety of emotional disorders. Occasionally a student will have truly exhausted, in another treatment, what's useful and relevant from some components of our comprehensive treatment, and these components can be de-emphasized or skipped in the test anxiety treatment. More commonly, discussing prior treatment will help tune the treater in to potential obstacles to watch out for in the test anxiety treatment (e.g., a student may report difficulty with completing practice between sessions, or may report that they dropped out of treatment because they didn't see fast enough results). In addition, at times, students have prior experience with ineffective interventions, or interventions that were not well-communicated. When we mention breathing exercises or even use the word "mindfulness," some students' skepticism flares, and we need to explain—without defensiveness—why the current treatment may be different from what the students have already been exposed to.

INDIVIDUAL AND GROUP MODALITIES

All modules of our test anxiety treatment can be used with individual students or with groups of students. Each treatment modality has its advantages. When working with a single student, it's easier to conduct a detailed assessment and then customize the treatment to the individual's profile, as described above. When time is constrained and you must be highly selective in what material from the modules you try to cover, it's especially helpful to be able to tailor the treatment uniquely to one student and adjust the pacing according to the student's response to different treatment components. Individual treatment also maximizes the treater's ability to ensure that the student remains engaged and participatory in every aspect of the treatment.

Group treatment can be tailored to some degree to the profiles of the students composing the group—especially when the group is small and fairly homogeneous—but compared to individual treatment, it is more likely to follow a preplanned agenda and pacing, with less room to adjust and optimize the relative emphasis on different treatment modules and components according to students' profiles and their responses to treatment. This can sometimes be a good thing, however. Compared to individual treatment, it's easier in group treatment to make sure that you don't get sidetracked by one-off problems that may be preoccupying a student at the time of their treatment session but that may have little bearing on the overall, lasting problems they experience related to test anxiety. While individual treatment may afford more ability to closely monitor a student's engagement, students sometimes show more accountability with between-session practice completion when they expect to be discussing this in the presence of other students at the next treatment session. Moreover, students often learn a great deal from each other when doing group treatment. Hearing about other students' test anxiety, and completing experiential exercises together with them, typically decreases stigma and increases students' confidence that their test anxiety need not limit their academic choices and achievement. Group treatment has the added benefit, naturally, of allowing more efficient use of limited treatment resources, insofar as multiple students can receive test anxiety treatment at once. In private practice settings, this can make the approach more financially accessible as well.

When time and resources allow for it, a combination of group and individual modalities can be ideal for delivering our test anxiety treatment. Indeed, the few comparisons of efficacy of different delivery methods support combining group and individual sessions (Hembree, 1988). Regular group meetings allow students to learn from and help one another, and the group format facilitates consistent pacing of the more didactic, skills-focused portions of treatment. Supplementary individual meetings can increase the treater's ability to closely monitor each student's level of engagement and learning and can provide extra time to emphasize those parts of treatment that are most relevant to each student's profile and goals.

A third treatment modality merits a mention: educating parents about test anxiety and its treatment. Especially for students who live with their parents—but sometimes even for students who are at college, or who go to a boarding school, but who frequently seek emotional support from their parents—this can be quite impactful. We have found that one or two meetings with parents, individually or in groups, provides enough time to cover the essentials of Module 1, educating parents about the signs and symptoms of test anxiety and about its normality and the fact that it does not *cause* poor test performance. It can be useful to give parents a broad overview of the procedures used in Module 2, 3, 4, and 5, as well. Equipped with all of this, parents can learn to validate and normalize students' experiences of test anxiety while praising students' use of the adaptive steps taught throughout the treatment, such as practicing exposure exercises and using the most effective strategies for studying. As Lebowitz et al. (2014) noted, parent-based treatment for child anxiety actually has numerous unique advantages. It can (1) address parental anxiety and parent behaviors that maintain child anxiety, (2) reach children in the real-world settings where anxiety is most present (e.g., preparing for a test while at home), and (3) help children who lack the time or willingness to attend a structured program of treatment.

BRIEFER AND LONGER TREATMENTS

The time available for treating test anxiety varies widely across settings. At one extreme, an educator may have just a single 30-minute block of time to deliver a classroomwide test anxiety intervention (see "Incorporating Treatment into Multi-Tiered Systems of Support" below). Even in a brief period like this, valuable information can be imparted—for example, students can learn about how anxiety doesn't harm test performance (from Module 1), or about studying techniques that will best prepare them for tests (from Module 4)—or a useful tool can be practiced (e.g., progressive muscle relaxation from Module 2). At the other extreme, a school counselor may be seeking activities to use with a student who has been guaranteed weekly individual counseling sessions as part of a special education plan.

When there's enough time to deliver a comprehensive test anxiety treatment, the proportion of time spent on different treatment modules will depend on the characteristics of the students in treatment (see "Tailoring Modular Treatment to the Student" above). However, to give clinicians a ballpark sense of how time might be apportioned, we provide here two examples. First, consider the case of leading a small group of students through four 60-minute treatment sessions. The first session may focus entirely on psychoeducation (Module 1), which often involves lively discussions in the group format as students learn about each other's experiences of test anxiety and about research on the topic. The second session may focus on mastering bodily anxiety (Module 2), with students practicing one exposure exercise (e.g., hyperventilation) and one relaxation exercise (e.g., slowed breathing). The third session may focus on mastering cognitive anxiety (Module 3), with in-session practice of worry journaling and (time permitting) the "leaves on a stream" exercise. The fourth session may include brief instruction in how to study effectively (Module 4) and then an overview of taking tests well (Module 5), using the sample test in Handout 10.3 as a basis for groupwide active learning. After each of the first three modules, between-session homework may be assigned, and then this may be reviewed at the start of the next session.

As an example of a longer treatment, consider the case of treating an individual student over the course of ten 45-minute sessions. Session 1 may be an intake, focused on assessment through rating scales and a semi-structured interview, as described in Chapter 3. Session 2 may cover psychoeducation (Module 1). Mastering bodily anxiety (Module 2) may be spread over Sessions 3 through 5, with Session 3 emphasizing exposure to bodily anxiety, Session 4 emphasizing relaxation exercises, and Session 5 further strengthening these focuses and expanding into exposures to anxiety in everyday life. Mastering cognitive anxiety (Module 3) may also be split into three sessions, with Session 6 focused on worry journaling and tactics for disempowering specific thoughts, Session 7 focused on non-reactive observation of thoughts, and Session 8 focused on formal and informal attention training strategies. Session 9 may focus on studying effectively, and Session 10 on best practices in test taking. Throughout a more extended course of treatment such as this, some homework assignments may be practiced and reviewed repeatedly across multiple weeks, depending on the focuses that are most valuable to the individual student.

MEASURING CHANGE

We strongly encourage practitioners to measure the efficacy of the treatment in a standardized way, and this is one reason to consider using quantitative rating scales like those described in Chapter 3. Unfortunately, as Romba et al. (2020) observed, "Although randomized controlled trials have implemented measurement-based care for years, its use is not yet common in clinical practice" (p. 645). Measurement-based care not only determines if a treatment has worked as intended (and if an alternative treatment is needed) but also conveys sincere interest in students' well-being, which in turn enhances the therapeutic alliance. Moreover, when treatment has been effective, completing rating scales can help to demonstrate those effects to students more powerfully, which itself increases self-confidence.

When treatment is brief, spanning no more than 5 or 6 sessions (see above), it is typically enough to conduct formal measurement at just two points in time, before the first session, and after the final session. We usually ask students to complete the Test Anxiety Inventory or the Multidimensional Test Anxiety Scale prior to the first session, using a web form, or else we administer it at the beginning of the first session via a paper form or web form. If a separate initial session is set aside for an intake, that session can include completion of rating scales as well. Post-treatment ratings on the same scale can be obtained at the end of the final session, before students depart. This approach is more likely to generate data than trying to get students to complete rating scales at a later date.

As with the initial assessment, thought should be given to the objects of measurement. As we noted in Chapter 3, symptoms of anxiety will generally decline with effective interventions such as the ones in our treatment modules, but because our treatment philosophy is less about anxiety reduction and more about learning to tolerate and even welcome anxiety, it is self-efficacy that may show a larger change than anxiety symptoms per se. The self-efficacy ratings discussed in Chapter 3 are very brief and can easily be added to an assessment battery.

Two other areas of formal assessment may be of interest to clinicians. First, engagement and enjoyment in educational settings can be rated or just described, to see whether addressing test anxiety has led to more positive attitudes toward settings that were formerly marred by exams. Second, since the treatments in our Modules 2 and 3 are helpful for anxiety more generally, it is possible to measure spillover effects of the treatment onto other kinds of anxiety. As we mentioned in Chapter 1, many students who have severe test anxiety will also have anxiety about other topics, at least those related to academics and performance.

We view measurement-based care as going beyond the use of rating scales, to refer more generally to techniques to measure change during therapy. Some of these techniques should be integrated into every session beyond the first one. It is helpful to start sessions by reviewing exams in the student's life. For a student in a typical academic setting, exams that have occurred since the last session or exams that are coming up should be discussed, along with how the student has been applying techniques from treatment and how helpful the student has found them to be. For a student preparing for a high-stakes test, it is appropriate to check in regarding the student's thoughts, feelings, and preparation strategies for that test in relation to therapy content. Therapists should explain why it's important for students to be candid about whether they have been using the techniques, as well as whether the techniques have been effective. To support such candor, of course, it's important to be nondefensive and show curiosity that is based on genuine concern for students' improvement. When a student reports either nonadherence or lack of effectiveness (and it is important to distinguish between those), this should generate a troubleshooting discussion to help the student either better adhere to recommendations or else consider alternative recommendations.

INCORPORATING TREATMENT INTO MULTI-TIERED SYSTEMS OF SUPPORT

Because test anxiety treatment can be effectively delivered in school settings, it is worth considering how the treatment fits into the multi-tiered systems of support (MTSS) structures that have become popular in school psychology and related fields (e.g., March & Mathur, 2020). MTSS structures often have three "tiers" of support modeled after three types of public health prevention/intervention strategies. Tier 1 represents universal interventions that are designed to prevent mental health problems in the first place. Social-emotional learning programs and evidence-based classroom management approaches are common examples of such interventions. In MTSS, school staff monitor students to see if these interventions have been effective. For students who are nevertheless showing problems, Tier 2 services are provided, with these comprising more intensive and targeted intervention strategies. These strategies are often provided in small group formats, and students are again monitored to determine their responses to the intervention. Finally, if these strategies are insufficient, a still more intense Tier 3 comprises individualized, highly intensive (in terms of school professionals' time and effort) interventions. This multi-tiered approach is designed to be both proactive and efficient.

Tier 1 Strategies

With respect to test anxiety, several elements from our treatment program are appropriate Tier 1 intervention strategies. For example, from our psychoeducation module (Chapter 6), all students should be aware that test anxiety is common and can even be rational and adaptive, increasing motivation and eliciting test preparation. Relatedly, students should be taught about the relationship between test anxiety and test performance, with emphasis on the fact that high test anxiety does not, by itself, prevent high performance. One appropriate delivery method for these Tier 1 interventions is "push in" lessons where a school psychologist, school counselor, or other mental health professional visits classrooms and provides a presentation and/or leads an interactive discussion on these issues.

Another method for delivering Tier 1 interventions uses teachers as interventionists. An in-service professional development training can model for teachers how lessons on test anxiety can be taught to students. Because teachers are often on the front lines of test anxiety, they can apply the information to their own grade level and subject area(s), and students may even view them as more credible information sources than unknown treaters. In-service trainings can also address teachers' own misconceptions about test anxiety and its effects, to ensure that teachers are not spreading messages that counter effective treatment. As with students and parents as audiences, we recommend that mental health professionals leading in-service trainings prepare for skepticism about the research on test anxiety's lack of direct effects on performance; many teachers have high levels of test anxiety themselves!

Another class of Tier 1 strategies focuses on teaching test preparation and test-taking skills from our Modules 4 and 5. Again, this can be done directly with students or via teacher training. Optimally, instruction on how to study and take tests would be part of education for all students, but in our experience, such instruction tends to be inconsistent at best. Finally, teachers often have minimal training in test design and how *they* can assist students in preparing for their tests, and benefit from in-service training and consultation about how to prepare both tests and students in ways that reduce unnecessary anxiety. For instance, some teachers use unnecessarily harsh fear-based appeals to motivate students to study (Putwain et al., 2021), refuse to provide students with information about what kinds of items they will see on upcoming tests, and write test items with confusing or imprecise language. These problems are not due to any malice but come from a lack of understanding that can be remedied through trainings.

Tier 2 and Tier 3 Strategies

MTSS approaches should always include a clear referral pathway from Tier 1 to Tier 2. In the case of test anxiety, teachers who see severe test anxiety symptoms, or who have students who report such symptoms, can refer the students to a school-based mental health professional for small-group treatment that includes Modules 2 and 3 while also reinforcing the messages from Modules 1, 4, and 5. Another referral pathway would involve administering a brief measure of test anxiety symptoms to all students, and identifying those with the highest scores, or scores above some criterion threshold, for more intensive treatment. Such emotional screenings have become popular in MTSS frameworks (Briesch et al., 2018). Of course, universal screening can seem logistically daunting, and even raises schools' concerns about liability for not effectively treating problems that they have themselves identified. Screening should be used when at least a proper Tier 2 program is available, and to ease logistics, very brief measures can be used (e.g., the 5-item short form of the Test Anxiety Inventory).

In MTSS, the Tier 2 versus Tier 3 distinction is not always clear, in terms of exactly which strategies are used in each tier. Often, Tier 2 interventions are presented in group formats, whereas Tier 3 interventions are delivered individually. This can be applied to test anxiety treatment, of course. Intensity can vary in other ways as well. For instance, for some students who present with physiological symptoms of test anxiety, relaxation strategies will be sufficient for symptom reduction, and student satisfaction with treatment will be high. This would be less intensive than interoceptive exposure exercises, which are easier to do in individual sessions and could be reserved for Tier 3 intervention.

Regardless of which strategies are placed where, the referral pathway from Tier 2 to Tier 3 should be based on measures of change during Tier 2 intervention programs. This is another reason why quantitative measures of change are so useful. Increasingly, school staff are asked to justify resource deployment by referencing data on which interventions have already been tried and failed (Alsalamah, 2022), and mental health professionals will comply best with such demands when they can point to scores on these measures.

CHAPTER 6

Learning About Test Anxiety

The more closely we study nervous people . . . the more surely we are impelled to the conclusion that, in very large part, the acute suffering as well as the chronic misery which goes by the name of nervousness is ultimately traceable to faulty education.
    —John Donley (1911, p. 4; in the public domain)

When we give workshops on the nature of test anxiety for teachers and mental health practitioners, a common reaction is "I wish I had known this when I was a student!" We agree, and our first therapy module teaches students key findings from the research literature on test anxiety. *Psychoeducation*—that is, directly teaching about relevant psychological topics—is a common strategy in counseling, one that originated in cases of severe mental illness (e.g., Anderson et al., 1980). Patients and their families often held serious misconceptions about the illnesses and were reassured and helped just by being provided accurate psychological information. Psychoeducation strategies are associated with less pathologizing of people's behaviors and experiences, and conceptualizing psychotherapy as a process of helping clients achieve goals rather than as treatment of illness per se (see e.g., Authier, 1977).

Psychoeducation has been especially popular in anxiety treatment, and with good effects. Often, psychoeducation is done in groups (the same format as most psychology classes), and one recent meta-analysis found group-based psychoeducation to reduce anxiety with a medium effect size ($d = -0.47$; Baourda et al., 2022). Psychoeducation may be particularly relevant in cases of anxiety because clients' beliefs *about* anxiety often aggravate their symptoms. Indeed, an entire model of psychotherapy for worry (metacognitive therapy) focuses on changing those beliefs (Wells, 2008).

In a full course of test anxiety treatment, we recommend spending one or two sessions just on psychoeducation. Of course, information about anxiety is actually scattered throughout all of our therapy modules, but we prefer to spend the first one or two sessions (after assessment) just doing psychoeducation. There are two broad goals to keep in mind.

First, there is specific factual information about test anxiety to convey. Students learn to view their test anxiety as normal and perfectly compatible with good academic functioning, instead of seeing it as unique, pathological, and harmful. Second, students should develop a sense of the treatment model as a whole, understanding *why* we would expect certain strategies to be effective in treating test anxiety. Psychoeducation helps instill hope in students and builds their motivation for practicing the exercises in Modules 2 and 3 (Chapters 7 and 8), and for changing study and test-taking behaviors, as presented in Modules 4 and 5 (Chapters 9 and 10).

NORMALIZING TEST ANXIETY

Some students with test anxiety feel that they are alone in their reactions to tests, or at least that their symptoms are fairly rare. These beliefs are especially common in certain client groups. For instance, male students are more likely to have a peer subculture in which talking about anxiety is discouraged, and young men who are open about their anxiety are perceived as weak and less masculine (Oransky & Marecek, 2009). Even though, as we discussed in Chapter 1, girls do experience more test anxiety on average, boys are still less likely to report the anxiety that they *do* feel to peers. A second group who may view their test anxiety as deviant is students whose test anxiety had a relatively late onset, such as in college. These students never experienced significant anxiety earlier, and never realized that many of their peers always did, so they think that something is wrong with them for experiencing it now. Finally, some students attend schools or are part of a family unit where there is pressure toward making high achievement look easy. Very high-achievement settings are associated with increased anxiety (e.g., Luthar et al., 2020), which can be especially problematic when there is a norm of pretending that everything is okay.

Even apart from these particular groups, we have found that students tend to underestimate how common test anxiety is in their peers. This is probably due to the fact that the symptoms of test anxiety aren't usually directly publicly observable to others—students can't see their peers' racing hearts or their worry thoughts, or, for that matter, associated avoidant behaviors, such as not taking practice tests while at home. Moreover, anxiety and other negative emotions occur more often when people are alone. Indeed, students tend to estimate that a range of negative emotional experiences are rarer in their peers than is actually the case (Jordan et al., 2011), which may cause them to fixate needlessly on these experiences. For any students who believe that test anxiety symptoms are rare or abnormal, accurate information can be a remedy. Sometimes this is as simple as the therapist making a general statement about how common test anxiety symptoms are:

STUDENT: I don't know why, but starting last year, I can no longer sleep the night before a big test.

THERAPIST: I'm sorry to hear that. It can be really frustrating when you can't get to sleep, especially the night before an important event.

STUDENT: It doesn't make any sense! I feel like everyone else comes into class ready for the exam, and there I am, working on three hours of sleep.

THERAPIST: Not being able to sleep before exams is actually a pretty common experience. But many students I meet with think they're the only one.

At other times, we bring out statistics like those reviewed in Chapter 1. For example, in a large study of university students, 99% of students endorsed at least one test anxiety symptom (Lovett et al., 2024). See Handout 6.1 for a compendium of relevant statistics. We sometimes ask students to guess the prevalence of test anxiety symptoms ahead of time to emphasize the discrepancy between perception and reality, and we discuss students' reaction to the latter. Furthermore, in the same way that students can feel relieved when they learn that their test anxiety is normal, they can also feel validated to learn that their underestimation of others' test anxiety is normal. We often point out to them how invisible other people's anxiety can be to us, which combines with people's curation of a positive public image (e.g., on social media) to leave us feeling alone in our own anxiety.

Before moving on, we should acknowledge that some students do *not* need much information about the prevalence of test anxiety. They may even be in environments where peers are very open about symptoms (sometimes there is a culture of co-rumination; see Spendelow et al., 2017), and although they are frustrated by the symptoms, they have no illusions about the rarity of the experience of test anxiety. In such cases, we still like to acknowledge and reinforce that information, but we focus more on other aspects of psychoeducation.

BREAKING TEST ANXIETY APART

When students think they're alone in their test anxiety, the anxiety feels more formidable and tends to affect their behavior in more deleterious ways (e.g., they may not take a challenging but useful class because they expect it will cause test anxiety). Emphasizing the commonness of test anxiety is a first step in defanging test anxiety. A second step is helping students dismantle the phenomenon of test anxiety into its constituent parts.

We usually begin with a very high-level overview of anxiety:

> *Everyone has pleasant and unpleasant emotions. Both kinds of feelings can be healthy and useful. Anxiety is an example of an uncomfortable feeling. When we feel anxious or fearful, it's often a useful sign that there might be a threat nearby, and it causes us to take action to deal with that threat. For example, if I'm outdoors and I hear thunder in the distance, I'll start to feel uneasy and think about how to escape a possible lightning storm. The unpleasant anxiety I feel will motivate me to take cover. Once I get indoors to a safe place, I feel less anxious.*
>
> *When have you felt anxious, nervous, or scared recently?*

After talking through one or two student-generated examples, emphasize that anxiety comes up commonly in academic settings, especially when a student is doing challenging things they haven't yet fully mastered. The possibility of failure can feel threatening. The idiom "getting outside your comfort zone" is apt—growing is, indeed, almost always a process that involves a degree of emotional discomfort.

Next, we introduce the idea that breaking down uncomfortable emotions into physical sensations, thoughts, and associated behaviors can help make the emotions feel less overwhelming, and instead they can become more manageable and endurable. Part of treating test anxiety is understanding it. If working one-to-one with a student, you might ask them to start talking about how test anxiety shows up in their body and mind and the behaviors associated with their test anxiety. If doing a group intervention, it can be helpful to have students first privately brainstorm their test anxiety symptoms using Handout 6.2, before leading a groupwide discussion of the three components of test anxiety. Handout 6.3 is a useful recap for students to take with them from session.

Physiological Component

When discussing physiological or "bodily" symptoms of test anxiety with students, it's helpful to describe these symptoms as a matter of the body getting "hyped up" to take action when there's something threatening in the environment. This reminds the students that anxiety is a functional, adaptive emotion in general, even if parts of the bodily response may not be especially useful when it comes to academic challenges and may mostly just be annoying to experience. Physiological symptoms of test anxiety can include quickened breathing, accelerated heart rate, sweating, gastrointestinal discomfort, nausea (and vomiting in extreme cases), diarrhea, an urge to urinate, feelings of cold or hotness, shakiness or trembling, lightheadedness, dizziness, muscle tension, dry mouth or throat, and general restlessness. The physiology of anxiety can also cause sleep disruption.

Cognitive Component

When discussing the thinking component (or cognitive symptoms) of test anxiety, students often find it helpful to consider the thoughts that show up before, during, and after a test. (Bodily symptoms, on the other hand, aren't differentiated as much by timing relative to anxiety-provoking exams.) In anticipation of a test, students may worry about failing or performing less well than they should; about future consequences of poor performance on the test (e.g., a disappointing overall grade in a class, or not getting into a college or graduate school); about how the test will be extremely difficult; about how their anxiety during the test will impede their performance; and about not meeting parents', teachers', or peers' expectations. During a test, students may experience any of these worries, and they may also think about how other students are doing better on the test than they are; about how they will run out of time and not finish the test; about how the test is unfair or impossible or at least not probing the things they studied; and about how they themselves are stupid, unable to cope with stress, or otherwise inadequate. Students may find these thoughts distracting, and they may worry that their memory, attention, and comprehension during the test is being impaired by their anxiety.

Even after the test is over, students may continue to entertain similar worries to those they experienced before and during the test (e.g., about how a low performance may affect their academic future and others' opinions of them). Test-anxious students are also prone to rumination after a test is over, trying to remember each of the items and their answers to the items, going over the questions again and again, and agonizing over whether their answers were correct. This can prevent students from mentally moving on to their next class or activity.

Problem Behaviors Associated with Test Anxiety

When discussing problem behaviors associated with test anxiety, we like to begin by noting that sometimes, feeling anxious about a test can motivate effective behaviors:

> *Ideally, feeling nervous about an upcoming test can be useful. To ease your discomfort, you might study more until you feel confident you have mastered the material reasonably well and are prepared for the test. If this was the only behavior associated with your bodily anxiety and worries about a test, we wouldn't call this behavior a problem at all, because it would work fine for you. It would be like finding indoor shelter when you hear thunder in the distance, and then feeling more comfortable. Well done—your anxiety went to work for you in a helpful way!*
>
> *But unfortunately, sometimes we develop problem behaviors related to test anxiety. These are behaviors that aren't so helpful. They are the equivalent of putting earplugs in your ears after hearing thunder in order to relieve your anxiety about being hurt in a lightning storm—you might feel safer, but you aren't actually any safer! Indeed, you might be less safe, if you now can't even hear if the thunder is getting nearer. Another example of an unhelpful anxiety-driven behavior would be trapping yourself inside a lightning-proof vault in your basement whenever you hear thunder. This might actually keep you really safe, but you'd be better off overall if you simply got indoors to ensure reasonable safety and then went about your day doing productive or enjoyable things, while tolerating whatever remaining anxiety you might have.*
>
> *What sorts of things do you do, related to your test anxiety, that aren't really so helpful for you, on the balance? These might be things you do before, during, or after tests that make you anxious.*
>
> *Another way of getting at the same question is: How do you think you'd behave differently, before, during, or after tests, if you didn't experience any anxiety about tests? This can give you a sense of which of your behaviors are related to test anxiety.*

Problem behaviors associated with test anxiety can include avoiding or procrastinating test preparation; avoiding practice tests or other studying methods that resemble testing; avoiding the test itself (e.g., feigning illness); rushing through parts of the test and not using the full time allotted for it; not fully reviewing and learning from feedback given on the test; and not meeting with teachers or attending special sessions to review the exam afterward, when these resources are available. Students may also engage in behaviors that help distract them from feelings of test anxiety, such as using substances, napping, binge eating, overusing social media, bingeing streaming media, shopping, or exercising excessively. Or students may seek to quell test anxiety by seeking reassurance from other people over and over. Some students try to eliminate their test anxiety by studying obsessively, well past the point of diminishing returns, and to the point that they lose sleep and balanced well-being in their lives, and may even harm their overall academic performance. On a larger scale, test-anxious students may select courses or even majors or schools that have fewer stressful tests, or may decline to take standardized tests even if doing so might restrict the desirable opportunities available to them.

After discussing the various aspects of test anxiety with students, consider asking them to monitor and record their experiences with test anxiety outside of session (a blank copy of Handout 6.2 helps keep some students organized in their recording). This can help students build further insight into how test anxiety shows up for them in its various forms, before, during, and after tests. Remind students, again, that disaggregating the test anxiety "beast" into its smaller, specific parts can also have a therapeutic impact by itself, decreasing the aversive power of test anxiety. The data that students collect through self-monitoring can also help you keep tailoring the treatment to meet their needs and preferences.

TEACHING THAT TEST ANXIETY ISN'T HARMFUL

It's typically easy to teach students that test anxiety is common, whereas it can take some work to persuade them that test anxiety does not harm test performance in the way that most students think it does. Students often resist this idea. In fact, we devoted a whole chapter of this book (Chapter 2) to persuading readers of this point. The benefits of understanding that test anxiety isn't dangerous are twofold. First, students often feel some immediate relief from anxiety once they believe that their anxiety is harmless. The pressure of a "relax, or you'll fail!" mindset greatly increases uncomfortable anxiety. Once test anxiety isn't experienced as such a threat, it doesn't grab students' attention as much. Second, students often feel empowered by the knowledge that test anxiety won't impair their performance, and this translates into their making choices according to their interests and aspirations rather than according to a limiting agenda of minimizing their anxiety (e.g., they may elect to take a challenging class, or an optional standardized test that may help them gain admission to college).

We begin by simply telling students that lots of research has shown that, contrary to common intuitions, test anxiety has a very weak relationship to test performance. That is, students who are more anxious during a test perform about the same as students who are less anxious. In fact, even quite high levels of anxiety are compatible with good performance. Ask students to comb their memories for personal examples supporting this point: "Have you ever been really anxious or keyed up about your performance and done well on a test or something else at school?" Students can also draw on other domains of performance (e.g., sports, music) when looking for personal evidence that they can do well when anxious. It's useful to have examples of elite performers who acknowledge high levels of performance-related anxiety. Emma Watson, the actor, said that before giving a speech, "I was very nervous. It wasn't an easy thing for me to do. It felt like: 'Am I going to have lunch with these people, or am I going to be eaten? Am I the lunch?'" (Candy, 2015). Harry Styles, the pop musician, was described by a colleague as getting "quite scared" before shows and going "through a period of throwing up before he went on stage." (McAfee, 2013).

Of course, students are likely to also easily generate examples of times when they felt test anxiety and didn't perform well on a test (or were nervous during a sports event and performed poorly, etc.), and they may take these examples as evidence that test anxiety can at least sometimes harm performance. This provides a good opportunity to prompt students to challenge the common assumption that test anxiety *causes* low performance: "Is it possible that things other than your anxiety might have contributed to your low performance?" Here, perhaps after some further gentle encouragement, students usually can recognize that a third variable, such as insufficient preparation for the test, might have caused both their anxiety and their performance problems—or maybe they'd have been anxious no matter how well-prepared they were, but it was still the poor preparation that accounted for the poor performance. Students may also point out that performance problems during a test can actually *cause* test anxiety. Sometimes both of these processes can be at play: A poorly prepared student may feel nervous going into a test, knowing they probably will find the test difficult, and then as they indeed have trouble on the test (because they are unprepared), they begin to feel even more anxious, worrying about how a low score may cause them to fail the class, or may disappoint their parents or teacher.

For many students, it's helpful to cite further research to back up the assertion that test anxiety doesn't impair test performance. We have found that students are especially impressed by the research studies using the SAT, described in Chapter 2. Middle school and high school students are usually familiar with the SAT as a prototypically high-stakes and anxiety-provoking test. The research findings can be stated simply:

> *One study looked at students' performance on a set of SAT problems that occurred during the real test, when most students were probably anxious, as well the same students' performance on a similar set of SAT problems that the students knew wouldn't count for anything. Students' performance was about the same on both sets of problems. They presumably felt much more nervous and worried when completing problems during the actual SAT administration, and yet they did just as well then as they did when working on SAT problems without anything at stake. So it doesn't seem like their anxiety level had an impact on their ability to succeed on SAT problems.*
>
> *In another study, students' anxiety was measured both before they began taking the SAT and after they finished taking the SAT. The students' anxiety levels before the test had almost no relationship to their performance on the test. But their anxiety levels after the test correlated more strongly with their test performance. So it seems like being nervous before the test didn't matter much for their performance, but doing poorly during the test did cause them to feel more nervous. If anything, test performance problems caused test anxiety, rather than test anxiety causing test performance problems.*

Answering Students' Objections

Sometimes students will push back by pointing out that it would seem hard to perform well on a test if a student were in a totally panicked meltdown, hyperventilating, crying, and vomiting during a test. It's appropriate to validate such an objection. If we take it to such an extreme, high anxiety could indeed impair performance. Similarly, if we looked at the absolute extreme opposite of high anxiety—a student who was in a stupor and maybe falling asleep—this state of over-relaxation would also not be compatible with high performance. But many research studies have shown that within the usual range of anxiety that students actually experience during real testing, there's little to no relationship between anxiety level and performance.

Students may also object that no matter what research studies say, it's difficult to shake off the commonsense intuition that test anxiety does impair their performance. Here it's useful to validate that there are good reasons most students believe that test anxiety harms performance. First, students may have vivid memories of some times when they were very anxious and performed very badly, and it's natural to infer from those experiences that the anxiety caused the bad performance. But remind students that it may have been their recognition of their poor test preparation, and their realization during the test that they were doing predictably poorly (given their preparation), that caused their anxiety to go into overdrive. The anxiety didn't cause the bad performance. Remind the students also that they probably have had some experiences where they were very anxious even during strong performance. Second, validate that students may have learned to fear test anxiety partly because of messages they'd received from other students, teachers, or parents. Other people who think that test anxiety impairs performance may have emphasized the importance of trying to take a deep breath and stay calm during exams, teaching students that test anxiety is something potentially harmful that must be guarded against.

CONNECTING STUDENTS' GOALS TO THE TREATMENT

After helping students normalize, disaggregate, and reappraise their test anxiety as compatible with high academic functioning, we recommend returning to the treatment goals that were identified during their initial assessment. Based on the further breakdown (during psychoeducation discussions, as above) of students' physiological and cognitive test anxiety symptoms, the associated problem behaviors, and the increased awareness of students' implicit theories of how test anxiety relates to test performance, you will be better able to evaluate with students how Modules 2, 3, 4, and 5 will fit into the overall picture of their test anxiety treatment, and where it will make sense to place relatively greater emphasis in the treatment.

Ask questions to sharpen students' motivations: "What are your short-term and long-term goals at school? Do you maybe even have career goals that involve certain academic requirements? How could you benefit from treating your test anxiety?" Reinforce the psychoeducation from the present chapter while discussing the students' goals and motivations. For example, if students suggest that treating their test anxiety will help them do better on an entrance exam for something they wish to do, remind them that test anxiety doesn't have much impact on test performance. Whereas if students state that they'll be more likely to take the entrance exam that makes them nervous if they have better tools to stay comfortable during the exam, or if they can get more comfortable with their anxiety, that's a more realistic framing.

Of course, at this stage, students don't yet know exactly what the test anxiety treatment will consist of. We recommend sharing a copy of Handout 6.4, which summarizes the test anxiety treatment modules, and reviewing this with students. Equipped with the understanding provided by the foregoing psychoeducation module, students will now be in a good position to digest this content and discuss how it connects with their treatment goals. In turn, you'll be well-positioned to fine-tune your plan for how extensively to emphasize the materials in Modules 2, 3, 4, and 5 for the rest of the treatment.

How Common Is Test Anxiety?

The following statistics are from research studies on test anxiety. See Chapter 1 of *Overcoming Test Anxiety* by Jordan and Lovett for more details and for citations supporting these figures.

- Among 335 3rd, 4th, and 5th graders, 55% endorsed moderate or high anxiety regarding classroom tests, and 68% endorsed moderate or high anxiety about a state assessment.

- Among 1,348 9th and 10th graders, the average student reported experiencing test anxiety with a frequency between "sometimes" and "often."

- Between 30% and 52% of college students report experiencing test anxiety "often" or "almost always" on the Test Anxiety Inventory, a widely used assessment of test anxiety.

- Among 183 graduate students in the healthcare professions, 51% of women and 38% of men had at least "moderately high" levels of test anxiety.

- Among almost 3,000 college students, about 99% reported having at least one test anxiety symptom, at least sometimes. Most students endorsed experiencing each of the following symptoms at least sometimes: feeling uneasy or upset during tests, difficulty concentrating on tests due to preoccupations with course grades, worrying a great deal prior to tests, and being unable to stop worrying about a test after it is over.

Breaking Test Anxiety Apart

How does test anxiety show up in your body? What are the physiological changes you notice when you experience test anxiety?

What sorts of thoughts and worries show up when you're experiencing test anxiety? Consider patterns of thinking that appear before, during, and after tests when you have test anxiety.

What problem behaviors are related to your test anxiety? What sorts of things do you do, related to your test anxiety, that aren't really so helpful for you, on the balance? These might be things you do before, during, or after tests.

The Three Components of Test Anxiety

The following are common examples of how test anxiety can show up for students.

ANXIETY IN THE BODY

- Faster breathing
- Discomfort in the gut
- Urgency to pee
- Lightheadedness
- Dry mouth or throat

- Faster heart rate
- Nausea
- Feeling hot or cold
- Dizziness
- Sleep disruption

- Sweating
- Diarrhea
- Feeling shaky
- Muscle tension

ANXIETY IN THE MIND

- Worrying that a test will be really hard
- Worrying that anxiety during the test will hurt performance
- Worrying about failing or performing poorly
- Worrying about not meeting parents', teachers', or peers' expectations
- Worrying that a low test score will lead to a poor overall class grade
- Worrying that a low test score will prevent admission to a college or graduate school
- Thinking that other students are doing better on the test than you are
- Thinking about how you will run out of time and not finish the test
- Thinking about how the test is unfair, too hard, or not testing what you studied
- Thinking you are stupid, unable to cope with stress, or otherwise inadequate
- Thinking over and over again about test items after the test is over

PROBLEM BEHAVIORS RELATED TO ANXIETY

- Avoiding or procrastinating test preparation
- Avoiding practice tests or other studying methods that resemble testing
- Avoiding the test itself (e.g., staying home from school)
- Rushing through parts of the test
- Not fully reviewing and learning from feedback given on the test
- Not meeting with teachers or going to review sessions after the exam, when offered
- Numbing or distracting from test anxiety through substance use, napping, binge eating, overusing social media, bingeing streaming media, shopping, or exercising excessively
- Seeking reassurance (e.g., about your performance in a class) excessively
- Studying obsessively, even after being prepared enough for the test
- Choosing classes, majors, or schools based on which ones have fewer stressful tests
- Not taking standardized tests even if doing so might increase your educational or career opportunities

Treating Test Anxiety

MASTERING BODILY ANXIETY

This treatment module will help you gain mastery over the nervousness you feel in your body when experiencing test anxiety. You'll complete physical exercises, such as breathing very quickly, that cause bodily feelings of anxiety. You'll learn to feel more welcoming of these sometimes uncomfortable bodily aspects of test anxiety. You'll also practice techniques, such as muscle relaxation, that may help calm the anxiety directly. Furthermore, you'll practice doing things in your everyday life that you might normally avoid due to the physical nervousness that doing those things brings on. And to further increase your confidence that you can deal with the physiological aspects of test anxiety, you'll complete mentally and physically challenging tasks after purposely revving up anxiety in the body.

FOCUSING THE MIND

In this module, you'll complete a series of exercises that help you get less tangled up with your test anxiety-related thoughts, increasing your bandwidth to focus on what really matters for you. You'll practice a writing exercise that helps you build distance from your worries and helps you take what's useful from them, while letting go of the excess. You'll also practice simply watching your own thinking unfold, with openness and curiosity. This will help you develop a more peaceful experience of your mind, even when you're experiencing thoughts related to test anxiety. Moreover, you'll learn tools (e.g., repeating a thought aloud until it sounds silly) for reducing the emotional power and the believability of unhelpful thoughts. Through formal and informal exercises, you'll build up your control over your attention, so that you can focus on studying, for example, without getting sidetracked by your test anxiety or other distractions in the environment.

STUDYING FOR SUCCESS

Here you will learn the most efficient and effective methods for mastering academic material. This will increase your confidence and your test performance, and as you more consistently do well on tests, your test anxiety will decrease over time. You'll learn that the best studying techniques are often the same ones that bring up some test anxiety—for example, taking a practice test, or trying to teach a friend what you've learned, without using any notes. You'll find these study methods more comfortable after strengthening your anxiety tolerance through the previous treatment modules. You'll also learn how to space out the timing of your study sessions to maximize learning. Additionally, you'll learn best practices for reducing distraction and procrastination when studying (e.g., getting sucked into your smartphone). Finally, you'll learn tools to improve your sleep. Studying and learning are much easier when you're well-rested!

DOING YOUR BEST ON TESTS

Students with test anxiety often worry that they are "bad test takers," unable to show their knowledge and abilities on exams as well as they should. This treatment module focuses on teaching you the most effective techniques for doing as well as possible on tests, given your level of preparation. You'll learn best practices for taking any sort of test, as well as a set of tactics that are specifically tailored to multiple-choice tests. To practice using these tactics, you'll work on a sample test with difficult problems that will require you to reach beyond your knowledge base to identify correct answers. After completing this module, you will feel even more confident about taking tests and more motivated to prepare for them, knowing that you have the skills to do as well as any other student who enters the exam with a similar mastery of relevant content.

CHAPTER 7

Mastering Bodily Anxiety

In the introductory psychoeducation component of our test anxiety treatment (see Chapter 6), students learn that feeling nervous does not, by itself, harm test performance. Contrary to common intuitions, students can do just as well on exams when their heart rate is fast as they can when it's slower. We have found that learning this fact alone can bring immediate benefits to students. Rather than fearing that anxiety they notice in their bodies will impair their performance—a fear that in turn causes more anxious arousal, in a feedback loop—students can interpret their heightened nervousness as normal when facing a challenging situation. They then feel more at ease overall with testing, and more accepting of variations in their anxiety levels.

Still, in our experience, the impact of intellectually grasping new facts can be limited. Even if students buy into the notion that anxiety won't wreck their performance, some students will continue to feel quite uncomfortable about taking tests, to the point that they show maladaptive avoidant behaviors such as declining to participate in optional practice test sessions that can efficiently improve their learning. In short, psychoeducation is not enough. Experiential exercises are crucial for developing mastery over test anxiety.

OVERVIEW OF PROCEDURES

In this treatment module, students learn more about how bodily manifestations of anxiety are safe and can actually be functional, and they learn that approaching rather than avoiding anxiety can make it more manageable. We then introduce exercises that help students build more comfort with and acceptance of the physiological aspects of their anxiety response. These exercises, called *exposures*, involve purposely inducing bodily anxiety and sticking with it. We also equip students with complementary tools that often help them to directly calm their bodies. Finally, we invite students to practice behaving flexibly in real-life situ-

TABLE 7.1. Summary of Procedures for Bodily Anxiety

General Strategies	Specific Tactics
Learning how bodily anxiety can be functional	Education about the fight-or-flight response Education about exposure versus avoidance
Getting used to bodily anxiety	Body scan practice Physical exercises that induce bodily anxiety
Calming the body	Slowed breathing Muscle relaxation
Building everyday courage	Seeking typically avoided real-world experiences that induce bodily anxiety Welcoming other forms of discomfort
Strengthening flexibility in the face of anxiety	Doing mental work while physically anxious Completing physical tasks while physically anxious

ations when they are feeling highly anxious, including with academic tasks. We summarize these interventions in Table 7.1.

Through all of these exercises, students build confidence. They also begin to feel more at ease when studying and taking tests, on average—even when bodily symptoms of anxiety happen. Making academic work a less painful and more pleasant part of students' everyday lives is, of course, a meaningful end in itself. On top of this, increased comfort with tests can decrease students' maladaptive avoidance behaviors, not just in the short-term (as in the practice tests example above), but in the long term as well. For example, students who are more comfortable with the bodily sensations associated with test anxiety are less likely to shy away from a preferred career path simply because of the volume of stressful tests that it may require.

SELECTION AND SEQUENCING OF PROCEDURES

As with the other components of our test anxiety treatment, therapists should use their judgment in adapting the materials in this chapter to the needs and developmental level of the specific students they are helping. For instance, if a student has had panic attacks related to their test anxiety, then a greater emphasis on bodily anxiety exposures may make sense. Or if a student's anxiety invariably increases rather than decreases when they focus on their breathing in any way, then muscle relaxation, rather than paced breathing, may deserve more focus as a calming tool. And the level of psychoeducation detail that interests and is comprehensible to students—about the autonomic nervous system, for example—will vary based on grade level.

The materials reviewed below do not need to be presented in the order in which they appear. When doing test anxiety interventions with groups of students, for example, there is a risk of students entering a more passive "listening to the lecture" mode if too much psychoeducation is done upfront. Hence, in a group format, we usually jump into a highly engaging experiential exercise such as hyperventilation exposures early on, to spur students' interest and get them talking with one another. That said, we do recommend one rule of thumb with the sequencing of procedures. If students are taught relaxation techniques, this ideally would occur after they have already had some practice with exposures for their anxiety. This helps to keep clear the message that anxiety cannot be avoided altogether in life, and that learning to embrace situations that may include bodily anxiety is paramount. It can be nice to also have tools that sometimes take the edge off of nervousness, but this is not the main goal of treatment. Starting off with relaxation exercises may inadvertently feed a student's unrealistic expectation of being able to control their bodily state at all times.

HOW ANXIETY SHOWS UP IN THE BODY

As discussed above, the amount of information about the physiology of anxiety that you choose to share with students will differ depending on their grade level and curiosity. For many students, a brief recap of the information presented in Chapter 6—a high-level overview of how specific aspects of anxiety in the body can be helpful in coping with some threats—will suffice. But we have found that even if you set out to keep this psychoeducation minimal, it's helpful to be prepared to answer students' questions, and we therefore recommend reviewing the information below.

Academic tests, like many other modern stressors, do not pose an immediate threat to a person's physical survival. However, as with other threats to esteem, status, and future prospects, a challenging test can nonetheless cause our bodies to react as if we were in danger. At a behavioral level, fear engages a system that helps mobilize people and other animals to escape threats (Gray, 1988; Gray & McNaughton, 2003). This *fight-or-flight* response system is especially sensitive in children and adolescents with a variety of anxiety disorders (Vervoot et al., 2010). When activated, this system causes us to scan the environment vigilantly and to either flee, if the threat is imminent enough, or to fight off the threat when nothing else works.

At a physiological level, the stress response to tests and other anxiety-inducing threats is underpinned by the autonomic nervous system. The autonomic nervous system regulates bodily functions that aren't under conscious, voluntarily control, such as the beating of the heart, and its activity constitutes a core part of emotions in general (Kriebig, 2010). Two of its divisions are key to understanding the stress response: the sympathetic and parasympathetic nervous systems.

Stressful situations that require fast behavioral responses activate the sympathetic nervous system. When the sympathetic nervous system is activated, adrenaline is released, and a familiar cascade of anxiety-related bodily changes occurs: heart rate increases; airways in the lungs expand; stored energy is released into the bloodstream; blood flow is diverted away from the gut and the skin and toward the heart, lungs, and skeletal muscles; perspiration increases; and the pupils dilate. Activation of the parasympathetic nervous system, on the other hand, is associated with times of rest and involves changes such as reduced heart rate and blood pressure and increased digestive processes. It is important for students to understand that the bodily changes produced by activation of the sympathetic nervous system are helpful in prototypically scary situations in which physical action is called for, such as when needing to flee from a dangerous animal. It is beneficial in such a scenario to have oxygen exchange and blood flow kicked into high gear and to have the muscles primed for action. Even in non-dangerous but anxiety-provoking situations involving strenuous physical exertion, such as participating in a high-stakes sports match, these bodily responses are useful and tend not to feel disruptive to us.

When sitting down with a stressful test, on the other hand—and in other situations in which putting one's energy into physically fighting or fleeing isn't a sensible option—bodily anxiety can be especially attention-grabbing and uncomfortable (cf. Ehrenreich et al., 2018). Bodily signs of anxiety can feel threatening in and of themselves (e.g., feeling as if one might go crazy, pass out, or have a heart attack), and can also amplify perceptions of threats in the environment ("something must be terribly wrong"—perhaps one's performance on a test?). It can feel as if it will be impossible to focus and perform well. Naturally, all of this discomfort can cause people to want to avoid anxiety-provoking situations such as tests.

HOW EXPOSURE WORKS

To introduce the idea of exposure therapy for mastering the sensations of anxiety in the body, we like to get students thinking about how fears in general are overcome:

> *Tests are inherently stressful, especially when they count for a lot. Just like with a major sports competition or musical performance, you'll probably always feel some nerves when you have an important exam coming up, and when you're sitting down to take the test. These are normal feelings when the body and mind are preparing for a challenge. But the bodily aspects of anxiety—like noticing your heart pounding or changes in your breathing—can be uncomfortable, and anxiety about feeling those bodily sensations can actually be a big part of test anxiety. If you're more comfortable with the bodily experience of anxiety, you'd probably find yourself feeling less worried and more confident about taking tests.*
>
> *So how do we overcome the fear of fear, so to speak? It can help to think about how we deal with other fears in life. Imagine you had a friend who was really afraid of dogs. They turn down social invitations when they expect dogs might be present, they turn around and find a different route when they run into dogs while walking, and so forth. How do you think your friend could get more comfortable with dogs?*

Students generate a variety of creative ideas in response to this question. Most of these ideas converge on the theme of *exposure*, or repeatedly approaching the thing that causes a person anxiety or fear. Common sense says, and research confirms, that if the friend spends enough time having safe experiences with dogs, their fears will eventually melt away. Moreover, if actually physically interacting with a dog is "too much, too soon" for the friend, they could start off by watching lots of dog videos. There are many ways that a person could encounter dog-related stimuli to build more positive (or at least benign) associations with canines.

Exposure therapy is highly effective for treating a variety of anxiety-related problems, and yet the majority of individuals in psychotherapy for these problems do not receive any formal exposure-based treatment (Kaplan & Tolin, 2011). It's helpful to share with students that exposure to the bodily aspects of anxiety can help not only with their test anxiety, but with many kinds of anxiety- and fear-related problems, as sensitivity to and avoidance of uncomfortable physiological sensations is a common feature of emotional disorders (Barlow et al., 2018; Boettcher et al., 2016; Boswell et al., 2013):

> *A great way to increase your courage across all sorts of anxiety-provoking settings, including with tests and other academic tasks, is to spend time purposely sitting with and observing your feelings of nervousness, until these feelings become less threatening. We're going to do exercises that bring up anxious feelings in the body when there isn't actually anything potentially threatening happening, like a high-stakes test. By doing this over and over, you'll learn to feel more comfortable with bodily anxiety, and you'll feel less compelled to avoid situations that bring up that anxiety. The feelings will become more tolerable and less like they mean anything catastrophic—more like a mild itch rather than a sharp pain.*

When conducting exposure therapy with students, it's a good idea to bear in mind key principles from contemporary research on how exposure works (e.g., Craske et al., 2008, 2014; Weisman & Rodebaugh, 2018):

- To learn that a situation, such as feeling anxiety in the body, is safe, it's important to root out and eventually remove any *safety behaviors* that might make attributions for one's safety ambiguous. For example, a student might check their pulse with their fingers while doing a hyperventilation exercise, to reassure themselves that their heart rate isn't getting too high. Or they may distract themselves from feelings of dizziness, when doing a spinning exercise, by listening to a podcast. These behaviors make it harder to learn that the stimuli themselves—a racing heart or dizzy sensations—are harmless, even without the assurance of counting one's pulse or the mitigation provided by music.
- Even after learning to feel safer with particular stimuli or situations, old feelings of threat associated with those things can surge back if the associations with mastery and safety aren't maintained actively. This is part of why we include, later in this chapter, instructions for students to make a long-term habit of seeking out experiences in everyday life that elicit bodily anxiety. A student could do all sorts of intensive exposure to bodily cues of anxiety for a few weeks during test anxiety treatment, but if they then revert to a lifestyle in which they try to minimize their encounters with the body's fight-or-flight response kicking into gear, the gains they made during treatment might be transient.
- Although it helps to provide an overarching rationale and positive expectations for exposure exercises, students will have the strongest learning experiences when they are allowed to harbor some natural trepidation beforehand. Hence, if a student asks before a spinning exercise whether they might get so dizzy that they need to vomit, it's best to encourage participation and curiosity without offering direct assurance—for example, calmly offering, "I guess we'll have to try it and find out what happens." Afterward, the student will be able to directly compare their negative expectation against the reality that followed, and the contrast they notice will maximize their learning.

- Linguistic processing of one's emotional experience can be helpful during exposure. That is, students may benefit from being encouraged to verbalize to themselves exactly what they notice during exposure exercises. This can help them stay grounded in the experience itself, observing nonjudgmentally what's happening here and now, and acknowledging that it can be tolerated, rather than becoming lost in anxious ideas about what the experience might become.
- Using a variety of stimuli in a variety of contexts can accelerate and strengthen the learning of safety through exposure. For example, going back to the dog example, a person will feel more robustly safe with dogs if they do exposure practice with different sizes and breeds of dogs, single dogs as well as groups of dogs, dogs in parks as well as dogs in houses, leashed and unleashed dogs, and so forth. This is why students are encouraged to combine multiple bodily anxiety exposure exercises, to do them in different settings, and to eventually combine them with other activities, including anxiety-provoking academic tasks.
- The intensity and duration of discomfort experienced during exposure exercises often declines between sessions more than within a given session. Students may find a given exercise equally challenging at the end of a 10-minute set of practices as they did at the beginning, but at the start of a new session of exposures the next day, that same exercise may feel markedly more doable.

PRACTICING EXPOSURE

For most students, we recommend jumping straight into the exercises for actively inducing bodily anxiety, called *interoceptive exposures* in behavioral therapy jargon. However, for students who are especially fearful or avoidant of bodily sensations of anxiety, it can help to warm up with the body scan exercise.

Body Scan

Readers, and some students, may be familiar with the notion of a body scan, which involves turning one's attention sequentially to sensations in all different body parts. It's commonly used as a mindfulness meditation exercise, to develop skill at nonjudgmental, curious observation of bodily feelings. However, most body scan scripts also include suggestive language that seems designed to instill relaxation, such as an emphasis on slow exhalations, relaxing any tensions located during the exercise, or visualizing the release of stress from the body. Body scan practice has been shown to offer immediate and longer-term benefits; for example, a single 10-minute body scan decreased distress related to chronic pain (Ussher et al., 2014), and six weeks of daily practice improved concentration and emotion regulation and increased self-compassion and life satisfaction.

In our test anxiety treatment, the body scan is not used as a relaxation tool, although the slowed breathing and muscle relaxation exercises described later in this chapter include much of what is likely calming in a typical body scan meditation. For our purposes, the body scan is used instead as a mild exposure to bodily sensations of all kinds, including those that are unpleasant. In the body scan script that we present below, we encourage attention to potentially aversive feelings that may be associated with anxiety (e.g., the pulse, digestive sensations), alongside other focuses such as sensations in the skin or skeletal muscles. While reading all or parts of this script aloud to students, try to use your normal, everyday cadence and tone, with approximately 10-second pauses between each instruction, and pauses of a few seconds within each instruction wherever it feels natural:

> *Begin by closing your eyes or casting them downward, so that you are undistracted by sights in the room.*
>
> *Notice the feeling of your feet on the floor. Are your shoes tight or loose? Do you feel pressure anywhere on your feet? Are they at all sweaty? Are there any small, involuntary movements of the muscles in your feet, as you pay attention to them? Notice how your legs feel supported by the soles of your feet, pressed flat against the floor.*
>
> *Next, turn attention to your legs. Are there any tingling sensations in your skin? Any muscles that are sore or cramping? Do you have urges to move your legs at all? Whatever you notice, just pay attention to it. There is no need to change anything—just notice the sensations, and stay with them.*
>
> *Now notice your abdomen and your lower back. Are you hunched over or sitting straight up? Which muscles are tensed, and which are relaxed? Do you feel any nausea, gurgling, or other sensations in your gut?*
>
> *Move your attention next to your lungs. Notice each breath entering and exiting your lungs. Follow the breath as it goes in and out, traveling through your nose, mouth, and throat. Feel the temperature of the air. Do you feel like you're getting the right amount of air into you, or are there any urges to slow down or speed up your breathing? When you breathe in, is there more expansion in your chest or in your belly?*
>
> *Next, notice your shoulders, arms, and hands. Where is there tension in your muscles? Where is there relaxation? How does your skin feel? Do you notice any itches or any numbness? Are the palms of your hands dry or sweaty? Do your limbs feel heavy or light? How are they supported? With all of these things, remember to just pay attention and stay with the sensations, no matter whether they are pleasant or unpleasant.*
>
> *Finally, turn attention to your face, head, and neck. How does your jaw feel? Do you have your cheeks or forehead or lip muscles tensed? Is your mouth dry or wet, open or closed? Where is your tongue resting? Do you notice any cold or allergy symptoms? How does your throat feel? Does breath flow easily through it, or does it feel constricted? Can you feel your pulse in your neck, or anywhere else in your body? How do your neck muscles feel? Do you notice any itching in your scalp?*

Scanning body sensations while walking is another exercise that can help students begin to feel more accepting of the wide range of feelings that might be happening in the body at any given time. Handout 7.1 includes the body scan instructions for students.

Exercises for Inducing Bodily Anxiety

Before guiding students through exercises designed to bring about bodily anxiety, make sure that the students don't have any health conditions that would make the exercises medically risky. Ideally, any students you guide through these exercises would first obtain clearance from their primary care provider. If in a group setting where it may not be possible to verify this with each individual student, you can at least ask students to skip any exercise if they aren't sure it would be medically safe for them given what they know about their physical health. For example, it may be unwise for students with heart or lung conditions, epilepsy, or severe asthma to purposely hyperventilate for extended periods. Students who have recent injuries or who have chronic musculoskeletal vulnerabilities may want to skip or modify exercises involving muscle tension, at least the part of an exercise focusing on a particular muscle group. And students who have a history of falling due to dizziness and balance problems would want to be careful with any exercises involving spinning. We should emphasize, however, that for the vast majority of students in most settings, all the exercises described below are quite benign medically. It's useful to remind students that if they are safely able to do things such as playing vigorous sports or going on rides at carnivals or amusement parks, then their bodies are evidently able to handle strong changes in breathing, balance signals, and other sensations.

It is helpful to briefly reiterate to students the rationale for exposures to bodily anxiety. Depending on the grade level of the students you are working with, you may wish to further abbreviate and simplify the following:

> *Feelings of anxiety in the body often happen in settings where it seems like something dangerous or bad might occur, like if we're waiting to go on a scary ride, or if a friend is angry and yelling at us. Because we experience bodily anxiety in connection with scary situations over and over in our lives, the anxiety feelings themselves often become frightening to us. It's almost like our brain thinks, "OK, the last time I felt this way something bad was happening, so I guess something bad is happening right now, too!" Things like feeling shaky or breathless can themselves seem threatening and can grab our attention. This is part of what can make test anxiety such an uncomfortable experience. When it feels like our bodies are in overdrive with nervous energy, it can rev up our sense that something is really wrong in the situation.*
>
> *The good news is that if we purposely and repeatedly bring up anxiety symptoms in our bodies at times we know we are safe, we can develop a friendlier, more familiar relationship with those symptoms. We learn from experience that there's nothing terrible about our hearts beating faster, for example. Physical feelings related to test anxiety become less of a big deal to us, and we grow more confident in our ability to deal with anxiety-provoking academic situations.*
>
> *We're going to try now a series of exercises that may bring up feelings in the body that you might have when you're anxious or scared, like when you're about to take an important test.*

For each of the following exercises, we recommend asking students how they expect it to be for them before trying the exercise. If working with an individual student or a small group, this can be discussed out loud. If working with a larger group of students, each student might write down their predictions about the exercises before trying them. Learning from exposure exercises is maximized when people explicitly notice how aspects of their expectations are violated by the actual experiences they have during the exposures. Test-anxious students usually overestimate how aversive or intolerable these exercises will be.

If time permits, we recommend having students try most or all of these exercises to determine which ones bring up bodily feelings that most closely resemble their naturally occurring anxiety reactions. Those exercises, then, are the ones you will want them to practice most often afterward to develop more mastery over the physiological component of their test anxiety. When trying the whole set of exercises for the first time, allow at least a minute or two between each exercise, to let students recenter and to discuss what they noticed during the exercise, before moving on to the next one.

When trying to elicit bodily anxiety, we have found that students respond most reliably to breathing-based exposure exercises. Anxiety tends to alter one's breathing patterns, which can then change perceptions of how much effort is needed to breathe, and of how hungry one is for air, both of which can engender further anxiety (Paulus, 2013). We therefore usually begin with one of the breathing exercises listed below, but there is no set order in which the exercises must be tried. If a student is unable to complete an exercise for the suggested duration, that is a pretty good sign that the sensations following from the exercise are fearful for the student, and it would be a good one to target with further exposure practice. Handout 7.2 includes the following exercises for students.

- Hyperventilating. Take rapid, deep breaths with your mouth open. Try to take in as much air as you can. Continue for 45–60 seconds. In introducing this and the other exercises below, use natural language with students. For example: *We're going to take deep breaths, but they're going to be really fast. We're going to breathe in and out through the mouth and the nose, quickly. Try to take in as much air as you can each time, and then get it out as quickly as you can and take another breath. Don't be afraid to make noise—that's exposure too! We're going to do it for a minute—I'm going to time us. Let's start . . . now!*
- Straw breathing. Close your mouth tightly around a narrow straw, such as the kind used to stir coffee. (Starting with a regular-sized straw is fine, too, for students who are sensitive to breathing sensations.) Squeeze your nostrils closed with your fingers. Breathe only through the straw for 60–90 seconds.
- Breath holding. Breathe in, and then simply try to hold your breath for 30 seconds.
- Running in place. Run in place as fast as you can, or do something else to get your heart pumping rapidly (e.g., jumping jacks) for 60–90 seconds.
- Chair spinning. Using a swivel office chair, spin in circles as fast as you can for 60 seconds. If no chair is available, this exercise can also be tried standing; just be careful about safety (e.g., do it in a space with soft surfaces all around, so that if you were to fall from dizziness, you would not get injured).
- Head shaking. Turn your head side to side, with your eyes open, at a moderate pace, for 30–45 seconds.
- Tensing muscles. Try to tense as many muscles in your body as you can, all at once, for 60 seconds. Another option is to maintain a pose that forces a lot of tension in your muscles (e.g., getting into a push-up position, or adopting a sitting posture with your back against a wall, or staying halfway up in an abdominal crunch while lying on the ground).
- Hand staring. Stare at a single spot on your hand. Try to minimize blinking. Hold your focus for 2 minutes. Unlike the exercises above, this one does not usually induce

strong somatic sensations such as lightheadedness, breathlessness, a racing heart, nausea, or dizziness. Instead, it can give students a discombobulated, surreal, weird feeling of detachment from the environment or their bodies, which can also be part of the embodied experience of test anxiety for some people.

Once students have identified exercises that effectively induce bodily anxiety sensations for them, we recommend introducing them to Handout 7.3, a form they will use to record exposure practice they do on their own. The available research does not indicate exactly which frequency of practice is ideal for developing mastery of bodily anxiety, but we recommend starting with at least five exposure workout sessions weekly, spread out across several days, and continuing until all exercises have become relatively comfortable, almost boring, for a student—or until, at the least, they find themselves much more accepting of the discomfort that comes with the exercises, without as much of a felt need to delay or stop the exercise. Within a practice session, it is best to repeat each exercise at least two to three times at relatively high intensity, with brief breaks of a minute or two between repetitions to record what one notices each time and to let most bodily sensations return back to baseline (Deacon et al., 2013). For students who are extremely sensitive to bodily sensations and who find themselves nearly panicking in response to particular exercises (e.g., hyperventilation), it is fine for them to begin the exercises at lower intensity, since the most important thing is for them to be willing to continue practicing. We have found that these students usually gain confidence within a week or two of practice and are able to ramp up the intensity quite rapidly.

If a student practices multiple bodily anxiety exposure exercises, once they have gained more mastery in each, they can consider combining them. For example, to more fully develop comfort with one's bodily anxiety, an exercise to increase heart rate (running in place) can be followed immediately by a dizziness induction (spinning). Or exercises can be done simultaneously, like breathing through a straw while tensing one's muscles. Students can be creative in other ways, too. If a college student likes to drink coffee, for example, they might choose to do their bodily anxiety exposure exercises after a cup of coffee, to amplify their sensitivity to bodily cues such as a faster heart rate, which might be exaggerated by their caffeine intake. To make the most of exposure practice, students should also be encouraged to try the exercises in varied settings (e.g., outdoors as well as indoors; at home as well as at school; in the morning as well as the afternoon). Deliberately varying the combinations of bodily anxiety sensations that one encounters, and the contexts in which they occur, helps to create a fuller and more durable peace with these sensations.

RELAXING THE BODY

Through exposure exercises, students will have learned at a deep, visceral level that their physiological anxiety responses are safe and that they can handle whatever comes up in their bodies during tests and other valued activities. Even while reinforcing students' growth in this respect, it is perfectly appropriate to acknowledge that they may sometimes wish they could enjoy more feelings of relaxation when preparing for or taking tests. Remind students that you did not ask them to get more comfortable with bodily signs of anxiety because of any macho ideology in which toughing out discomfort is valorized as an end in itself. If there were a way to wipe out all aversive experiences of test anxiety (beyond whatever is needed to get students motivated and energized to prepare), of course we would eagerly offer this to students! But emotion regulation does not work that way. Pressured attempts to suppress our feelings can actually inflame them, as the following hypothetical scenario (adapted from the polygraph metaphor in ACT; Hayes et al., 2011) can impress upon students:

> *Imagine that during your next big test, you were hooked up to equipment that could detect if your body showed any signs of anxiety. For example, you wore a device that measured your heart rate, and another device that measured whether your hands got sweaty. Now imagine that you were told that you'd fail the test if you showed any signs of nervousness during it. If your heart rate went up at all, you would fail automatically!*
>
> *How do you think you would do in this situation? Would you be able to keep your hands dry and your heart rate slow and steady?*
>
> *Clearly this would be a setup for failure. Any person in this scenario would feel so much pressure to stay calm, so fearful of getting anxious at all, that they'd get nervous right away and set off the machines measuring heart rate and so forth.*
>
> *This is why it's helpful to develop acceptance of a variety of anxious responses that might come up in the body, as you've been doing with the exercises involving things like breathing through a straw. Sometimes you're just going to feel nervous in life, with tests and other things. There's no way to eliminate this completely. And if you're strongly attached to an agenda of getting rid of all your anxiety, you may actually make yourself more anxious, ironically.*
>
> *The good news is that there are techniques that can help you feel more comfortable and relaxed some of the time. Again, it's crucial to realize that these techniques won't always work in the ways you expect, or work as completely as you'd like. But many people do find them useful for developing more of a sense of calm in the body overall.*

The techniques we review below are thought to produce a calmer energy in the body through activation of the parasympathetic nervous system, the effects of which are largely opposite those of the sympathetic nervous system responsible for the fight-or-flight response. Several interventions for test anxiety have used training in bodily relaxation techniques to good effect, including paced breathing, muscle relaxation, guided imagery, and other tactics (e.g., Gregor, 2005; Larson et al., 2010; Putwain & Pescod, 2018). Direct comparisons between the effectiveness of such tactics have been very limited (e.g., Toussaint et al., 2021), so we recommend that, if time permits, students try both the breathing and muscle relaxation exercises we describe to determine how they affect them as individuals.

For both exercises, students should understand that practice is required to maximize benefits. Practice with these exercises tends to increase their efficiency as well as their effectiveness. With dedication, students may be able to eventually produce a welcome relaxation response in the body with just a minute or two of effort, and they may be able to do so even in higher stress situations, whereas, at the start, they may find bodily relaxation tools inaccessible or at least ineffective in situations where they are especially captured by anxiety. We suggest that students practice bodily relaxation tools for at least five minutes per day, five days per week, to begin. If they start to find the tools helpful—and not every student does, which is fine—then they will often begin to incorporate them into the natural rhythms of their daily life, without any need for deliberate, scheduled practice. Some students like to use the tools to produce pleasant, focused respites in their day, such as going through a muscle relaxation sequence before sleep. Other times, students may find the tools helpful for taking the edge off of aversive levels of anxiety (e.g., slowed breathing when feeling uncomfortably nervous before an exam).

Breathing Calmly

Intentionally altering one's breathing patterns has long been a core part of meditation, yoga, tai chi, and contemplative traditions around the world. For achieving relaxation, emphasis is usually placed on slowing the pace of breathing, lengthening the duration of exhalation compared to inhalation, and diaphragmatic ("belly") contraction. These alterations may activate the parasympathetic nervous system (the "rest and digest" system) through vagus nerve stimulation (Chang et al., 2015; Gerritsen & Band, 2018). Regular practice with calm breathing can reduce stress, anxiety, and negative emotions, and improve attention (Ma et al., 2017; Salyers et al., 2011). However, when starting out, there can sometimes be a short-term spike in physiological anxiety (e.g., Toussaint et al., 2021), perhaps because people may actually tend to inadvertently over-breathe (hyperventilate) when first paying deliberate attention to their breathing patterns.

When guiding students through an example of calm breathing, you may invite them to audiorecord your instructions, so that they can then use the same guidance when practicing on their own afterward. Encourage them to seek out other variations, too, if they wish to, to see what works best for them. YouTube has many free guided breathing exercises designed for relaxation, for example. Below is a script that we have found appeals to most students. We recommend using your typical speaking tone, rhythm, and volume when guiding students through the exercise, rather than affecting something more stereotypically meditative, to help students understand that this is a practical tool, nothing esoteric that requires them to enter a trance-like state.

It is fine to abbreviate this script (e.g., skipping much of the first two paragraphs) when time is limited:

> *Begin by getting comfortable in your seat. Place your feet flat against the floor. Feel how your legs are fully supported by the floor under your feet, and by the chair [or sofa, or whatever the student may be sitting on] beneath your thighs. Similarly, rest your arms wherever is comfortable, against your lap, or the arms of your chair, or whatever, their weight fully supported. Let your shoulders hang loose, relaxed. Notice any tension in your face or jaw, and release that tension too. You can close your eyes or at least lower your gaze gently. [Pause for 5–10 seconds.]*
>
> *Now, with your body at ease, turn attention to your breath. For a few breaths, just pay attention to what's happening naturally. Is your chest or your belly expanding in or out with each breath? Are you breathing through your nose or your mouth? What's the pace of your breathing? [Pause for 15–20 seconds.]*
>
> *We are now going to practice a specific kind of breathing that can often help your whole body and mind relax. It can lower your heart rate and your blood pressure. It's*

called belly breathing, or sometimes diaphragmatic breathing. In this kind of breathing, you'll notice your belly expanding outward with each breath in, and then contracting back inward with each breath out. Your chest won't rise or fall much. You'll breathe slowly, especially when exhaling.

Begin by placing one of your hands on your upper chest, and your other hand on your belly, just below the bottom of your ribs. As we go through this exercise, the hand on your chest should stay relatively still, while the hand on your belly should move outward when you inhale, and then fall inward again when you exhale. [Illustrate this with hands on your own chest and belly, showing how your belly pushes out and then in when inhaling and exhaling, respectively.]

Now you're going to be breathing in slowly through your nose, holding your breath briefly, and then exhaling slowly. When I say "in," you'll start breathing in through your nose. I'll count to 4, and then say "hold it." A couple seconds later, I'll say "out," and that will be your cue to start exhaling through your mouth. I'll count to 6, and then we'll start the cycle again. Ready?

In . . . 2 . . . 3 . . . 4 . . . Hold it . . . [Wait 2 seconds.] Out . . . 2 . . . 3 . . . 4 . . . 5 . . . 6.
In . . . 2 . . . 3 . . . 4 . . . Hold it . . . [Wait 2 seconds.] Out . . . 2 . . . 3 . . . 4 . . . 5 . . . 6.
In . . . 2 . . . 3 . . . 4 . . . Hold it . . . [Wait 2 seconds.] Out . . . 2 . . . 3 . . . 4 . . . 5 . . . 6.
In . . . 2 . . . 3 . . . 4 . . . Hold it . . . [Wait 2 seconds.] Out . . . 2 . . . 3 . . . 4 . . . 5 . . . 6.

Good job! Remember, you should feel your belly expanding out and in with each breath, and you should be breathing in through your nose, and out through your mouth. Now you'll do some cycles of this slow belly breathing on your own. You can continue to count at a pace of 4 seconds in, 2 seconds holding the breath, and 6 seconds out, or you can adjust the pace a bit if that's more comfortable for you. Just try to keep focused on slow, deliberate, full breathing. Let's begin. [Wait for 60 seconds.]

With each breath in, feel the cool air entering through your nostrils. As you hold your breath for a couple of seconds, with your lungs filled, visualize any stress in your body gathering up into that air in your lungs, and then expel that warm air outward, slowly, through your mouth. [Wait for 30 seconds.]

Now, turning attention back to the environment around you, you can open your eyes.

Handout 7.4 features an adapted version of this script for students.

When reviewing students' experiences with the calm breathing exercise, emphasize that although such breathing often causes feelings of relaxation, it may also sometimes cause anxiety. Even when the latter happens, there can still be therapeutic value in the exercise; encourage students to frame it as another opportunity to practice sitting with bodily sensations that are not always comfortable. Encourage students to approach their daily calm breathing practice with curiosity and an open mind and heart. They can record what they notice using Handout 7.5. Remind them once more that calm breathing is a skill and becomes easier and more effective with practice. Eventually they may be able to make good use of it even when they are not sitting or lying still and when they are not able to devote full attention to it.

Releasing Muscle Tension

The psychologist Edmund Jacobson developed in the early 1900s a method of relaxing the body that centered on releasing muscular tension (e.g., Jacobson, 1938). *Progressive muscle relaxation*, as he called it, has proven effective for reducing overall anxiety (Hayes-Skelton et al., 2013; Manzoni et al., 2008) and the experience of test anxiety specifically (Tamayo-Toro, 2019; Zargarzadeh & Shirazi, 2014), although it remains unclear exactly *how* muscular relaxation translates into more general emotional ease (e.g., Conrad & Roth, 2007; Pifarre et al., 2015). Some authors have suggested that reversing the muscular tension component of the body's stress response may cause deactivation of other aspects of the stress response. Building confidence in one's ability to relax muscles throughout the whole body may also boost one's sense of mastery over bodily states in general (Torales, 2020).

We recommend illustrating each step of the muscle relaxation sequence by doing it with your own body as you narrate the instructions. As with the breathing exercise above, you can invite students to audiorecord your progressive muscle relaxation instructions, for use outside of the treatment session. They can also find a variety of guidance on YouTube and on meditation and mindfulness apps. As with the breathing exercise, again, we recommend using your normal, natural voice when walking students through the following script, which can be amended and abbreviated (or lengthened) as you see fit for your particular students:

> *When we feel anxious, one of the most common changes in our bodies is tension in our muscles, from head to toe. For example, we often clench our jaws or tense our shoulders or neck without even realizing it.*
>
> *When we can get our bodies fully relaxed, our minds tend to follow. Anxiety often melts away when muscle tension is released. There's a really effective way to make this happen. It involves first winding up the tension in each muscle group, and then releasing that tension. We're going to try this out with all the muscles in the body. This technique is called progressive muscle relaxation.*
>
> *If you have any injuries or other issues in your body that might make any step in this exercise physically painful, please skip that part. For example, if you are healing a tendon injury in your forearm, maybe you know it's not a good idea to tense your arm muscles as hard as possible right now. Use your best judgment.*
>
> *We'll begin by making fists with our hands, squeezing them tight as if we were trying to get juice out of a lemon. At the same time, bend your wrists inward or outward to create tension in your forearms. Feel the tension in your hands and forearms. [Wait 5 seconds.] Now relax—release the tension. Notice the difference between tension and relaxation. Maybe there's some warmth or tingling now in your hand and arm muscles. [Wait another 5–10 seconds.]*
>
> *Now bend your elbows at a 90-degree angle, and squeeze your upper arm muscles hard. At the same time, press your elbows down into the sides of your body, so that you also have tension in your shoulders and even your back. Notice how all that tension feels. [Wait 5 seconds.] Now relax. Let go of all the tension in your arms, hands, shoulders, and back. Let your arms hang heavy and loose, totally at ease. Notice the sensations of relaxation. [Wait 5–10 seconds.]*
>
> *Next, turning attention to the lower legs, lift your toes up toward your knees, while keeping your heels on the ground. You should feel a stretch in your ankles and your Achilles tendon and calves, and tension in your shin muscles. Squeeze those muscles hard. [Wait 5 seconds.] Now let go, letting your feet fall flat on the ground again. Notice how different this relaxation feels, your feet and ankle, as well as your legs, totally at ease. [Wait 5–10 seconds.]*

Now, turning attention to the upper legs, lift your feet off the ground, and extend your legs straight out. Feel the tension and effort in your upper leg muscles, at the front of your thighs. [Wait 5 seconds.] Now let go. Relax. Let your feet fall flat on the ground, your legs fully supported by the floor and your chair. Notice the relaxation and warmth radiating through your whole legs, down into your toes, and the continued relaxation throughout your whole arms, all the way into your fingers. [Wait 5–10 seconds.]

Next, pull your shoulders up toward your ears, and your chin down toward your chest, as if you were a turtle pulling its head down into its shell. Feel the tension in your shoulders, your neck, and your back. [Wait 5 seconds.] Relax. Let go of the tension. Notice how heavy and loose your limbs feel, and how easily and comfortably your neck supports your head. Study the difference between tension and relaxation in these parts. [Wait 5–10 seconds.]

Now we'll turn attention to the face. We often carry muscle tension in our face without realizing it. Let's make a funny face. Try either raising or lowering your eyebrows, and try squeezing your eyes shut. Clench your jaw tight, too, and purse your lips closed. Squeeze all those different muscles in your face. [Wait 5 seconds.] Now let go. Relax. Notice how smooth your forehead feels, and how relaxed the muscles around your eyes are. Let your jaw hang a little loose, and feel the difference between that and tension in your jaw. Your whole face is at ease. [Wait 5–10 seconds.]

Finally, let's turn attention to the center, our cores. Expand your chest while taking a deep breath in, and then tense all your abdominal muscles, as if you were doing a crunch. [Wait 5 seconds.] Now relax. Release that tension. Let your belly expand forward as you take another slow breath in, all your abdominal muscles relaxed. [Wait 5–10 seconds.]

With each breath in and out, repeat to yourself the word "relax" silently, and let a pleasant, peaceful relaxation wash over your whole body. [Wait about 30 seconds.]

Handout 7.6 features an adapted version of this script in a reproducible handout for students. Students can record their practice using the form in Handout 7.7.

EMBRACING EMOTIONAL CHALLENGES

Our emphases so far have been on (1) directly inducing bodily anxiety symptoms, to get more comfortable with these and less reactive to them, and (2) practicing techniques that can often produce more relaxation in the body. In both cases, we have been focusing on physiological sensations, relatively divorced from any real-world context, such as a test, that might be causing anxiety or other emotional states. This has been deliberate, to help students recognize how much of the aversiveness of test anxiety is rooted simply in natural variations in bodily states, and then to help them build mastery over these states—both an ability to tolerate and even welcome intense feelings in the body, and an ability to sometimes modulate these to be more comfortable.

Ultimately, the point of mastering bodily anxiety is to promote the development of more flexible behavior in everyday life, including in academic pursuits. In addition to the *interoceptive* exposures described earlier (e.g., hyperventilation), we recommend that students pursue *in vivo* exposures in which they deliberately seek out academic and other experiences that naturally elicit anxiety for them. Ideally, they will begin such practice while actively in treatment for their test anxiety, and they will find it rewarding enough (e.g., in terms of increased feelings of self-confidence) that they will adopt a lasting lifestyle in which they face their fears willingly on a regular basis.

A good way to brainstorm ideas for such exposures is to ask students the following:

> *Imagine there were a way to magically turn off all uncomfortable experiences of anxiety. You could just take a pill, or flip a switch, and you could be freed from fear. What would you do differently tomorrow if you didn't have to worry about feeling nervous? Is there anything you'd do differently in terms of schoolwork, test preparation, or test taking?*

This straightforward question gets students to reflect on where they behave avoidantly, and out of alignment with their values, because of their anxiety. Whatever students come up with, encourage them to consider whether they could begin to work toward these behavior changes *even while they still have anxiety.*

Ideally students will generate testing-related examples. For example, a chronic over-preparer might say that if they were not so anxious about tests, they would stop their studying at a more reasonable point and do something more enjoyable or health-promoting instead (e.g., socializing, reading a book, playing a video game, sleeping), knowing that any further test preparation would merely be to quell their feelings of anxiety, and would not likely enhance performance significantly. A chronic under-preparer might, on the other hand, state that if they did not feel so uncomfortably anxious, then they would solve more practice problems in advance of a test, knowing that this will enhance their learning and performance but would normally elicit nervousness during the practice. With these two students, the recommendation would be to gradually begin studying less or studying more, respectively, even while these behaviors will, in the short-term, increase anxiety. As they reap the rewards (e.g., more life balance and well-being, and greater success on tests, respectively), likely without any big downsides, their preferences and behaviors will shift in a more adaptive direction.

Some students will generate ideas that aren't directly about testing but are about academic anxiety more broadly. For instance, a student might name challenging quantitative courses they would take if they didn't feel so math-phobic. This would be a fine target for everyday exposure. Apart from behaviors directly bearing on test anxiety and schooling, encourage students to practice any other safe but anxiety-provoking thing that interests them. Students often come up with ideas related to practicing more extraversion, despite some social anxiety. Here, too, facing their fears will get them more comfortable with the bodily experience of anxiety in a real-world setting, and will help build their general self-efficacy and their sense that their behavior choices can be independent of anticipated emotional reactions.

For students who showed enthusiasm about the benefits of the bodily anxiety mastery exercises used earlier in this treatment module, you can recommend practicing more naturalistic behaviors that strengthen their acceptance of aversive bodily states beyond anxiety per se—behaviors that can be worked into their everyday repertoires for the long term. The pioneering American psychologist William James (1890/1983) articulated well the rationale for this kind of practice: "Keep the faculty of effort alive in you by a little gratuitous exercise every day. That is, be systematically ascetic or heroic in little unnecessary points, do every day or two something for no other reason than that you would rather not do it, so that when the hour of dire need draws nigh, it may find you not unnerved and untrained to stand the test" (p. 130). For example, a student might practice going for short walks outside in the cold without warm clothing or turning the water cold for a couple of minutes during their showers. Or they might build up a practice of more intense physical exercise than usual, or select a day each week during which they eat only very bland foods. (As always, take into account the particulars of the students you're working with; the latter ideas would be contraindicated for students with restrictive eating disorders.)

The purpose of such practices is not to cultivate masochism, but rather to build up greater flexibility around aversive bodily states, whether we might label such states anxiety, coldness, exertion, or hunger. As William James suggested, a general-purpose fortitude and willingness can be developed through everyday choices to do things you're afraid of or that you simply don't feel like doing. Through such practice, students often find that their threshold for what constitutes stress changes, so that states such as test anxiety have even less power over their behavioral choices. They begin to see themselves as brave and capable. They notice that their behavior is governed more by wishes to approach opportunities that interest them (e.g., taking an optional standardized test that could grant them access to a program they'd like to do), and less by wishes to avoid anxiety or other uncomfortable bodily states that might accompany those opportunities.

Students can record their practice leaning into everyday sources of anxiety, and other sorts of discomfort, using Handout 7.8.

PERFORMING WHILE ANXIOUS

In the foregoing section, we recommended that students translate their improved mastery over bodily anxiety into changes in everyday behaviors that will help them move toward their academic goals and that will continue to teach them that anxiety and other aversive bodily states are tolerable and manageable. To further strengthen students' confidence and courage, a last practice we recommend is doing challenging tasks (e.g., doing SAT practice problems of a difficulty level that matches a student's current abilities) after ramping up bodily anxiety past what might occur naturally. Students can use the exercises reviewed earlier to induce bodily anxiety (e.g., running in place until one's heart is pounding) and then do the kinds of academic work that they might fear would be inhibited by their anxiety. Compared to impersonal psychoeducation, this direct experiential evidence is especially persuasive for most students, teaching them that they can perform even while feeling physiological symptoms of anxiety.

The confidence that students gain from this exercise can be bolstered through practicing other daily tasks, too, aside from those directly related to academics and testing, while in an anxious state. For example, a student might make a phone call after having done a dizziness induction, or might make artwork or play a game on their phone after having held their breath or hyperventilated. The more that students directly learn, from a wide variety of experiences, that their mental and physical faculties are intact even when bodily anxiety is present, the more assurance they feel that test anxiety need not limit their academic pursuits and achievement.

Students can record their practice using Handout 7.9.

SUMMARY

Test anxiety often has a strong physiological component, manifesting in sensations such as shortness of breath, shakiness, a fast heartbeat, and lightheadedness for some students. In this chapter, we presented several procedures that therapists can use to help students master the bodily aspects of test anxiety. During this treatment module, students practice physical exercises that directly induce the physiological symptoms of test anxiety, but without any testing situation present, which helps students to habituate to these feelings and to regard them not as fearful but instead as merely representing the activation of an adaptive part of the nervous system, uncomfortable though the symptoms may be. Students also practice slowed breathing and muscle relaxation exercises that can help them to achieve some level of control over uncomfortable anxiety symptoms and to produce a calmer bodily state. Finally, students adopt a variety of practices to do more things that they are scared of and to get used to performing when they are feeling nervous.

After completing this module of our test anxiety treatment, students should be more knowledgeable about how test anxiety shows up in the body, more comfortable with that bodily anxiety, more capable of producing calm states in their body when desired, more willing to do what it takes to pursue their academic goals even when bodily anxiety may show up in the process, and more confident that their performance will not suffer as a result of their test anxiety.

Body Scan Instructions

Begin by closing your eyes or casting them downward, so that you are undistracted by sights in the room.

Notice the feeling of your feet on the floor. Are your shoes tight or loose? Do you feel pressure anywhere on your feet? Are they at all sweaty? Are there any small, involuntary movements of the muscles in your feet, as you pay attention to them? Notice how your legs feel supported by the soles of your feet, pressed flat against the floor.

Next, turn attention to your legs. Are there any tingling sensations in your skin? Any muscles that are sore or cramping? Do you have urges to move your legs at all? Whatever you notice, just pay attention to it. There is no need to change anything—just notice the sensations, and stay with them.

Now notice your abdomen and your lower back. Are you hunched over or sitting straight up? Which muscles are tensed, and which are relaxed? Do you feel any nausea, gurgling, or other sensations in your gut?

Move your attention next to your lungs. Notice each breath entering and exiting your lungs. Follow the breath as it goes in and out, traveling through your nose, mouth, and throat. Feel the temperature of the air. Do you feel like you're getting the right amount of air into you, or are there any urges to slow down or speed up your breathing? When you breathe in, is there more expansion in your chest or in your belly?

Next, notice your shoulders, arms, and hands. Where is there tension in your muscles? Where is there relaxation? How does your skin feel? Do you notice any itches or any numbness? Are the palms of your hands dry or sweaty? Do your limbs feel heavy or light? How are they supported? With all of these things, remember to just pay attention and stay with the sensations, no matter whether they are pleasant or unpleasant.

Finally, turn attention to your face, head, and neck. How does your jaw feel? Do you have your cheeks or forehead or lip muscles tensed? Is your mouth dry or wet, open or closed? Where is your tongue resting? Do you notice any cold or allergy symptoms? How does your throat feel? Does breath flow easily through it, or does it feel constricted? Can you feel your pulse in your neck, or anywhere else in your body? How do your neck muscles feel? Do you notice any itching in your scalp?

Exercises for Exposure to Anxiety Sensations

- *Hyperventilating.* Take rapid, deep breaths with your mouth open. Try to take in as much air as you can. Continue for 45–60 seconds.

- *Straw breathing.* Close your mouth tightly around a narrow straw, such as the kind used to stir coffee. (Starting with a regular-sized straw is fine, too, if you are especially sensitive to breathing sensations.) Squeeze your nostrils closed with your fingers. Breathe only through the straw for 60–90 seconds.

- *Breath holding.* Breathe in, and then simply try to hold your breath for 30 seconds.

- *Running in place.* Run in place as fast as you can, or do something else to get your heart pumping rapidly (e.g., jumping jacks), for 60–90 seconds.

- *Chair spinning.* Using a swivel office chair, spin in circles as fast as you can for 60 seconds. If no chair is available, this exercise can also be tried standing; just be careful about safety (e.g., do it in a space with soft surfaces all around, so that if you were to fall from dizziness, you would not be injured).

- *Head shaking.* Turn your head side to side, with your eyes open, at a moderate pace, for 30–45 seconds.

- *Tensing muscles.* Try to tense as many muscles in your body as you can, all at once, for 60 seconds. Another option is to maintain a pose that forces a lot of tension in your muscles (e.g., getting into a push-up position, or adopting a sitting posture with your back against a wall, or staying halfway up in an abdominal crunch while lying on the ground).

- *Hand staring.* Stare at a single spot on your hand. Try to minimize blinking. Hold your focus for 2 minutes. Unlike the exercises above, this one does not usually induce strong bodily sensations such as lightheadedness, breathlessness, a racing heart, nausea, or dizziness. Instead, it might give you a discombobulated, surreal, weird feeling of detachment from the environment or your body, which can also be part of the experience of test anxiety for some students.

Practicing Exposure to Anxiety Sensations

At least five times weekly, ideally on separate days, practice the exercises from Handout 7.1 that are most uncomfortable for you. Within each "workout," practice each exercise at least twice, with a brief break between exercises to take notes and let your body return to its usual state. When you do an exercise more than once in a single workout, use separate rows to take notes on each repetition.

Date	Exercise	Duration (seconds)	Notes (What did you notice? And what was your maximum discomfort, on a 0–10 scale?)

Calm Breathing Instructions

Begin by getting comfortable in your seat. Place your feet flat against the floor. Feel how your legs are fully supported by the floor under your feet, and by the chair (or sofa, or whatever you may be sitting on) beneath your thighs. Similarly, rest your arms wherever is comfortable, against your lap, or the arms of your chair, or whatever, their weight fully supported. Let your shoulders hang loose, relaxed. Notice any tension in your face or jaw, and release that tension too.

Now, with your body at ease, turn attention to your breath. For a few breaths, just pay attention to what's happening naturally. Is your chest or your belly expanding in or out with each breath? Are you breathing through your nose or your mouth? What's the pace of your breathing?

You are now going to practice a specific kind of breathing that can often help your whole body and mind relax. It can lower your heart rate and your blood pressure. It's called belly breathing, or sometimes diaphragmatic breathing. In this kind of breathing, you'll notice your belly expanding outward with each breath in, and then contracting back inward with each breath out. Your chest won't rise or fall much. You'll breathe slowly, especially when exhaling.

Begin by placing one of your hands on your upper chest, and your other hand on your belly, just below the bottom of your ribs. As you go through this exercise, the hand on your chest should stay relatively still, while the hand on your belly should move outward when you inhale, and then fall inward again when you exhale.

Now you're going to be breathing in slowly through your nose, holding your breath briefly, and then exhaling slowly. You'll be breathing in through your nose for a count of 4 seconds, and then holding your breath for a count of 2 seconds, and then exhaling through your mouth for a count of 6 seconds. And then you'll start the cycle again.

Follow along with the pacing below to get the hang of it:

Inhale through nose . . . 1 . . . 2 . . . 3 . . . 4 . . .
Hold breath . . . 1 . . . 2 . . .
Exhale through mouth . . . 1 . . . 2 . . . 3 . . . 4 . . . 5 . . . 6 . . .
Inhale through nose . . . 1 . . . 2 . . . 3 . . . 4 . . .
Hold breath . . . 1 . . . 2 . . .
Exhale through mouth . . . 1 . . . 2 . . . 3 . . . 4 . . . 5 . . . 6 . . .

Remember, you should feel your belly expanding out and in with each breath, and you should be breathing in through your nose, and out through your mouth. Feel free to adjust the pace a bit if some other count is more comfortable for you (e.g., a slower inhalation). Just try to keep focused on slow, deliberate, full breathing.

Now try repeating several times through the whole calm breathing cycle.

If you feel like adding another layer of relaxation to the exercise, try adding the following visualization. With each breath in, feel the cool air entering through your nostrils. As you hold your breath for a couple of seconds, with your lungs filled, visualize any stress in your body gathering up into that air in your lungs, and then expel that warm air outward, slowly, through your mouth.

Practicing Calm Breathing

Spend at least a few minutes on most days practicing calm breathing. You can follow the instructions in Handout 7.4, or you can find another script you prefer to follow along to by searching YouTube for slowed breathing exercises or using a meditation app.

Date	Lenth of practice (minutes)	Anxiety level (0–10) beforehand	Anxiety level (0–10) afterward	Notes (What did you notice? What kind of calm breathing practice did you do?)

Muscle Relaxation Instructions

When we feel anxious, one of the most common changes in our bodies is tension in our muscles, from head to toe. For example, we often clench our jaws or tense our shoulders or neck without even realizing it.

When we can get our bodies fully relaxed, our minds tend to follow. Anxiety often melts away when muscle tension is released. To do this, it helps to first wind up the tension in each muscle group, and then release that tension. Doing this with all the muscles in the body is a technique called progressive muscle relaxation.

If you have any injuries or other issues in your body that might make any step in this exercise physically painful or otherwise a bad idea, please skip that part. Use your best judgment.

Begin by making fists with your hands, squeezing them tight as if you were trying to get juice out of a lemon. At the same time, bend your wrists inward or outward to create tension in your forearms. Feel the tension in your hands and forearms. Hold this for 5 seconds.

Now relax—release the tension. Notice the difference between tension and relaxation. Maybe there's some warmth or tingling now in your hand and arm muscles. Study these feelings for 5–10 seconds.

Now bend your elbows at a 90-degree angle, and squeeze your upper arm muscles hard. At the same time, press your elbows down into the sides of your body, so that you also have tension in your shoulders and even your back. Notice how all that tension feels. Hold this for 5 seconds.

Now relax. Let go of all the tension in your arms, hands, shoulders, and back. Let your arms hang heavy and loose, totally at ease. Notice the sensations of relaxation. Study these for 5–10 seconds.

Next, turn your attention to your lower legs. Lift your toes up toward your knees, while keeping your heels on the ground. You should feel a stretch in your ankles and your Achilles tendon and calves, and tension in your shin muscles. Squeeze those muscles hard. Hold this for 5 seconds.

Now let go, letting your feet fall flat on the ground again. Notice how different this relaxation feels, your feet and ankle, as well as your legs, totally at ease. Study these feelings for 5–10 seconds.

Now, turn your attention to your upper legs. Lift your feet off the ground, and extend your legs straight out. Feel the tension and effort in your upper leg muscles, at the front of your thighs. Hold this for 5 seconds.

Now let go. Relax. Let your feet fall flat on the ground, your legs fully supported by the floor and your chair. Notice the relaxation and warmth radiating through your whole legs, down into your toes, and the continued relaxation throughout your whole arms, all the way into your fingers. Study these feelings for 5–10 seconds.

Next, pull your shoulders up toward your ears, and your chin down toward your chest, as if you were a turtle pulling its head down into its shell. Feel the tension in your shoulders, your neck, and your back. Hold this for 5 seconds.

Relax. Let go of the tension. Notice how heavy and loose your limbs feel, and how easily and comfortably your neck supports your head. Study the difference between tension and relaxation in these parts, for 5–10 seconds.

Now turn your attention to your face. We often carry muscle tension in our face without realizing it. Make a funny face. Try either raising or lowering your eyebrows, and try squeezing your eyes shut. Clench your jaw tight, too, and purse your lips closed. Squeeze all those different muscles in your face. Hold this for 5 seconds.

Now let go. Relax. Notice how smooth your forehead feels, and how relaxed the muscles around your eyes are. Let your jaw hang a little loose, and feel the difference between that and tension in your jaw. Your whole face is at ease. Study these feelings for 5–10 seconds.

Finally, turn your attention to your core muscles. Expand your chest while taking a deep breath in, and then tense all your abdominal muscles, as if you were doing a crunch. Hold this for 5 seconds.

Now relax. Release that tension. Let your belly expand forward as you take another slow breath in, all your abdominal muscles relaxed. Study these feelings for 5–10 seconds.

With each breath in and out, repeat to yourself the word "relax" silently, and let a pleasant, peaceful relaxation wash over your whole body. Repeat this for another minute or two.

Practicing Muscle Relaxation

Try practicing progressive muscle relaxation at least a few times per week, ideally on separate days. You can follow the instructions in Handout 7.6, or you can find another script you prefer to follow along to by searching YouTube for progressive muscle relaxation exercises or using a meditation app.

Date	Anxiety level (0–10) beforehand	Anxiety level (0–10) afterward	Notes (What did you notice? What kind of muscle relaxation practice did you do?)

Practicing Everyday Courage

Try every day to do something that you expect will make you feel at least somewhat anxious, especially if it's something that you think would be valuable to do but that you would normally want to avoid because of the anxiety. It's okay if some of the behaviors you choose aren't directly related to your test anxiety or other academic issues. You can also use this form to record times when you practice embracing other sorts of discomfort in everyday life, besides anxiety.

Date	What did you do?	Notes (What did you notice? How did you feel after completing the activity?)

Practicing Performing While Anxious

A few times each week, try purposely revving up your bodily anxiety using exercises from Handout 7.2, and then tackle academic material (e.g., solve homework problems). You can also try completing other everyday tasks after revving up your anxiety in this way, to get used to doing various things even while there may be anxiety symptoms in the background.

Date	Exercises to cause anxiety (including duration)	What you did while anxious	Notes (What did you notice? How did you feel after completing the activity?)

CHAPTER 8

Focusing the Mind

In Chapter 7, we reviewed some exercises that can help students attain a more relaxed and comfortable bodily state at baseline, but our main aim was developing students' willingness to experience the opposite—physiological anxiety. The friendlier and more familiar students can get with the heightened anxious arousal that inevitably accompanies some important academic tasks, and the more they can practice approaching rather than avoiding their anxiety, the more flexibly they can function, choosing what's best for reaching their academic goals.

In this chapter, we build upon this approach, turning attention to the cognitive rather than physiological dimension of test anxiety. We review practical tools that strengthen students' ability to tolerate and work effectively with all kinds of thoughts they may experience, including anxious worries (e.g., that they will fail a test), without getting too derailed by those worries. We teach students how to keep a healthy distance from the chatter of their own minds, recognizing their thoughts as simply thoughts, not necessarily as facts that urgently demand further processing or a behavioral response. And through formal and informal attention training practices, students bolster their capacity to concentrate on what matters most to them in any academic situation (e.g., listening in class, or writing an essay on an exam), even while their minds may generate competing noise such as worries.

Students can get hooked by and preoccupied with their anxious thoughts (e.g., about failure, or being stupid or lazy, or not meeting peers' or parents' or teachers' expectations, or the future consequences of low performance), and their engagement with these thoughts can actually divert them away from behaviors that maximize learning and performance, such as fully using all of the time allotted to them on an exam. Students who are chronic worriers may even develop a superstitious sense that their worrying helps protect them from feared academic outcomes, or they may use worrying to try to prepare themselves emotionally for potential bad outcomes. Our treatment helps students begin to hold their thoughts at arm's length and to decide freely what's most effective for them to do in the present moment, no matter what thoughts their minds may be generating about the past, present, or future. Our overall conceptual framework for this chapter is inspired by, and many of our specific interventions and experiential exercises are drawn from, several leading contemporary behavioral therapies, including acceptance and commitment therapy (ACT; Hayes, Strosahl, & Wilson, 2011), dialectical behavioral therapy (DBT; Linehan, 2014), the unified protocol for transdiagnostic treatment of emotional disorders (UP; Barlow et al., 2017), and Roemer and Orsillo's (2009, 2020) synthesis of mindfulness- and acceptance-based behavioral therapies.

As with all components of our test anxiety treatment, therapists should, in individual treatment, tailor the materials in this chapter to the student they are helping. As we discussed in Chapter 3, test anxiety problems are quite variable, and if an initial assessment indicates, for example, that a student struggles much more with physiological anxiety than cognitive anxiety, then it is fine to de-emphasize or to skip over some of the strategies described below. We understand that the time available for intervention—not to mention students' span of attention and interest—can be quite limited in some settings, and we encourage therapists to err on the side of flexibility rather than rigidity in using whatever is most relevant for the particular student with whom they are working. Of course, in group or classroom settings, therapists should also use their best judgment about how to match these materials to the students' developmental stage and their most common problems related to test anxiety. Our goal is to present several research-tested strategies to choose from.

TRADITIONAL COGNITIVE APPROACHES

Some prior test anxiety treatments (e.g., Gregor, 2005) have included interventions derived from traditional Beckian cognitive therapy, such as recording and systematically challenging negative automatic thoughts. In these treatments, students are encouraged to notice distortions in their anxious thinking (e.g., jumping to conclusions, or catastrophizing) and to replace negative thoughts with more positive, balanced, or rational thoughts. Although there is some evidence that such cognitive restructuring can reduce students' reported levels of test anxiety, it is unclear whether this is due to the challenging of negative thoughts *per se*, or to a more general process of disentangling from one's thinking— and building a more flexible relationship with it—that comes from monitoring, writing down, and studying one's thoughts with some objective distance from them.

Our treatment does not include restructuring of the anxious thoughts that students experience related to tests. We've excluded cognitive restructuring as a treatment ingredient for a few reasons. First, some research indicates that, as suggested above, the benefits of traditional cognitive therapy may accrue mainly from learning not to buy into or get hooked by the thoughts that one's mind generates, and there are more direct and efficient ways of loosening up one's relationship to one's thoughts, in this respect, than to rigorously, comprehensively put thoughts on trial. Second, in our experience, many of the anxious thoughts that students experience related to testing are actually rationally grounded. For example, a student may think, "If I don't have nearly perfect grades, I'll have no chance of admission to Harvard." In fact, at least to a first approximation, this belief is reasonable, and challenging it is unlikely to be effective. Third, effortfully combating anxious thoughts contradicts the overall ethos of our treatment, implying that worries are dangerous in some way and must be actively fought at every turn. This may confuse students and dilute the impact of the rest of the treatment. We are aiming to help students feel (and be) less reactive in response to their test anxiety—to move toward a more nonjudgmental and compassionate acceptance of their internal experiences—rather than encouraging a more adversarial relationship with their anxiety. Actively disputing negative thoughts implies that emotional thought content is more causally powerful than it needs to be.

Still, some aspects of our treatment are consistent with a conventional cognitive approach, in the sense that we do hope to impart certain true and useful beliefs to students. As described in Chapter 6, a central component of the treatment is psychoeducation about the nature of test anxiety—in particular, how common it is, how it functions, and how it relates to test performance. A more accurate understanding of test anxiety can encourage students to adopt growth-promoting behaviors. For example, when students learn that physiological anxiety does not predict low test performance, and they come to view anxious reactions instead as transient, relatively harmless phenomena, they may be less likely to avoid school on a day when they feel very nervous about an exam—a maladaptive avoidance behavior that provides short-term relief at the cost of long-term learning. The notion that test anxiety doesn't necessarily inhibit performance will challenge some students' prior beliefs, and there are times when the therapist may use traditional cognitive therapy techniques such as Socratic questioning during the psychoeducation phase. For example, when a student insists that test anxiety invariably wrecks their performance, the therapist might ask them whether they can remember any times that they did well on a test despite being convinced, before or during, that they were going to bomb it. However, the whole purpose of challenging this particular cognition is to free students up from the notion that their anxious cognitions, and other aspects of test anxiety, need to be eliminated or otherwise controlled for them to achieve their academic goals!

A NOTE ON NOMENCLATURE

When introducing the various practices described in this chapter to students, we tend to avoid using the broad term *mindfulness*, which has become an overused buzzword in contemporary popular culture (Grossman, 2019). Instead, we prefer to describe the therapeutic activities using language specifically describing each task, like "watching your thoughts" and "training your attention" (which might, loosely, be regarded as related to open monitoring meditation, such as vipassana, and focused attention meditation, such as zen, respectively). We do this for two reasons. First, some students can be distracted or turned off by spiritual or esoteric connotations they may associate with mindfulness. Second, we prefer that students not bring preconceptions to the exercises based on prior times they may have encountered instruction in something called mindfulness (e.g., "that stupid breathing thing that Dad tells me to do when I'm upset!"), which may or may not resemble what we intend to offer. If students comment that a particular component of the treatment reminds them of mindfulness practice, it is of course fine to acknowledge that indeed, some of the exercises in this treatment program involve learning to *pay attention to the present moment without judgment*, as mindfulness is often defined.

OVERVIEW OF PROCEDURES

Paralleling our approach to physiological anxiety in Chapter 7, we begin by reminding students of the limited direct control they have over their anxiety, including their anxious thoughts, and the ways in which trying to get rid of anxiety can actually sometimes exacerbate the problem. Next, we introduce strategies that aim to help students build a friendlier and more productive relationship with their anxious thoughts. Analogous to the exposure procedures for physiological anxiety, we include an exercise in which students directly face their worries in a sustained but contained way. Building on this, we provide exercises in which students learn to simply watch the varieties of thoughts (and feelings) that may visit them in a variety of settings, without enacting any behaviors to change their experience, even when uncomfortable. Next, we turn to change-based strategies that can ultimately help students free up cognitive resources and better focus their minds. While continuing to acknowledge that the mind will always generate some anxious thoughts, we instruct students in techniques that can help them hold these thoughts at arm's length and can help them think flexibly regardless of how they are feeling. Finally, to help students learn and take tests most effectively, we instruct them in tactics for developing their ability to stay focused on what matters to them. As with the relaxation exercises in Chapter 7, we emphasize that our change-oriented strategies are not a panacea but can often help students feel more comfortable and think more clearly, and can help them develop confidence about their ability to perform academically even when anxious.

We summarize these interventions in Table 8.1.

TABLE 8.1. Summary of Procedures for Anxious Thinking

General Strategies	Specific Tactics
Recognizing limited cognitive control through experiential exercises	Thought suppression experiment Forced forgetting experiment "Brain reader" thought experiment
Making space for worries	Worry journaling Postponing worries to worry time Noticing and taking constructive actions
Watching thoughts nonreactively	Narrating one's thinking (with emotions activated) Leaves on a stream and other imagery-based exercises
Disempowering specific thoughts	Thought repetition Acting opposite the thought Affirmatively welcoming the thought
Building flexibility around automatic thoughts	Brainstorming interpretations of pictures
Training attention	Informal focusing practice with everyday activities Formal focusing exercises (e.g., breath, food, body sensations) Selective attention, switching attention, and divided attention with sounds or music Reading in noisy environments

THE MIND HAS A MIND OF ITS OWN

We like to begin with a brief experiential exercise or two that help students understand the limited control they have over the thoughts their minds generate. Playful exercises inspired by ACT can generate vivid and memorable insights in students. The following examples can be modified with content that is specific to the student(s) seeking help:

- *For the next minute, don't think at all about whether the colleges you applied to will accept or reject you. You can think about anything else, but make sure your mind doesn't wander to anything related to college admissions. How did that go for you?*
- *Remember a class you didn't do as well in as you had hoped—something where you received a grade that disappointed you. Now forget about it altogether. Just shove it out of your mind completely, like deleting a picture from the camera roll on your phone, so that you can't remember it anymore. How did you do?*
- *Imagine that during your next test at school, you're hooked up to a fancy brain imaging machine that can detect when you're having any anxious thoughts. If you do experience any anxious thoughts, then you'll receive painful electric shocks as punishment. All you have to do is only have calm thoughts, and you'll be fine. How do you think that will go?*

What's striking in all these examples is that being motivated and trying harder are not enough to exert complete control over one's mind. Ask students whether offering them a billion-dollar reward would help them erase permanently from their memories the disappointing grade they received. Of course this is not at all helpful—and indeed, in the "think no anxious thoughts" example, it is even harder to control anxiety when the motivating threat of painful shocks is present. Research has also shown that trying hard to suppress unwanted thoughts can lead ironically to a surge in those very thoughts. This is in stark contrast to controlling one's outward behavior—what a person says and does. For example, for a big enough reward (or to avert a big enough punishment), even the most math-phobic student might be willing and able to spend a dozen extra hours a week studying algebra—but they could not will themselves to begin spontaneously experiencing nothing but positive, passionate, excited thoughts about a subject that they loathe. This difference between controlling private mental events (thoughts, feelings, urges) and publicly visible actions is worth emphasizing to students.

Trying to fight off anxious thoughts is sometimes compared to a tug of war with a monster that pulls back harder the harder you pull. The best recourse is sometimes to drop the rope and walk away from the struggle and turn to a more rewarding enterprise. In the case of test anxiety, that can mean doing more productive studying or just enjoying other activities. However, this is easier said than done. After students have developed a strong intuitive sense of how vanquishing anxious thoughts completely is unlikely to work, we remind students of how purposeful exposures to bodily anxiety had helped reduce their preoccupation with such anxiety, and we preview for them that they will be practicing analogous exercises for their anxious thinking in this treatment module. We begin with worry journaling, which may not eliminate students' worries but can help with taking a step back and not getting so caught up in them, and can guide them to more constructive actions. Worries can begin to be experienced only as thoughts that the brain automatically generates, not necessarily as truths or wisdom that requires any further response. When students can engage with their anxious thoughts in a more contained way, this ultimately increases their ability to focus on valued activities in the world.

WORRYING WELL

The human mind is prone to time traveling. People do lots of thinking about both the past and the future, and for students with high levels of anxiety, much of that thinking is worrying. Students with test anxiety think about tests before they are even announced by teachers, and when the exam is finally in the past, the students may not be able to stop thinking about how they might have done. There is nothing inherently bad or dysfunctional about reviewing the past or imagining the future. Reflecting on joyful memories or fantasizing about a bright future can help people build positive emotions. Studying past mistakes can help people avoid making similar mistakes again. Worrying about possible unwanted events in the future can mobilize people to proactively develop solutions to problems, even problems that have not yet presented themselves (see Suddendorf et al., 2022). It is appropriate and entirely adaptive for a student who is unprepared for a test later this week to think about how poorly things may go, and for this worry to then propel them to focus on their studies. Imagining things that might go wrong in the future means that we do not always have to simply react to threats in real-time and improvise when problems arise.

Sometimes, however, worry spins out of control. It takes up significant mental bandwidth, and it paralyzes a person more than it mobilizes them. Some people have trouble terminating cycles of worrying—at the extreme, such individuals might be diagnosed with generalized anxiety disorder—and the worrying can start to function more like ceaseless avoidance of life problems rather than a trigger to productive problem solving. When worrying about test performance and academic achievement goes into overdrive, time and energy can be diverted away from the activities that actually help students prepare for and overcome their academic challenges. For example, a student might spend an hour texting with a peer, sharing worries about a class they both find difficult, rather than doing extra problem sets to enhance their competencies in the class. Recent research (Newman et al., 2014) suggests that worrying may, in part, function as an emotional preparation strategy. If a student is already feeling lousy most of the time because of ceaseless worrying, then when something bad befalls them, like a low grade, the impact may be less intense than if they had been in a more positive emotional state. However, this emotional preparation comes at the expense of actual academic preparation, insofar as the worrying takes up time that could have been devoted to studying.

When students' worries about tests and other academic issues have become more harmful than helpful, an intervention for generalized anxiety called *worry time* or *worry journaling* can be useful. In introducing this intervention to students, it is important to emphasize that the goal is not to get rid of worries. Preparatory psychoeducation about the universality of worrying, as we provide above, is critical. We have found it helpful to ask students to consider the possible costs of having no worries at all about academic performance. Typically, they recognize how problematic this would be, much like if their bodies never felt pain when injured. Conversely, for students who are attached to worrying as a way to buffer themselves against disappointment if things do not go well on a test, ask them to consider the costs of this intentionally indulged, ritualistic worrying—both the ways it can turn their attention away from behaviors that could objectively decrease the chances of a poor outcome (e.g., taking more practice tests, or sleeping at night) and the ways it can eat up time that students could use on enjoyable activities, when they are already as prepared as they wish to be for an exam. Insightful students will sometimes also recognize that if they never try experimenting with mixing up their worrying routines, so to speak, they will never have the opportunity to discover what is and is not useful in their worrying.

The goal is not for students to eliminate worrying but to develop a healthier relationship with their worries and to put their worrying to good use when possible—to worry well, we sometimes say. The intervention can be introduced in this way:

> *Worry journaling involves setting aside and scheduling a block of time each day, maybe 10 minutes, and devoting yourself entirely during this time to writing out (or typing up) all the worries that your mind generates, including worries about tests or other academic issues. At the end of the writing period, review what you've written and identify the main themes of your worries, the problems or future threats that most concern you. Then, for each problem, consider whether you have any current influence or control over it. If there's nothing you can do about the issue (e.g., whether you'll get into a particular college, after you've completed the application), fine; but if you do have influence over the issue (e.g., whether you'll pass an upcoming history test), find one small action step you can take today or tomorrow to help address the problem (e.g., make a plan with a friend to study for the test), and take it.*

Presenting a rationale for this exercise is critical for getting students on board, because worry journaling can be counterintuitive at first:

> *Worry journaling helps you discharge your mind's rehearsal loop. Imagine that you needed to do a dozen different things after our session today, but you didn't have them recorded anywhere. Your mind would keep reminding you of these important tasks you need to deal with, and it would be hard to focus on anything else. Your attention would get disrupted repeatedly. But if you had all these tasks recorded in a list on your phone, you'd be able to stay present much more effectively. That's the way that it goes with worries—when you write them out each day, your mind gradually begins to nag you with the worries less often at other times of day, when you're trying to accomplish other things.*
>
> *And when your mind does start worrying at other times of day—like when you're preparing for bed, let's say—if you've been practicing worry journaling, you can say, "Thanks, mind, for that reminder—I'll be dealing with it again during my worry time tomorrow at 3:00pm." Or if you notice your mind is worrying about something completely*

new, you can quickly jot it down in your worry journal and then return to it during your designated daily worry time. It's easier to shift your attention back to whatever matters most to you at present, and not get tangled up with spontaneously intruding worries, when you know you'll be dealing with your worries at a scheduled time each day.

Worry journaling also helps you get more comfortable with your worries. When you purposely spend time each day looking at the content of your worries, writing them out, this robs them of their power over you, similar to how the hyperventilation exercise we tried last week [see Chapter 7], if you practice it regularly, makes the physiological symptoms of anxiety less attention-grabbing and bothersome when they visit you at other times. When you first start worry journaling, it might be a slightly stressful exercise, but with practice, you may actually find yourself getting so comfortable and familiar with your worries that they bore you! When you see your worries on the page—or on the screen—you recognize them for what they are: a series of words that your brain generates automatically, and the images these evoke in you—previews of things that might go wrong, which are sometimes useful to you, sometimes less useful, but never harmful in themselves.

Finally, worry journaling helps you organize your worries and identify key action steps you can take to solve problems where you have some control. In other words, worry journaling helps you zero in on what's useful in your mind's worrying, and harness this for good. Instead of worries being the enemy, and draining you, or being something you need to keep engaging with in order to emotionally brace yourself against worst possible outcomes, they become just another source of information you can look to as you decide how to spend your days and where to devote your time and energy. Worry journaling frees you up to take effective actions aligned with your values and goals.

We have found that having students practice worry journaling in session for 10 minutes increases the chances that they will practice daily outside of session. Open-ended prompts asking about their experience with the exercise in session—"What did you notice?"—helps to cultivate a curious, open, nonjudgmental attitude about their worries. Handout 8.1 features a form that students can use to record their daily worry journaling practice.

Sometimes students ask whether they will need to keep practicing worry journaling forever. Although some people find worry journaling helpful as a long-term practice, we have found that even very worry-prone students can often maintain the benefits of the practice while transitioning eventually to a modified version in which they simply reserve a short period of time each day and use that time for worry journaling *only if they think it would be useful* that day (cf. Wells, 2009). Through worry journaling practice, students learn to generally postpone rather than immediately indulge the further processing of worries that pop up throughout the day, and they also learn that processing worries is typically useful only insofar as it leads to practical, task-focused coping tactics (problem-solving action steps). The result is that students begin spending less time worrying about academic issues and more time dealing with them constructively through action. As students achieve this change, many of them find that when their designated worry time arrives each day, their worries no longer feel urgently important, and they may choose instead to spend the time externally focused on a directly productive activity such as reading a textbook. This overall shift from worrying to action also helps to free up students from any notion that extensive time spent worrying is necessary to their emotional survival of the occasional poor test outcome, or, on the other hand, to their achievement of excellent outcomes.

EXPERIENCING THOUGHTS AS THOUGHTS, NOT FACTS

In our treatment, we do not generally encourage students to try to rationally dispute their anxious thoughts related to tests and other academic issues. To do so often means getting further caught up in the mind's chatter. The path to greater freedom instead involves a degree of acceptance that the mind is an anxiety- and judgment-producing machine. It is always spitting up the bits of language that people call thoughts, and it will always do so. Some of these thoughts can be annoying and distracting, but there are a range of practical tools students can use to keep a healthy distance from their thinking. Thoughts can come to be regarded less as a series of factual pronouncements that must be paid great heed and more as a podcast playing in the background, filled with a mix of opinions, judgments, predictions, recollections, and innuendos.

Observing and Describing the Stream of Consciousness

A practice we recommend to most students with test anxiety—and that is central to many mindfulness- and acceptance-based therapies such as ACT and DBT—is systematically observing and describing thoughts, feelings, and urges. This means explicitly labeling thoughts *as* thoughts, feelings *as* feelings, and urges *as* urges. As with most techniques in our treatment, we would advise practicing this exercise with students in session, asking them to narrate aloud, or silently to themselves, what happens in their stream of consciousness for a couple of minutes. There are lots of ways you might lead students into this exercise; below is just one example.

> THERAPIST: Imagine that you're watching a great horror movie, with the lights off and the volume up. You're drawn into the story, as if everything in it were really happening, and you feel scared, to the point that it's hard to pay attention to much else in the environment. If you wanted to take a step back emotionally and free up your mind, one thing you could do is to actually just name to yourself each of the cinematic elements unfolding. You could explicitly describe the changes in background music occurring, the choppy and frenetically paced editing—
>
> STUDENT: —The trembling in the actor's voice, the close-up shots of the fear on their face.
>
> THERAPIST: Exactly! Just describing verbally each of these things you're seeing and hearing, in a piecemeal fashion, as they play out on the screen, pulls you out of the movie. You're removed from the illusion. Through a similar practice, you can learn to step back from your own mind and not be so prone to fully buying into the thoughts and feelings that pass through you, which might sometimes indeed feel

like a familiar horror movie, like when you feel totally lost on a hard exam question and grow convinced you're going to fail the test and maybe even the whole class, and then not be able to get into college, and then not be able to get a job, and so on and so on.

STUDENT: Yup, I've seen that movie before!

THERAPIST: The amazing thing is, if you practice watching the operations of your own mind, and labeling the thoughts and feelings that come and go, you can get more freedom from those thoughts and feelings. Your mind will still busily tell you all sorts of things, but you recognize this as your mind's chatter and not necessarily as a deep signal of anything terribly important. For a minute, I want you to say out loud whatever thoughts and feelings come up for you—but be sure to label them as thoughts and feelings. For example, "I'm noticing a thought that I should be dealing with that email my boss sent me earlier. I'm noticing an urge to go get my favorite sandwich at Starbucks." Make sense?

STUDENT: Sure, yeah, I can try that. Um . . . I'm having the thought that I'm not sure what to say here, and now I'm having a feeling of anxiety. Now I'm having the thought that this exercise won't work for me and that I'm not doing it right.

THERAPIST: Yes! That's what our minds do—they cast doubt, they judge, they're always evaluating what we're doing or not doing. Totally natural. Keep going—let's see what kind of noise your mind produces in the next minute or two.

Listening to emotionally evocative music, as recommended in the Unified Protocol, can further enhance the exercise of watching one's own mind, broadening the range of thoughts and feelings that students might notice during the practice. By playing pieces of music that trigger feelings of tension, sadness, or excitement in them, students can create an opportunity to observe, describe, and build greater acceptance of the range of thoughts their minds might visit when these emotions arise in the wild, in their everyday lives. Of course, in the context of helping students with test anxiety, music that elicits negative emotion may be most useful for students to practice with.

An especially reliable way to inject strong emotion into in-session practice is to place a test in front of students. Using free online resources, the therapist could print a quiz in a subject that they know is especially aversive for a student. Alternatively, students could be asked to close their eyes and vividly imagine an anxiety-provoking test situation that they have experienced in the past, or that they anticipate in the future (e.g., sitting for the SAT). Either way, this should provide students with a good window through which to watch the typical operations of their minds when feeling academic stress.

With enough regular practice describing what happens in their own minds as an outside observer might, students notice they are able to inhabit this new perspective even during prototypical real-life academic anxiety situations. For example, what might have been experienced as a series of facts about the world—"This class is impossible, and I'm never going to be able to pass the test. There's no point in studying any more. I'm an idiot"—can now be experienced instead as, "I am having feelings of frustration and not being good enough. I'm noticing worries about how I'll do on the exam. I'm having an urge to give up."

This more distanced perspective on what's happening in the mind can reduce students' reactivity and leave them with more of a sense of freedom to choose what to do, behaviorally, in this anxiety-provoking situation.

Imagining the Inner Environment as Outer

Some students prefer to use visual imagery when engaging this kind of exercise. One well-known example from ACT involves visualizing leaves floating down a stream, and then placing each thought, feeling, urge, and sensation that arises in consciousness on a leaf, and watching it float down the stream. A quick search online will yield several "leaves on a stream" scripts and videos that the therapist might study for inspiration in instructing students in this exercise. Other popular visualizations include placing thoughts on billboards that pass by while driving down the highway, imagining thoughts as incoming texts or emails that pop up but don't require a response, placing thoughts on clouds that move through the sky, placing thoughts on suitcases that are circulating on a conveyor belt at the airport, or imagining thoughts inscribed onto the sand of a beach and then washed away with each crashing wave. With all of these visualizations, the idea is simply to practice observing thoughts (as well as feelings, urges, and sensations—and any other contents of consciousness) at a distance, to notice how they come and go and sometimes come back again, and to do so without trying to push away certain thoughts, or to hold on to others—to practice acceptance and nonjudgment of, and non-reactivity to, one's own thoughts.

If you choose to read aloud a "leaves on a stream" or related script, we agree with Roemer and Orsillo (2020) that you don't need to adopt the gentle, hypnotic, slow manner of speech that is stereotypically associated with mindfulness instruction. Maintaining your more typical tone, rhythm, and volume of speech helps to ensure that students aren't thrown off by perceptions of affectation, and it also helps to prevent any misunderstanding that the exercise is intended to induce relaxation. The exercise is about observing rather than changing the contents of one's mind.

Regardless of whether students prefer to use specific visual imagery to practice observing their inner experiences without judgment, regular practice is required to change one's relationship with one's thoughts. We have found that this bears emphasis for students, who often respond well to analogies with performance in athletic or artistic settings:

> *To not get too caught up in your anxious thinking during challenging, stressful situations such as a test at school, when your thoughts may be loud and insistent and emotionally compelling and may feel quite factual, it's crucial to start having a more distanced relationship with thoughts during ordinary times, when your emotional temperature is lower. It's like shooting hoops or playing piano. You have to regularly practice a new way of operating for it to become automatic and something your mind or body can engage even when under pressure. So in the next week, please set aside at least two or three minutes each day to practice watching your stream of consciousness. You can use imagery, like we did in the leaves on a stream exercise, or you can just watch your thoughts and feelings as they pop up, labeling each one and noticing how they come and go on their own. We'll talk at our next meeting about what you noticed during this exercise throughout the week.*

As always, letting students know in advance that you'll be checking in about their practice is crucial for keeping them accountable and committed. It's also helpful for their motivation levels to remind them that daily, formal practice is not a rest-of-their-lives commitment. The goal is to develop a skill—nonreactive observation of their own thinking—that will begin to be incorporated into how they conduct themselves each day automatically, so that no intentional efforts are required to keep the skill strong. Handout 8.2 features a form that students can use to record their daily practice.

When discussing students' experiences with watching their thoughts, be ready to validate a range of reactions they might have, from enjoyment to annoyance. Remind them that the judgments their minds generate about their engagement in the exercise (e.g., "I screwed it up," "I can't wait to do this again," or even "This is stupid") are just more thoughts to be observed.

FREER, MORE FLEXIBLE THINKING

After helping students gain an appreciation for the benefits of structured, purposeful engagement with their worry thoughts, and their stream of consciousness more generally, we turn attention to tools they can use to free themselves emotionally from particularly unhelpful thoughts, to build up more flexibility in their thinking, and to focus their minds on the task at hand.

Unhooking from Unhelpful Thoughts

Students sometimes report getting especially caught up with particular thoughts. For example, suppose a student notices how often they experience and buy into the thought, "I just can't do math," and how they get behaviorally derailed when this happens (e.g., giving up on practice problem sets, or submitting a test early, when stuck on difficult problems). We describe below a few ACT techniques that can be used to help drain particular recurring thoughts of their behavioral impact:

- The student can try repeating aloud, many times in a row, the emotionally salient essence of the thought ("I'm bad at math"). Eventually the semantic content fades away (this phenomenon was perhaps first recorded in Titchener, 1916), and the thought is revealed to be just a series of sounds produced by the brain (and the tongue). It can begin to feel as if the thought were in a language that the speaker doesn't know, where even the most insulting statements or words could not have any emotional impact. Studies have shown that repeating thoughts over and over decreases their reflexive believability and emotional effect (e.g., Masuda et al., 2010). Another, related way of defamiliarizing the thought and attenuating its attention-grabbing power is to try singing it to a familiar song or saying it in a goofy voice that isn't one's own.
- The student can try saying the thought to themselves repeatedly while acting contrary to the thought. In this example, they could purposely keep reminding them-

selves that they "can't do math," while completing some math problems that are within their current grasp. Thinking one thing while doing the opposite reminds students that their thoughts are unreliable guides to reality, consisting of noise as well as signal, and helps unhook them from their own thinking. Of course, with some thoughts that students get stuck on, an opposite action may not be readily available. Students might still benefit in a generalized way, as part of their practice for distancing from their thinking, from choosing some arbitrary thought (e.g., "I can't see blue things!") and enacting the opposite (scanning the environment for blue objects).

- The student can practice welcoming the thought every time it occurs: "Thank you, mind, for the reminder of next week's exam!" By explicitly making space for the thought, perhaps even telling themselves that they *want* to have the thought, the student's adversarial, fearful relationship with the anxious thought diminishes. As noted above, it is our resistance to thoughts (e.g., attempts to suppress them) that ironically often worsens their persistence and feeds their power over our behavior. Students might even consider, while welcoming the thoughts that hook them, purposely adopting a physical posture of willingness, as described in DBT: a half-smile, relaxed jaw, uncrossed arms, open hands, and so forth.

One Picture, Many Interpretations

Aside from tools to defuse the impact of particular thoughts, students can benefit from building up general-purpose flexibility in their thinking, so that any automatic interpretation of a situation doesn't feel like the only possible interpretation. For example, a student might be expecting to be notified electronically of their exam grade at a given time, but they haven't yet received any notification. They might assume the worst—that their teacher is waiting to tell them about a failing grade in person instead, because it has such dire implications for their ability to pass the course altogether. This kind of thought, in turn, can engender a lot of distracting anxiety. (And anxiety inclines the student toward rigid, negative interpretations of situations like this in the first place!) At a time like this, it can be helpful for students to be practiced in recognizing how much uncertainty there often is in our first interpretations and thoughts in response to many different situations, and to be able to consider other possible understandings (e.g., that the teacher may just be falling behind in their own grading process).

To reduce attachment to first thoughts and interpretations in general, a good exercise is generating as many different appraisals of the same ambiguous stimulus as possible. Especially effective in group treatment settings, this exercise, drawn from Barlow's Unified Protocol, involves showing students a picture of a scene that isn't clearly defined, and then asking them their thoughts about what's going on in the scene. Students' automatic, immediate interpretations of the scene will usually vary somewhat, and when prompted to, students will be able to develop plenty of other ideas about what might be happening. The exercise is a test in itself (albeit a projective one), and we recommend using a picture that can be interpreted as showing a student taking a test. Ask students questions about what's happening in the picture, what led up to this, what's going to happen next, and what thoughts and feelings are being experienced by the person in the picture. Some students will see discouragement or frustration on the student's face; others will see boredom, wistfulness, or creative reflection. Some students will think the student is completing an exam, while others may imagine the student is doodling or writing a personal note.

This same exercise can be repeated with as many pictures as you like, of course, and can be done in dialogue with an individual student in addition to the group setting. Practice in generating a wide variety of thoughts consistent with the same situation reminds students that no single thought their minds produce should be regarded as 100% reliable. It is a good idea to reinforce this message when wrapping up this exercise:

> So you can see how the same picture we're all looking at can yield tons of different interpretations. Everyday life is that way, too. We experience things in the world, and our minds are constantly generating all sorts of subjective, automatic judgments and assumptions, yet we hardly notice them that way—instead, it seems like we are just seeing the facts as they are, objectively.
>
> When we're stressed out, we're especially prone to interpret things in a negative and threatening light. It's sort of like the opposite of those Instagram filters that make everything look more beautiful. For example, in class, when you feel anxious about your performance and confused by the material, you might look around at other students' calm-looking faces, and consider their lack of questions for the teacher, and think, "I'm the only one who doesn't get it." And of course this interpretation could be right—but there are other possibilities too, such as that your peers are also confused and too embarrassed to speak up and ask the teacher for clarification.
>
> Remembering the exercise we did with the ambiguous picture can help you develop more flexibility around your automatic interpretations, recognizing them as just hypotheses, not certainties, and helping you distinguish your mind's thoughts from hard facts about the world. This helps you stay focused on what's important to you in any situation, rather than being drawn into needless rabbit holes of worrying and over-analyzing. In the example I just mentioned, you can notice your interpretation of the situation—that you're falling behind peers in your class—but not get too wrapped up in the implications of this possibility, holding it at arm's length as just one interpretation, not THE reality. You can better stay focused on what's effective for your learning in that moment—specifically, asking the teacher some clarifying questions.

TRAINING ATTENTION

The preceding sections were devoted to practices that help students to gain some observing distance from the ever-unfolding cascade of thoughts that their minds produce, to distinguish these thoughts from facts about the world, and to recognize their freedom to behave consistently or inconsistently with whatever their minds might be telling them. After regularly practicing these exercises, students find that their attention is less dominated by the spontaneous, anxious chatter that their minds generate. When attention is not grabbed as much by worries about future outcomes (or ruminations on past experiences, for that matter), there's naturally a greater ability to concentrate on tasks in the present. Staying tuned in to the present also enables students to learn while in the classroom and while studying at home and to demonstrate their mastery when taking exams (see Chapters 9 and 10 for additional behavioral strategies to boost concentration while studying and to enhance test-taking skills). Moreover, attunement to the present can deepen students' enjoyment of their nonacademic time, unburdened from distraction by worries and other thoughts about the past or future. Students may be interested to learn that happiness tends to increase when the mind is focused on whatever task is at hand, rather than wandering to other things (Killingsworth & Gilbert, 2010).

Even with lots of practice building up nonreactive acceptance of the whole range of thoughts that their minds conjure up, students will still sometimes find their attention diminished during anxiety-provoking academic situations. Deliberate, repeated practice keeping attention narrowly trained can help students to strengthen their focusing capacities for these situations. Indeed, intentionally practicing focused attention is a central component of several evidence-supported treatments for anxiety, such as metacognitive therapy (Wells, 2009), mindfulness-based stress reduction (Kabat-Zinn, 1990), and mindfulness-based cognitive therapy (Segal et al., 2002). We discuss two types of attention training exercises that students can practice.

Built-In Practice

As the notion of building focused attention through regular exercises is introduced, students sometimes understandably object that they just don't have time to add another deliberate practice to their daily routines:

> STUDENT: I thought this treatment was supposed to help me with my test anxiety. Part of why I get anxious is that I'm drowning in homework and exams to study for. I'm really not looking for any more "homework."

> THERAPIST: I get it—you have a lot on your plate already. You're right. Thankfully, it's possible to train your attention during activities you're already doing every day. For instance, tell me what you do in the morning before going to school.

> STUDENT: Well, I usually don't have time for breakfast, but I do shower every day—I can't wake up without it.

> THERAPIST: Perfect. During your daily shower, you could practice focusing entirely on the washing process. Whenever you notice that your attention has wandered to something else, to any other thoughts your mind generates, like how you did on yesterday's English test, you would simply bring your attention back to the feeling of the soap on your skin, the warmth of the water, the scent of the shampoo, the sound of the fan overhead, and so forth—the immediate experience of the shower itself.

> STUDENT: I don't know that I could do that at 7:00am. I'm half-asleep still.

> THERAPIST: You might be surprised by the degree to which you can build up your capacity for sustained attention, like a muscle you exercise daily. But fine—maybe that's not your preferred practice. Flexibility is important. What do you do after school?

STUDENT: Most days, I work a shift at a store after school, sorting the clothing racks.

THERAPIST: And how do you get to the store?

STUDENT: I take the bus.

THERAPIST. Okay. So during your bus ride to work, you could try keeping your attention focused on the sounds of the bus's engine for the whole ride, or on the conditions of the sidewalks on the route.

STUDENT: But I like having that time to zone out and listen to music or look at social media.

THERAPIST. Makes sense—again, so much of your day is already eaten up by various obligations and to-do's. But of course, if the exercise I'm prescribing can actually strengthen your ability over time to pay attention to other things during the day, like if you can stay more fully present in your chemistry class, without losing focus to ruminations about yesterday's English test, then you may actually be able to reclaim time in your day. Would you be willing to try out this practice for four weeks, during your bus rides to work? We can revisit at that point how it's going for you.

STUDENT: Sure, that sounds fair. It's worth a shot.

All sorts of repetitive chores can make great opportunities for practicing focused attention: doing the laundry, folding clothes, washing dishes, scrubbing a bathtub, or mowing the lawn, for example. Exercising, cooking, and eating are also common daily activities during which a student might choose to focus deliberately on what they are seeing, hearing, feeling, smelling, and/or tasting in the present moment. Clinical research has demonstrated that informal attention training may be even more effective than formal meditation practices for maintaining decreases in distress and dysfunction resulting from mindfulness-based treatment for anxiety (Morgan et al., 2014).

Regardless of what a student decides to focus on, it's important to remind them that their attention will invariably wander away repeatedly during their practice. All they need do is bring it back to what they've chosen to attend to, over and over, as many times as needed. Encourage students by framing the attention strengthening as happening every time they notice their focus shift away from the intended object, and then they shift it back again. If their mind wanders 100 times, that means they get to complete 100 repetitions of attention strengthening practice!

Adding a Formal Practice

Despite time constraints, some students choose to add to their daily routines at least a few minutes exclusively devoted to practice of focused attention. Research has shown that even relatively brief practice sessions can yield improvements in attention and decreases in anxiety (e.g., Basso et al., 2019; Hoffman et al., 2010). Students might choose to focus on their breathing, as in many traditional formal mindfulness practices, or they might slowly scan their entire body and notice any physical sensations or urges to act (e.g., to scratch an itch) in each body part. The progressive muscle relaxation exercise from Chapter 7 can also function similarly as an attention training exercise (Hayes-Skelton et al., 2013). Or students might choose to closely examine and describe to themselves, as if for the very first time, a familiar everyday object, such as a water bottle or a pen. In a group treatment setting, a fun exercise can be handing out similar-looking oranges (or some other object we typically label and then cease to pay attention to, such as a blank piece of paper), one to each student, asking each student to study their orange carefully for a minute. Then take back all the oranges, mix them up, and ask students to identify their own. Students will often express surprise about how quickly and easily they can discriminate the object that was theirs at the start of the exercise—a testament to how much can be noticed with just a bit of sustained, focused attention.

As with exercises in which students practice observing and describing their free-ranging stream of consciousness, some students may experience anxiety during these focused-attention practices. This can be especially so for paying attention to breathing. Doing so can lead to over-breathing, even if the exercise involves trying to keep a slow rhythm of inhalation and exhalation, and as reviewed in the last chapter, hyperventilation can engender a variety of anxiety symptoms. In any case, simply remind students that there is no goal of feeling relaxed during the exercise. If the mind wanders to the thought, "I'm feeling anxious," or "my heart is racing," just notice this wandering and bring attention back to the chosen object of attention.

Tuning In to a Signal amid Noise

Students should by this point be familiar enough with the default workings of their minds to understand the following analogy:

> *The mind's chattering never stops. It's like an endless playlist on Spotify or YouTube, sometimes jumping around from track to track or video to video in random order, sometimes playing tracks to completion but often stopping mid-stream and jumping to another track, and also returning over and over again to certain tracks or videos, often ones that bring a lot of discomfort or distress—such as worries about how you'll do in a class that's challenging you, or on a high-stakes standardized test coming up.*

Because most people experience their stream of consciousness auditorily, an especially powerful way to build up the capacity to attend to a task at hand (e.g., a test) even while dealing with the distractions of one's thinking is to practice paying selective attention to a particular audio source while other sources are present.

As part of a broader metacognitive therapy for emotional disorders, Wells (2009) included an attention training technique that entails exactly this challenge. The attention training technique has been applied effectively to test anxiety (Fergus & Limbers, 2019), and can be introduced to students straightforwardly:

> *The good news is, it's possible through repeated training to develop your ability to stay tuned in to what matters most to you in any given situation, like taking a test at*

school, even while your mind's playlist of anxious thoughts might continue in the back-ground—thoughts like "all the other students are breezing through this test," "I'm going to run out of time and won't be able to finish," "the test questions are unfair," or "I just can't wait to be done and get away from this stress." In fact, research has shown that the tech-nique we're about to try can be helpful specifically for test anxiety when students practice it regularly. During this exercise, all you need to do is follow my instructions. I'll be asking you to pay attention to particular sounds in the environment. To keep you focused on this task and avoid visual distractions, I'll ask you to keep looking at [name something unin-teresting in the environment] throughout the exercise. Now remember, even as you make an earnest effort to follow my directions and keep attention focused where I ask you to do so, it's natural that unrelated thoughts and feelings, what we called the mind's playlist, might enter your awareness. This just increases the challenge level of the exercise a bit, enhancing the opportunity to strengthen your attentional control. Regard your thoughts during this exercise as just another ambient sound in the environment, a noise that you don't have to pay heed to.

To guide students through the 12- to 15-minute exercise, it's best to have at least six distinct sounds audible from the room in which the practice is occurring. There should be three sounds in the immediate vicinity (e.g., a clock ticking, a fan or air purifier running, the therapist's hand tapping a table) and between three and six sounds more faintly audible from outside the practice room (e.g., a white noise machine in the hallway, a radio playing in the waiting area, traffic outside a city office). If, as in many therapy offices, there aren't many sounds naturally audible in the distance, it's fine to introduce low-volume sounds in the office as substitutes (e.g., playing the audio from a YouTube video that includes a few different nature sounds combined).

The attention training technique includes three progressively more challenging phases. In the first (5–6 minutes) phase—selective attention—the therapist instructs students to pay attention to a single sound among the many competing sounds. Begin with the most obvious, loudest sound, and escalate the difficulty every 30–60 seconds by asking students to now turn their attention to a different sound, slightly less salient in the environment. After students have paid selective attention to each of the sounds present, the second (5–6 minutes) phase of the exercise begins. This part involves switching attention more rapidly between the different sounds. The pace of the attention switching should increase through-out the phase (e.g., from 10–15 seconds for each sound at the start, to just a couple of sec-onds between switches toward the end), as the therapist randomly calls out which sound the students should turn their attention to. Finally, in the third phase (2–3 minutes) of the attention training technique, students practice divided attention. Here they are asked to expand their awareness and focus on hearing all of the sounds at once.

Students who are ambitious about building their capacity for focused attention, even in the context of intense test anxiety, can benefit from practicing the attention training tech-nique at least once daily for several weeks. Once they have practiced it in-session a couple of times and are familiar with the sequence of selective attention, switching attention, and divided attention tasks, they should be able to recreate the same exercise on their own, in any environment with enough distinct sounds present. Alternatively, students can search online for attention training technique audio recordings, which include an appropriate set of sounds and instructions guiding them through the exercise. As of the time of this book's writing, such recordings were freely available on some websites and apps (e.g., the Afternoon Break channel on YouTube). Therapists might also choose to use these recordings in place of providing the required sounds and instructions themselves in session. Research studies have used audio recordings of the attention training technique to good effect (e.g., Murray et al., 2016, 2018).

We also encourage students to adopt informal practices that are analogous to the attention training technique that has been most thoroughly tested in the empirical literature. For example, when students listen to music, they can practice selective attention, switching attention, and divided attention with respect to specific instruments or other elements of the song. Or they can practice listening to podcasts on earbuds in environments in which there are many people talking around them, or television voices competing for their attention. Reading while in auditorily busy environments can also help build their capacity to stay tuned in to one source of information when others might compete for their attention. It's important to emphasize that their performance will not always be perfect—some environments are very difficult to direct attention in—but that students' attentional skills will improve over time, even in environments that are far more distracting than a typical test environment. Handout 8.3 features a form that students can use to record their daily practice with training their attention.

SUMMARY

Test anxiety has physiological and cognitive components, as well as behavioral correlates. In this chapter, we presented a variety of techniques that therapists can introduce to students to help them manage the cognitive aspect of their test anxiety. The overarching goal is to help students develop distance from the anxious thoughts their minds emit, so that they can more effectively stay tuned in to the present. After completing this module of our test anxiety treatment, students typically report that they spend less time and energy grappling with their worries and other anxious thoughts, and that they can reinvest these freed-up resources into the behavioral routines—inside and outside the classroom—that help them achieve as they hope to academically.

The techniques described in this chapter need not be used strictly in the sequence we present them, but we have found that including worry journaling early in this module helps to build credibility with students. They usually are intrigued by this counterintuitive practice, and they often find immediate benefit from practicing it. Worry journaling also helps to prime a mindset that is amplified by the rest of the techniques in the chapter—namely, that anxious thoughts are not inherently harmful and need not be aggressively pushed away, but that it's also typically unhelpful to purposely indulge them through extensive processing, which takes attention and time away from the outward-directed, sometimes anxiety-provoking activities that actually propel students toward valued academic goals. Thought experiments build up students' understanding of the limited returns on trying to exert control over their internal thoughts and feelings (e.g., expectations of how they might do on a test) rather than their outward behaviors (e.g., preparations for that test). The practices we presented for nonjudgmentally observing and describing the stream of consciousness develop students' capacity to tolerate unpleasant mental content, including recurrent anxious thoughts, without getting too caught up in it. The ambiguous picture interpretation exercise reminds them of the fallibility and sometimes arbitrariness of their own thinking, which helps them to emotionally disengage a bit from the automatic thoughts their minds generate and to think more flexibly. Finally, we present techniques that students can practice to increase their ability to pay attention to whatever matters most to them in a given moment, including during testing, even when there is inevitably some background noise, such as their own anxious thinking, coexisting alongside the task at hand. That final set of exercises serves as a useful segue to training in study and test-taking techniques, which we cover in the next two chapters.

Worry Journaling

Schedule a 10-minute block of time into the day, during which you will write out all the worries your mind generates, including worries about tests and other academic issues. After doing this free writing, write below the main themes or problems that emerged in your worrying. For each issue, decide whether you have any influence over the problem. If you do, identify a manageable action step you can take today or tomorrow to help address the problem, and then complete this step. Return to the final column ("Did you complete this action step?") the next day, to track your problem-solving follow-through.

Date:

Problem	Do you have any influence over it? (Yes/No)	If yes, what's one action step you can take to help address the problem?	Did you complete this action step? (Yes/No)

Observing and Describing the Stream of Consciousness

Set aside at least two minutes daily to nonjudgmentally observe and describe whatever thoughts, feelings, sensations, urges, and so on arise in your mind. You can do this practice while in an emotionally neutral state, or you can try it after doing something anxiety-producing, like studying for a test. You can use imagery as you notice your thoughts (e.g., the "leaves on a stream" practice), or you can simply verbally label things without any specific imagery.

Date	Type of practice (What was the situation? Did you use any imagery?)	Length of practice (minutes)	Notes (What did you notice?)

Training Attention to the Present

Practice keeping your attention trained on just one thing at a time, whether it's an everyday activity you already do (e.g., walking to school), a formal practice you're starting (e.g., mindful breathing), or the attention training technique in which you focus on one source of sound at a time, switch your focus between sounds, and then focus on all sounds at once. No matter what you choose to focus on, your attention will wander away at times; simply redirect it to your intended target when this happens.

Date	Type of practice (An everyday activity or a formal practice? The attention training technique?)	Length of practice (minutes)	Notes (What did you notice?)

CHAPTER 9

Studying for Success

Inadequate preparation for exams is both a cause and a consequence of test anxiety. When students haven't studied well, they are more likely to perform poorly on a test, which in turn can increase their nervousness about future tests. And when test anxiety is high, sitting down to study for a test can be nerve-racking and therefore might be avoided. Studying by taking practice tests can be especially uncomfortable for students who are test-anxious, and as we will review in this chapter, this may be the most effective kind of test preparation. So even for perfectionistic students who study compulsively, rather than avoid studying altogether, because of their test anxiety, there may be excessive time spent on inefficient study methods such as rereading materials over and over.

Test-anxious students can thus get stuck in a cycle of poor test performance and avoidance of effective studying, or they may spend needless hours on inefficient studying even if their test performance is adequate. Earlier modules in our test anxiety treatment were focused on enhancing students' willingness to experience anxiety and developing their ability to manage its physiological and cognitive components (see Chapters 7 and 8). In this chapter and the next one, we go beyond improving students' relationship to their anxiety and aim directly at augmenting their studying and test-taking skills. After all, most students want not only to feel more comfortable with tests and other aspects of academic functioning, but also to do well on tests and to be able to prepare for them efficiently. When students develop more mastery of academic materials, their anxiety about testing tends to drop naturally (Faber, 2010).

Many treatments that have had the largest impact on test anxiety have included instruction in studying and test-taking skills alongside intervention components targeting students' test anxiety more directly (Ergene, 2003; Hembree, 1988; Huntley et al., 2019), but this instruction has not always been based on the strongest research evidence (Huntley et al., 2019). Our treatment teaches students those study strategies that have been proven most effective by modern cognitive science.

A PRIMER ON STUDY STRATEGY RESEARCH

To teach students how to get more out of their studying, it helps to have some background knowledge on the research surrounding this topic. This allows the clinician to answer common questions and to be more persuasive in getting students to adopt new study techniques. Oddly enough, educational psychology textbooks rarely cover the relative effectiveness of various study strategies, despite the apparent centrality of this topic to educators and anyone interested in how students learn (Dunlosky et al., 2013).

Once students reach the stage where they are expected to self-regulate much of their own learning via studying outside the classroom—typically around high school—possessing good study strategies can be crucial for achieving one's potential. Unfortunately, even after reaching college, most students know little about which approaches to studying facilitate learning the most; practical instruction in how memory and learning work can correct this deficit (McCabe, 2011). Without formal instruction in science-backed study strategies, students gravitate toward study approaches that give them a sense that their knowledge of the academic material is rapidly improving and that they understand what they need to (Soderstrom & Bjork, 2015). For example, in one survey of college students, a majority ranked repeatedly rereading their notes or textbook as their foremost study strategy (Karpicke et al., 2009). Quickly the material can begin to feel highly familiar, as if one were ready to take an exam on it, but research has shown clearly that this is one of the least effective ways to prepare for a test. We review below the studying techniques that are most strongly supported by empirical research (Dunlosky, 2013).

Practice Testing

Academic tests are a measurement of students' learning. Some kinds of measures have no effect on the thing measured, while others can profoundly impact the attributes one is measuring. For example, suppose that you wanted to build up your back and arm muscles and wished to measure your progress. You could, on the one hand, use a tape measure to track the growth in the size of these muscles. Regardless of how often you used this measurement, it would have no direct effect on muscle size or strength. On the other hand, you could measure your progress by seeing how many pull-ups you could do. If you measure yourself frequently enough using *this* method, it will by itself cause growth in muscular strength and size.

Which kind of measurement is an academic test? Is it more like a tape measure—an inert indicator of one's current level of learning—or is it more like an exercise that not only tests but strengthens one's current learning? The science is clear that testing promotes and doesn't just evaluate students' learning (e.g., Roediger & Karpicke, 2006). Retrieving one's knowledge, as in practice testing, solidifies that knowledge. Part of this effect is probably due to the fact that when trying to recall information, other knowledge in one's long-term stores is also activated, which then strengthens associations with the target information, making it easier to recall the target knowledge in the future (Carpenter, 2009). For instance, if you're asked who the 42nd US president was (Bill Clinton), you'll likely need to recall the names and order of presidents before and after Clinton, and that other information also gets rehearsed. Even when a student fails to recall relevant information or is unable to solve a problem during practice testing, this may facilitate learning. Gaps in the student's knowledge become more salient to them, and this may cause the student to keep studying in a focused way more than they might have if they didn't realize, through practice testing, their insufficient preparation for the actual exam (Vojdanoska et al., 2010).

The learning advantage afforded by retrieving knowledge—the central feature of practice testing—is very large, comparing it to some other common study techniques. In one representative study, undergraduate students were assigned to either (1) read material once, (2) read it repeatedly, (3) read it repeatedly and map out key concepts afterward each time, or (4) read it repeatedly and try to freely recall as much as they could afterward each time (Karpicke & Blunt, 2011). As measured by a test one week later, repeated reading, as well as repeated reading with the elaboration engendered by concept mapping, led to greater learning compared to reading the material just once. But contrary to students' predictions, it was the condition in which students tried to recall what they had just read after each round of studying that led to the greatest learning. In fact, test performance was about 50% higher in this condition than in the conditions in which students merely reread the material repeatedly or mapped out the key concepts after each rereading. This performance boost from the repeated retrieval practice (self-testing, essentially) held true for both verbatim recall of the information studied, a week later, and for questions that required deeper inference from the new knowledge. Indeed, even when the test involved mapping out key concepts, students who had done repeated retrieval during the studying phase outperformed those who had done concept mapping during their studying! Other research has indicated that students higher in test anxiety benefit from practice testing just as much as students lower in test anxiety do (Yang et al., 2020).

In addition to teaching students how to use practice testing for their own learning, educators would do well to offer frequent quizzes in class, for credit or just for practice, to boost students' learning and to teach them experientially the benefits of practice testing. Studies suggest that administering weekly tests, rather than having only a midterm and a final exam, not only boosts students' learning but also increases their satisfaction with a class and their liking of frequent testing (Banger-Drowns et al., 1991).

Distributed Practice

Research has long established that spacing out one's studying into multiple sessions, rather than cramming all studying into a single session, improves learning. Moreover, lengthening the intervals between study sessions leads to superior long-term retention of new knowledge, when holding the total quantity of studying constant (e.g., Benjamin & Tullis, 2010; Delaney et al., 2010). This idea of extending studying across numerous sessions has been called "distributed practice." Like any other schedule of studying, distributed practice can be applied to various study techniques, including practice testing, as described above. This means that if a student were to study for four hours total for a history exam, their long-term learning would be stronger if they studied in four one-hour increments, each spaced a week apart, compared to studying in four one-hour increments spaced only a day apart; and they'd learn less still if they simply studied in a single four-hour session.

Unfortunately, left to their own devices, students often do the opposite of distributed practice. Due to procrastination, students sometimes engage in a single, massive cramming session, which they may also find rewarding because it can give them a fuller feeling of mastery within the session, compared to the more incremental gains in knowledge they would experience within any given smaller study session. When students repeatedly study the same material without much or any lag between repetitions, they tend to overestimate how well they know the material already, and how long their newfound learning will last (Bahrick & Hall, 2005). On the other hand, when studying is spaced out, students are more apt to realize how little of what they've studied is actually in their long-term storage, which can motivate them to continue studying more until they've truly mastered the material. Studies have shown that students don't recognize that longer lags between their study sessions benefit their long-term learning (Wissman et al., 2012), indicating again the importance of teaching students research-based methods of exam preparation.

Interleaving

Interleaving refers to mixing up the types of material studied within a single study session. For example, within a 60-minute study session, a student might repeatedly alternate between 10 minutes of practicing Spanish vocabulary and 10 minutes of solving physics problems, rather than simply studying Spanish for 30 minutes and then physics for 30 minutes. Or, within a single subject such as arithmetic, a student might alternate between multiplication, division, subtraction, and addition problems throughout their study session, rather than practicing a big chunk of multiplication problems, followed by a big chunk of division problems, and so forth.

Research has shown that interleaving results in superior long-term learning, compared to studying topics or problem types in large, segregated blocks (Dunlosky, 2013). This is unsurprising when considering that interleaving can be understood as a kind of distributed practice within a single study session. The student returns repeatedly to each type of material to be studied, with intervals of time away from each within the session. The student thus has to repeatedly retrieve from their long-term memory relevant information for mastery (e.g., methods for solving particular problem types; Taylor & Rohrer, 2010), rather than simply keeping this information in their working memory, as may happen if their study session does not alternate between different kinds of material.

Students may naturally gravitate away from interleaving for the same reason they may avoid practice testing and distributed practice: it tends to alert them to deficits in their learning, which can be stressful in the moment, but is, of course, ultimately adaptive if it promotes adequate studying to achieve mastery. When a student studies the same set of vocabulary for 30 minutes straight, they may overestimate how solidly the words are in long-term storage, whereas when they spread that same 30 minutes of vocabulary practice out over a couple of hours, interspersed with other types of studying (e.g., biology, history), they will recognize that some of their apparent mastery of new words decays quickly once they turn attention elsewhere for a few minutes. Anxiety can make it more difficult for learners to shift back and forth from one activity to another (Shi et al., 2019), but putting forth the extra effort to interleave different study materials still pays off at the time of the real test! If interleaving feels too difficult or unpleasant, it can be introduced gradually, as with any activity that is avoided out of anxiety.

Elaborative Interrogation and Self-Explanation

Some research indicates that students benefit from being encouraged to ask themselves probing questions about new knowledge they're trying to assimilate. For example, if a student had just learned what interleaving is and that it improves learning, they might challenge themselves to explain how interleaving confers its benefits. If they had previously learned about how distributed practice enhances learning, they might come up with the explanation we offered above. In doing so, the student would have activated other existing knowledge in their long-term memory and associated it with their new knowledge, bolstering this knowledge and strengthening their ability to retrieve it in the future (Willoughby & Wood, 1994).

In addition to asking "why" questions about what explains new facts that they're learning, students can benefit from more generally elaborating on the material they're studying in terms of other things they know about. For example, when learning about a war, they might ask themselves the parallels and differences with another war that they had previously studied. Or when studying a novel, students might ask themselves how the characters and their motivations relate to those contained in another novel by the same author. Any tactic like this increases the depth of integration of new knowledge with existing knowledge.

TEACHING STUDENTS SCIENCE-BACKED STUDY SKILLS

We find it helpful to get students talking right away about their studying behavior. Start by asking them how they tend to study for tests, and if it's difficult for a student to give a generalized answer, consider asking them to give several examples of tests that they've taken in the past month. For many students in high school and college, their study techniques will vary somewhat depending on the subject matter, instructors, and so forth.

Once you have a sense of how students study for tests, explore the relationship between anxiety and study behavior. Ask students directly how they think test anxiety relates to their own studying, and to their peers' study habits too. In individual or group treatment settings, natural conversation along these lines tends to draw out the idea that anxiety about tests can cause students to feel it's important to prepare for tests, but can also make that preparation really uncomfortable, especially when it involves doing things similar to what's expected on the test itself. Students might therefore avoid or procrastinate their studying, or selectively use comfortable study techniques such as rereading chapters or reviewing homework problems they had previously solved. Students typically also have an intuitive grasp of how insufficient or ineffective studying can impair their test performance, which can make them even more nervous about future tests. Developing more effective and efficient study skills is typically not a hard sell!

Exploring Students' Preferred Study Methods

To teach students better ways of studying, it helps to have concrete examples of materials that students might be tasked with learning. Presenting students with such materials also affords an opportunity to get them thinking about all the different ways that studying might be approached, and to recognize the study methods they currently favor. We recommend sharing a couple of Wikipedia pages, or excerpts from Wikipedia pages, with students. For example, you might share articles on wheat and Buddhism, or on Miles Davis and artificial intelligence. Students can view the pages via print-outs or electronic devices. For younger students, the Simple English version of Wikipedia is appropriate. This version features simpler vocabulary and syntax and more straightforward articles.

Ask students how they would try to learn the material in the articles, if they were going to be taking an exam on the two topics two weeks from now. The exam might include multiple choice items, short answers, essays, and so forth—anything that might appear on tests they typically take in school. Engage students in discussion of methods of studying—such as rereading, taking notes, summarizing, highlighting, underlining, or making flash cards—as well as timing of studying, such as whether they might cram the night before the exam versus spread out their efforts over the two weeks.

At this stage, you do not need to provide evaluative feedback about which methods of studying are more or less likely to lead to retention and deep comprehension of the materials. Instead, reinforce students simply for thinking broadly about all the different ways they could prepare, and for reflecting on which tactics and timing they tend to prefer, and why they prefer these. If students demonstrate insight into their preference for certain study methods because they are less stressful (e.g., rereading highlighted parts of the article versus summarizing aloud what they remember from it, without notes), use this as an opportunity for validation: "Of course! We all lean toward those things that are less anxiety-provoking. For example, if I'm teaching something new, I might find it more comfortable to keep rereading my teaching notes rather than standing up and seeing what I can recall without notes."

How to Study to Learn the Most

At this point, we suggest transitioning into a more didactic, directive mode with students:

> *A necessary first step in learning what's in those Wikipedia articles is to read them, of course. Many times, the next step students take is to reread them, and maybe to underline or highlight key parts of the articles on printed-out versions. Or students might take notes on what they're reading or even copy the text verbatim.*
>
> *These kinds of study methods are rewarding in the short term. When you keep rereading the same passages, they become familiar, and it quickly feels like you know the material. Unfortunately, this feeling often proves to be an illusion. Passively rereading material over and over, or even slightly more active variations on this, like highlighting the material or taking notes on it, may help you learn, but not as effectively as when combined with other study methods that we'll focus on soon.*

Reading an article again and again to learn the material is sort of like trying to learn a skateboard trick, a piano song, or a video game by watching YouTube videos of people doing these things. Sooner or later you need to test yourself and try to do it on your own! Growing your knowledge so that you can do well on tests isn't exactly like learning the motor skills needed for sports, music, or video games, but it's still the case that active performance, rather than passive observation, is what best develops your abilities.

Specifically, when studying, the strategies that help you learn the most are those that most closely resemble actually taking a test on the material you're studying. Whenever you try to retrieve from your memory what you've learned after reading one of those Wikipedia articles, you're actually strengthening what's in your memory. And when you realize that certain things haven't yet made it into your memory bank, you are more alert to what you need to pay attention to when you go back to the material and review it again.

Here it may make sense to invite students back into the discussion: "What are some ways that you can test your knowledge when studying? How could this apply to learning the content in the Wikipedia articles we looked at?" See whether students can help generate the following methods, or whether they have ever tried them:

- *After reading one of the Wikipedia articles, or even after reading each section in it, put away the article and try to recall from memory as much of the content as you can. Whatever you can remember, put into writing or speak aloud.*
- *After learning something new from the article, challenge yourself to go deeper by asking why what you just learned is true, or how it relates to other things you know about. This causes you to retrieve your new knowledge and also to get it linked up to other existing knowledge in your brain, which actually makes it easier to pull out of storage the next time you test yourself. For example, if learning about the planet Saturn, you might ask yourself how the facts you've learned about it (e.g., size, temperature, composition, moons) compare to those of other planets you already know about.*
- *Create practice tests for yourself, and take them. Come up with questions about the material you're reading as you read it, and then, when done reviewing, try to answer those questions, either in writing or while speaking aloud, without consulting the articles or any notes you have on them. In your normal classes, when there are ready-made practice tests available, in your textbook or from your teacher, these are great to use, too!*
- *Create and use flash cards to test your knowledge. A flash card is traditionally an index card where you write some information or a question on one side, and then an answer you're trying to remember on the other side. You then review the set of cards, looking at only one side of each card and trying to recall what's on the other side, before checking to see if you're right. So for example, if you were studying vocabulary, you'd put a word on one side, and its definition on the other. Or if you were studying a new language, you'd put a word in that language on one side, and the translation in your native language on the other side. Or if you were learning state capitals, you'd put a state name on one side, and the capital on the other side. There are various phone apps and software package for computers that allow you to*

create flash cards in electronic format, if you prefer that to paper. Of course, if you find yourself getting distracted by other things when using your phone or computer, try using old-fashioned index cards!

- *Try teaching a peer or family member about what you're learning. Tell them all about the topic, and try to answer any questions they have. Ask them to give you feedback on anything they didn't understand in your teaching.*

Validate for students that these kinds of study methods may be anxiety-provoking. That's part of why students tend to avoid them! It's stressful to realize, through all this simulating of testing, that you haven't yet fully mastered all the material. But this recognition of knowledge gaps helps guide students to more effectively review their readings and notes, and get more out of each rereading, before testing themselves again.

Point out to students that if they can show themselves through practice testing that they thoroughly know what they need to for the test itself, they will go into the test with less anxiety and more confidence. Practice testing also acts as repeated exposure that can help ease test anxiety in general.

Handout 9.1 includes a practical summary of effective study methods.

When to Study to Learn the Most

Explaining the best timing for one's studying is relatively straightforward:

> *When it comes to the timing of your studying, your best strategy is simple: Space it out. Even if you can learn by cramming for hours during a single big study session, cramming is less efficient than studying in a spaced-out fashion, and your learning from cramming tends to fade quickly. Again, studying an academic topic isn't totally different from learning to play a sport, a musical instrument, or a video game. Most people know from experience that they'll develop more as an athlete or musician if they practice for an hour per day, five days of the week, compared to if they just practice for five hours straight on one day of the week.*
>
> *Let's return to the example of the two Wikipedia articles we looked at. We stipulated that you'd be tested on their content in two weeks. Suppose you're going to study for four hours total between now and the day of the test. Keeping the principle of spacing out your studying in mind, you'd be better off studying for 20 minutes on 12 different days rather than studying for 60 minutes per day for the last four days before the test, or worse yet, studying in one big four-hour block. The deeper learning you'll achieve with the spaced-out studying will become especially apparent in the weeks, months, and years after the test itself. People tend to remember very little from cramming sessions in the long term. Spaced-out studying, on the other hand, can cause more enduring gains in your knowledge.*
>
> *A second simple point about spacing will also enhance the effectiveness of your studying. Within a study session, you'll benefit from mixing up particular topics you're reviewing, so that you keep repeatedly returning to each topic in a spaced-out way. For example, if your two Wikipedia articles were on wheat and Buddhism, you'll learn more if you alternate between these two subjects within each study session, rather than devoting each session exclusively to one topic or the other. And even if you were studying just*

one general subject, you'd be best off mixing up different aspects of that subject within each study session, so that your focus on any particular part of the subject is spaced out throughout the session. So rather than doing a bunch of flash cards about the botanical aspects of wheat, and then a bunch of flash cards about the history of human uses of wheat, you'd learn more by mixing up both kinds of flash cards.

Handout 9.2 includes a practical summary of how students can space out their studying.

Putting Good Study Skills into Practice

For creating real change in the way that test-anxious students study, the next step is the most crucial: mapping out their current studying challenges, and creating a concrete, specific plan for applying evidence-based study skills to their weekly schedule. Consider with students what they need to focus on learning outside their classroom time. Then help them look at their calendars and commit to regular, spaced-out blocks of time during which they can accomplish their learning tasks. For each content area they need to learn, think with them about how they can make their studying resemble testing more, in terms of regularly trying to retrieve what they've learned without looking at their notes or readings (e.g., using flash cards, or explaining concepts to a friend). Consider how they can use interleaving to their advantage, as well. Where possible, return repeatedly to students' study habits, week after week, and keep supporting them in developing more effective strategies that will maximize their learning and increase their confidence and performance on tests.

Handout 9.3 provides a worksheet for students to plan the timing and methods of their studying in advance. This includes a space for them to take notes on how the studying went for them, to help them refine their plans for future studying.

IMPROVING INSUFFICIENT-BUT-POPULAR STUDY STRATEGIES

In settings where time allows, it can be useful to also talk briefly with students about making the most of study strategies that they and their peers will probably continue using, even once they learn that the effectiveness of these strategies will be limited if they aren't combined with techniques that resemble practice testing, as reviewed above. Miyatsu et al. (2018) provided a useful summary of how to maximize students' benefits from the most popular study tactics. For each of the following studying techniques, we recommend beginning by asking students how they think the technique can be used more or less effectively. This gets them to continue to think actively and flexibly about all the different ways that one might study, and also causes them to retrieve and reflect on what they have already learned about effective study strategies.

- *Rereading.* Nearly all students reread chapters, articles, notes from class, and so forth as part of their studying, if they study at all. As previously mentioned, reading the same materials over and over, uninterrupted, can quickly give students a sense of fluency and familiarity that can cause them to overestimate how well they've absorbed the material. To maximize gains from rereading, students should (1) test what they've learned after each time reading, such as by writing down everything they remember from the reading; and (2) space out their rereading of the same material, both within and between study sessions. These same principles apply to rereading marked-up text as well as notes or outlines that students create in response to a text (see below).

- *Underlining and highlighting.* The act of marking up text by underlining or highlighting key passages can increase students' level of active processing of the information they're reading, since they have to determine what is most important among all the material. Secondarily, marking up text may help students focus their rereading efforts on the most important material, increasing the efficiency of their studying. To use underling and highlighting well, the most important thing is for students to refrain from marking the text the first time they read through it, when they are liable to poor judgment about what warrants emphasis. Only after having read all the material and gotten a sense of what's most important in it should students consider going back and rereading the text with a highlighter or pencil in hand.

- *Note-taking.* Taking notes while reading a text, like marking up the text, can increase students' active elaboration of the content they're trying to absorb, which can in turn facilitate later retrieval. Research has shown that even more so than with marking up text, taking notes can make later review of the material more efficient and effective. Some research has suggested that taking notes by hand may be more effective than typing them on a computer, since the slowness and effortfulness of handwriting may cause students to write sparser notes, which can require more active engagement with the material compared to quickly copying material verbatim. However, this research has not replicated consistently, and we would encourage focusing students mainly on the same point that applied to marking up text: refrain from taking notes until at least a second read-through of the text, to improve the cogency of those notes.

- *Outlining.* Outlining is similar to taking notes on a text but requires a student to determine a reasonable way to represent the hierarchy of information communicated in a text—the main overarching points, subpoints to these points, and so forth. As with marking up text and taking notes, this can improve the depth of their learning and the efficiency of their later review of material. And as with those two study methods, students should be advised to delay outlining until at least their second time reading through material, to increase the likelihood that they will create an outline that actually captures central themes in the text and is helpful for further studying.

Handout 9.4 includes a practical summary of how to use common study methods optimally.

MINIMIZING DISTRACTION AND PROCRASTINATION

For many students, knowing how and when to study is only half the battle. Common problems of distraction and procrastination can thwart even the best-laid plans for implementing evidence-based study strategies. We have found that behavioral techniques developed for adolescents and adults with attention deficit hyperactivity disorder (ADHD) and other executive functioning problems can help many students, regardless of their neurotypicality. Choosing from the following interventions can be based on the individual profiles of students with whom you're working. It can be useful to informally discuss how well students focus during study sessions and the extent to which they can remain organized with academic tasks. This can help to gauge the appropriateness of the following interventions.

Creating a Good Study Environment

Modifying aspects of the physical environment can improve students' ability to focus on their studying (Safren et al., 2017; Solanto, 2011). Mobile phones may be the biggest source of distraction for most students today. We have found that completely powering down one's phone, and ideally placing it in a separate room, provides a strong buffer against compulsive checking of texts, social media, news, and so forth. There are also "phone jails" or lock boxes with timers that students can purchase to keep their phones inaccessible for periods of time. Merely silencing alerts, on the other hand, while keeping the phone powered on and within arm's reach, rarely helps students whose studying is interrupted often by phone-checking. In fact, some students look at their phones even *more* frequently when their alerts are silenced, since they then never know whether there might be new, interesting content (e.g., incoming texts or social media updates) available when they unlock their phones and look at relevant apps.

When studying requires students to be on a computer, and distraction may again result from checking email, social media, and so forth, there are more intensive measures that can be taken, if the student is willing. Namely, the student can disable Internet access if it isn't required for the work (e.g., if a student is simply typing up practice test questions for a chapter they're reading). This can be done, for example, by using a laptop computer somewhere where there is no free WiFi signal available. Some students even choose to use a computer without a WiFi adapter built into it, or they remove the one that came installed on their computer. When Internet access is needed, a USB-based WiFi adapter can be plugged in. At other times, that adapter can be kept far away from where the student is trying to study. Software-based solutions are also available. Various Internet-blocking software packages can be installed, and some of these have the ability to selectively block access to specific problem distractors (e.g., Instagram), whether on a computer or on a mobile phone. If students need only a small amount of help in staying off distracting websites or web-based email, they can simply log out of all sites at the start of their study session, so that if they do open up a web browser, there's at least a small buffer of effort and time required—during which they can choose to abort mission—before they can compulsively check all the usual-suspect websites. Even disconnecting from the WiFi network can be helpful in this way.

Beyond phone- and computer-mediated distractions, some students find their attention pulled away from their studying by visual and auditory stimuli in their environment. If in a library, students might do well to position themselves so that their sightline does not include other students walking by. In terms of auditory distractors, anything involving speech tends to be most likely to disrupt attention, including music with lyrics.

Students should consider whether having friends or other peers present when studying increases or decreases their ability to focus. For some students, the sense of mutual social accountability ("they will see if I'm messing around on my phone rather than using my flash cards") keeps them on task. The enjoyment of friends' company can also make studying less aversive. Other times, students may find that they get so caught up in face-to-face socializing that they are unable to get any studying done.

Handout 9.5 includes a practical summary of how to optimize the study environment to stay focused.

Preventing Diversion into Other Tasks

Regardless of whether students restrict their phone or Internet access or have friends in the immediate vicinity with whom they might socialize, there are always ways they can get diverted into non-studying tasks. During studying or any other effortful activity, people's minds generate all sorts of other to-do's (e.g., searching for something random online, getting a snack, personal grooming, posting a picture to social media). After getting distracted and pulled into these tasks, people often feel, in retrospect, as if some of these tasks were just avoidant procrastination, even if they felt compelling at the time that their minds generated the urge to divert from their intended focus.

The *distractibility delay technique* (Safren et al., 2017) can help guard students from diverting away from their studying toward other seemingly urgent, but possibly questionable, to-do's. This technique is somewhat reminiscent of the worry journaling (see Chapter 8) with which students are already familiar.

The first step is to set a timer for an arbitrary duration during which the student intends to study uninterrupted, such as 30 minutes. During that period, every time the student notices the urge to do something else besides their intended studying, they write down that to-do on a list, and then they return to their studying. When the timer ends, the student reviews the full list of distracting to-do's that came to mind during the interval. If, at this point, any items on the list truly seem like something that should be done immediately, then the student does them, and then crosses them off the list. Other items will seem clearly like mere procrastinatory distractions, and students can cross these items off the list right away. Still other items might be deemed worth doing, but not immediately; these can be left on the list.

The student again sets their timer for another interval of time, and during this time, follows the same procedure, writing down anything that threatens to pull them away from their studying. And when this timer ends, the student goes through the same process to winnow down the list. This process is repeated until the student's study session is finished. Whatever items remains on the to-do list (i.e., those that the student regards as worth doing, but not right away), the student will transfer to the task list they keep for tracking all their daily to-do's (see below).

Handout 9.6 includes a practical summary of how to use the distractibility delay technique.

Keeping an Organized Calendar and Task List

Many students' academic functioning increases, and their test anxiety decreases, when they learn to maintain a single calendar containing all relevant assignment deadlines and test dates, as well as a single task list that contains all their to-do's. Whether in electronic or paper form, the calendar should be kept with them all the time, and they should record any new items in it immediately, rather than assuming that they'll remember to edit their calendar later (Safren et al., 2017). As students practice spacing out their study sessions, they should schedule each one in their calendar in advance. Students should also be encouraged to make a habit of checking their calendars at regular times every day, so that they don't lose track of obligations. To do so, it helps to pair the calendar checking with other behaviors that are already deeply ingrained habits; for example, a student might check their calendar every morning (look at today's schedule) and evening (looking ahead to the next day's schedule) after brushing their teeth (Solanto, 2011).

Students should also keep with them their task list, in electronic or paper form. This includes all of the things they need to remember to do, small or large. It can be helpful for them to assign each task a priority level, such as A, B, or C, to designate its urgency. For the highest priority items, it makes sense for students to make sure that the tasks, or the smaller subtasks needed to make progress on the bigger overall tasks, are entered into specific times in their calendar so that they chip away at them each day rather than procrastinating.

PROMOTING SLEEP

Unfortunately, almost everyone has firsthand experience with the way that anxiety can interfere with sleep. Sleep problems also predict the onset of worsened anxiety (e.g., Orchard et al., 2020), and American adolescents have grown much more sleep-deprived in recent decades (Twenge et al., 2017). Improving students' sleep may help ameliorate their test anxiety and may also help them get the most out of their studying. In our experience, sleepiness is a major disruptor of students' studying. Inefficient studying due to tiredness can mean that students require more hours to learn the same amount, which in turn can leave students with fewer hours to rest at night, in a vicious cycle.

For students who report sleep problems, we suggest sharing the following recommendations, largely derived from cognitive-behavioral therapy for insomnia (e.g., Carney & Manber, 2009; Perlis et al., 2005), to help develop a behavior change plan to promote better sleep:

- Ensure that the bedroom environment is conducive to sleep at night.
    - For adolescents, the most important measure here may be the removal of smartphones and other electronic devices, as access to social media and other Internet-mediated content is likely the biggest contributor to recent upticks in sleep loss in this age group (Hysing et al., 2015; Twenge et al., 2017). If students are willing to power down their phones and leave them outside their rooms overnight, this greatly reduces the chances of getting caught up in stimulating content before sleep or when waking during the night. As reviewed above ("Creating a Good Study Environment"), turning off alerts but leaving a phone powered on and within arm's reach can actually increase rather than decrease students' reflexive

checking of their phones, as they never know when they'll be rewarded with new content when they check their texts and favorite apps. For students who are willing to remove phones from their bedrooms at night, a conventional alarm clock will be needed to replace that function.

- A cool, dark, quiet environment is ideal. People generally sleep best in the 60–67 degrees Fahrenheit (15–20 degrees Celsius) temperature range. Blackout curtains can help block light; if these are unavailable, affixing aluminum foil to windows can also be highly effective and reduces heat buildup if strong sunlight hits the windows during the day. If ambient noise is a problem, running a fan or white noise generator can help obscure other sounds; earplugs can also help.

- Create a buffer zone of at least 30 minutes before bed, during which only low-stress, low-stimulation activities are engaged (e.g., showering, toothbrushing, reading an unexciting book, listening to a mellow podcast). Try to keep lights relatively dim during this time, too, and for an additional hour or two before bed if possible. Most important, try not to introduce any new, potentially stressful information during the buffer time before bed; for example, don't read news or check texts or social media.

- During the morning and afternoon, try to increase physical exercise and other activity levels, and get some bright light (e.g., sunshine) exposure if possible. The more active students are during the day, the stronger their appetite for sleep will be at night, and the better their circadian rhythm (i.e., their internal, 24-hour clock) will function. Unfortunately, when chronically sleep-deprived, students may feel exhausted and less inclined to be active during the day than they otherwise would be, which can perpetuate a weak drive for sleep and thus can increase the likelihood of poor sleep. Social accountability can help—for example, agreeing to meet up with a friend to exercise after school, if a student isn't currently playing a sport.

- Limit daytime caffeine intake and napping.
  - Students often underestimate how long-lasting the sleep-inhibiting effects of caffeine can be. If a student has even a modest-sized (by modern standards) cup of coffee at 12:00 noon, the effects on their nighttime sleep will be similar to those they'd experience if they ingested a 12-ounce can of cola or a cup of green tea at 8:00 P.M. or at 12:00 midnight (depending on how fast the student metabolizes caffeine). Moreover, many students don't realize that falling asleep without any problem doesn't mean that caffeine isn't affecting their rest. For many people, frequent waking at night, or an inability to fall back asleep when waking during the night, or an early final waking, are the main effects of excess caffeine intake.
  - Some students nap after getting home from school and extracurricular activities, exhausted from their accumulated sleep deprivation. Napping satisfies the sleep appetite, which feels good in the short term but often then interferes with the ability to sleep at night a few hours later, similar to how snacking may ruin one's appetite for the next meal. If students are having trouble with sleep at night, it is best to eliminate daytime napping.

- Limit sleeping-in on the weekend. This is a tough one to persuade students to implement, but we have found that some sufficiently motivated students are willing to try it out. The principle here is similar to that around napping. Sleep-starved students may sleep late on the weekend (e.g., 11:00 A.M.), fully satiating their sleep appetite and leaving them with very little drive for sleep when their preferred weeknight bedtime (e.g., 10:00 P.M., if waking at 6:00 A.M. for school) rolls around after they've been awake for not even 12 hours. Many students get caught in a cycle of sleeping poorly on Sunday nights, setting them up for tiredness throughout the school week, leading to another round of oversleeping the next weekend.

- Use the bed only for sleeping. A lot of students have heard this idea and try to avoid using their beds to do things during the daytime such as watching cliffhanger television, playing hyper-stimulating video games, or engaging in an emotionally charged text exchange. They understand that doing so can lead their minds to associate the bed with high levels of emotional arousal rather than tranquility. However, what most students don't realize is that the most toxic thing they can do in bed, vis-à-vis their sleep, is tossing and turning at night *trying to sleep*. This is maybe the most powerful way that insomnia can become self-reinforcing. When people spend hours in bed anxious or frustrated about their sleep, or feeling lonely, sad, depressed, or worried (as often happens when alone in bed at night, restless!), this can set them up to expect another torturous experience the following night, which the mind then sometimes creates for them. It is therefore extremely important, when having trouble with sleep, for students to give up the struggle if they know sleep isn't coming soon, and to get up and do something else that is more pleasant, calming, and/or productive with their time. For example, they might read a book or work on a coloring book under dim lighting. If they get tired again, it's fine to return to bed and see whether they can return to sleep.

- Recognize that short-term sleep loss won't cause any catastrophes. Emphasize to students that it's perfectly possible to perform fine on tests, for example, even if they have trouble sleeping the night before. Anxiety about the consequences of poor sleep is a common contributor to insomnia. Students should obviously be careful to minimize driving or do other activities that could be dangerous if reflexes are slowed when they have had a sleepless night—and a few students may have medical conditions for which short-term sleep deprivation could be more of a problem, such as bipolar disorder or a seizure disorder—but for most students, most of the time, accepting occasional trouble with sleep can actually help prevent developing chronic insomnia.

- Consider whether devices or apps that assess one's sleep at night actually contribute to sleep trouble. Some students use electronic devices (sometimes wearable) or use apps on their phone (which should ideally be out of the bedroom at night) that evaluate the quality and quantity of their overnight sleep. We have found that scrutinizing the data output from these apps and devices can actually cause students to get more anxious about their sleep, in many cases. Ideally, sleeping can be one daily activity for which students don't feel the need to strive for ever-better grades!

Handout 9.7 includes a practical summary of behavior changes to improve sleep.

SUMMARY

In this chapter, the focus has been on helping students develop highly effective study strategies and habits. Too often, students choose less effective methods of studying, and they don't fully master the knowledge and skills they need before tests. And then when they do worse than they would like on exams, they misattribute their performance to the fact that they felt nervous during the test, whereas in reality, the more important contributor to their suboptimal results was inadequate preparation.

In the treatment module presented in this chapter, students learn about how they can master academic material best by repeatedly, actively practicing retrieval of their knowledge—such as by teaching others what they've learned, or by testing themselves using flash cards. They also learn how to make the most of more commonly used, if less effective, study techniques such as taking notes on readings. They learn about the importance of spacing out the timing of study sessions, rather than cramming all at once, to maximize their learning and especially the duration of the knowledge they gain. Students develop strategies for minimizing their distraction when studying, such as by implementing various methods to limit Internet and smartphone access, thoughtfully choosing and modifying the study environment, and using a technique that prevents them from getting derailed into momentary, procrastinatory impulses to do other things. Finally, students learn how to improve their sleep habits, which in turn can enhance their daytime alertness and the effectiveness of their studying.

By mastering and applying the material in this module, students can improve their learning and their performance on tests. This improves their confidence and decreases their test anxiety directly. In the next chapter, we present a treatment module focused on optimizing students' test-taking skills, which serves to further bolster their confidence and ensure that their test performance accurately reflects their level of knowledge and preparation.

Studying Smart

Students often study by reading and rereading material and maybe highlighting, underlining, and taking notes on it. This is certainly more effective than not studying at all, but learning is greatly increased when you also actively exercise your memory and skills. These are ways you can do so:

- After reading new material or refreshing your memory with old materials (e.g., reviewing your notes from class, or rereading an assigned chapter), put away all the materials. Then write down all of the most important information that you can remember from what you just reviewed, or say it all out loud. Now look back over the material again and see what you left out when you tried to recall it. Repeat the process until you are able to freely recall everything that you think is important to remember.
- When you learn something new and apparently important in your reading, or you're reminded of it when reviewing material, try to draw connections between this new knowledge and other things you know about. For example, ask yourself how the war you've just learned about is similar to and how it's different from other wars that you've studied. Or how the main character in a novel you finished compares to protagonists from other novels you've read recently. Or ask yourself *why* questions—for example, why the war you're studying was fought (this helps connect the war to other things you know about the same historical period), or why the novelist might have crafted a character like the one in the book you just read (this helps connect the novel to things you know about its author or the cultural context in which the author was writing).
- As you read or review material, create practice test questions, such as short answer prompts or essay questions, or practice problems that rely on a new concept (such as in a math class). When you're done reading or reviewing the section of material, take your own practice test, without consulting any of your readings or notes. If you have trouble with anything on the practice test, go back and review the relevant materials, and then put them away and try those parts of the test again, until you have mastered all the problems you created. Of course, if the teacher or a textbook provides ready-made practice tests, be sure to use these fully!
- As you read or review material, create flash cards that represent key learning points. A flash card is a piece of paper, such as an index card, where you write some information or a question on one side (e.g., a vocabulary word), and the answer you're trying to remember on the other side (e.g., the definition of the word). When you have a stack of flash cards, flip through them repeatedly, until you're able to easily deliver the correct answer to every question or prompt on the cards. Make sure to shuffle the order of the flash cards between each time you try them out.
- Try teaching a friend or family member about what you're learning. Tell them all about the topic, and try to answer any questions they have. Ask them to give you feedback on anything they didn't understand in your teaching. Teaching other people effectively requires a strong understanding of material! Take notes on anything you were unable to explain well, and then review that material, and try teaching it again.

All of these study methods may cause more anxiety than just rereading materials over and over again, because these methods will cause you to recognize gaps in your current mastery of the material. However, wherever you feel uneasy about your current mastery of material, that's your signal to keep practicing until you know everything fluently! Remember: it's better to identify your areas of ignorance *before* the test, while you still have time to keep studying effectively, rather than *during* the test itself.

Spacing Out Your Studying

Handout 9.1 reminds you of *how* to study most effectively. With regard to *when* to study, use these key principles to maximize your results:

- Space out your studying rather than cramming at the last minute (or last day!) before a test. For example, if you have a test in two weeks, it's better to review the material in several short periods spread out over those two weeks, rather than review it repeatedly in one or two long study sessions shortly before the test. Remember to refer to Handout 9.1 for study methods that will help you make the most of each study session!

- To motivate yourself to space out your studying, remember that committing new academic material solidly to memory is a lot like developing new skills in things like sports, music, or video games. If you were trying to improve your softball pitch, your playing of a difficult passage of music on your instrument, or your ability to beat friends at a new computer game, would you be better off practicing all day, once a month, or practicing in short sessions multiple times every week? Even if the total hours spent practicing were the same, you'd make much better and longer-lasting gains in your skills if you spaced out the practice over many sessions, rather than trying to cram it into one marathon practice session.

- You'll also benefit from spacing out studying of specific materials *within* each study session. You can do this by alternating your focus between different topics in a study session. For example, you could spend 15 minutes practicing a language, then spend 15 minutes solving math problems, then go back to the language for 15 minutes, and end with another 15 minutes of math. And even within a single subject, you can alternate focuses so that you get some spaced-out repetition within a single study session. For instance, if you had an upcoming physics test that covered both rotational motion and thermodynamics, you could solve practice problems that alternated between the topics (one rotational motion problem, followed by a thermodynamics problem, followed by a rotational motion problem, etc.).

Planning for Studying

Use this form to plan your studying in advance, to be sure you spread out your learning (see Handout 9.2) and use highly effective methods for studying (see Handout 9.1). Check your calendar to make sure you're scheduling your studying for times of day that are practical for you. Use the last column to record notes on how different study methods went for you, for different subjects. This will help you keep refining your plan for future studying.

Date	Time of day	Study topics and methods	How did it go? Anything you noticed?

Improving Common Study Methods

The highly active study methods described in Handout 9.1 are the most effective ones for ensuring you really understand and can retrieve material. But an early step in your studying, before doing things like practice testing, will likely continue to be reading assigned readings and/or reviewing notes from class. These are ways that you can make the most of these processes:

- When rereading chapters, articles, notes from class, and so forth, space out rereading of the same materials, both within and between study sessions.

- Don't underline or highlight text the first time you read through something. Instead, wait until you have read through the full chapter, article, or other reading at least once before you go back to the text to underline or highlight the material that is most critical for you to understand and commit to memory. If you try to underline or highlight during your first time reading through, it will be hard for you to make good judgments about what material is most important.

- For the same reason, don't take notes on the text you are reading until at least the second time you read through it. This way, you'll remain fully focused on digesting the full text the first time you read it, and you'll have an opportunity to get a sense of the overall thrust of the material, and what's most central to it. Then when you go back through it again, you'll take notes more efficiently and effectively.

- Outlining readings can be an active way to take notes. Outlining requires you to identify the overall structure of material you're learning, such as which points are the most important ones, and which points are subordinate to these. As with underlining, highlighting, and note-taking, just be sure that you don't begin the outlining process until at least your second read-through of the material.

- To reiterate the theme of the first bullet point: When reviewing your notes, outlines, or underlined/ highlighted portions of texts, it's most effective to space out your reviewing of them, rather than looking them over repeatedly in rapid succession, without turning your attention to anything else between repeats.

A Study Environment That Helps You Stay Focused

These are some steps you can take to reduce your distractions when you sit down to study:

- Power off your smartphone completely. Better still, power it off and place it in another room. Although you could still go to the other room and power your phone back on if you wanted to check social media, texts, and so forth, the greater time and effort that will be required to do so, compared to keeping your phone on and within arm's reach, will discourage compulsive checking. There are also "phone jails" or lock boxes with timers that you can purchase to keep your phone inaccessible for periods of time. Some students simply silence their phone notifications when studying, but this sometimes isn't enough to reduce phone use—in fact, some students check their phone even more in this case, since they never know whether there could be more content available if they were to check their phone again.

- If you're using a computer while studying and you get distracted by looking at social media or other websites, find ways to restrict your access. If you don't absolutely need the Internet to complete your current study tasks, take steps that make it take more time and effort to get online, which will reduce compulsive use. For example, even just disconnecting from the WiFi network may help. Or you could take your laptop computer to a location where you don't have access to a WiFi network. Or you can designate a specific computer for schoolwork, and remove the WiFi adapter from its hardware, so that you can only get online if you plug in something like a USB-based WiFi adapter; when you don't need to use the Internet, place this adapter far away from where you're studying, just as you do with your smartphone. If you need help staying off just certain websites to stay focused, you could try milder restriction methods, such as Internet-blocking software packages that allow you to ban access to specific URLs, or you can at least log out from those websites at the start of your study session, so that using them would require you to log back in.

- Apart from distractions involving your smartphone or computer, what sorts of sights and sounds in the environment pull your attention away from your studying? For many students, any audible speech can be distracting, so if you listen to music, music without lyrics would probably be best. If there are unavoidable voices in the background where you're trying to study (e.g., a family member talking on the phone in a nearby room), consider using earplugs or a white noise generator to mask the voices. If you're in an environment where seeing other people might distract you (e.g., in a library), try positioning yourself so that your sightline is unlikely to include people walking by.

- Consider whether having a friend or friends or other people nearby you might help you stay focused better or might be more likely to distract you. For example, some students feel more accountable to stay on task if they are visible to other people. Maybe you'd be less likely to scroll on social media, and more likely to practice math problems, if you study in a living room where other family members can see what you're doing, rather than working alone in your bedroom with the door closed. Or maybe you enjoy studying more when you do it with a friend, and this makes you more likely to stick to your studying calendar. Of course, you'll want to keep an eye on whether you end up socializing so much that your study sessions take much longer than planned, without as much accomplished as you were hoping for! Many students are happier and more productive when they make an agreement with their friends, if studying together, to stay focused on the studying for a set period of time (e.g., 60 minutes) before taking a planned break for socializing.

Keeping on Task When Studying

Even when you create a good environment conducive to focused studying (see Handout 9.5), it's always possible to get derailed from your study session. When there's a challenging or anxiety-provoking task, it's common that your mind might generate ideas for other things you should do, such as getting a snack, shopping for something online, posting on social media, or even completing chores or errands you wouldn't normally want to deal with. It's easy to get sucked into these other tasks and lose your focus. Here's one good way to improve your odds of staying on task when studying:

1. First, set a timer for a period of time you want to keep your focus on studying, without any interruption. For example, you could set a timer for 30 minutes.

2. Now, during this time period, every time you notice the urge to do something else besides your intended studying, write down that to-do on a list, and then return to your studying.

3. When the timer ends, you can now review the full list of distracting to-do's that came to mind during the interval. Decide which of three categories each item fits into:
   a. If, at this point, any items on the list truly seem like something that should be done immediately, then you should do them, and then cross them off the list.
   b. Other items will seem clearly like mere procrastinatory distractions, and you can simply cross these items off the list right away.
   c. Still other items might be worth doing, but not immediately. These can be left on the list.

4. Now you can set your timer for another interval of time, and during this time, follow the same process, writing down anything that threatens to pull you away from your studying. And when this timer ends, you can go through the same procedure to winnow down the list.

5. Keep repeating this process until your study session is finished. Whatever items remain on the to-do list (i.e., those that you think are worth doing, but not right away), you will transfer to whatever task list you keep for tracking all your daily to-do's (e.g., an electronic calendar).

Getting Better Sleep

Anxiety can make it harder to fall and stay asleep, whether that anxiety is related to school or something else. Using the strategies below can improve your chances of getting good sleep:

- During the morning and afternoon, try to increase physical exercise and other activity levels, and get some bright light (e.g., sunshine) exposure if possible. The more active you are during the day, the stronger your appetite for sleep will be at night. Daytime activity will also tend to enhance your daytime energy and mood, improving your overall circadian rhythm, and should help dampen your anxiety during both day and night.

- Minimize your use of caffeine and napping. If you've been having any trouble falling or staying asleep at night, try to limit your consumption of caffeinated beverages (e.g., coffee, tea, energy drinks, cola) to one small beverage per day, and have it before mid-morning. Caffeine can stay in you for a very long time and can interfere with sleep all night. If you want to maximize your ability to sleep well at night, it's best to cut out daytime naps. Napping satisfies the sleep appetite when you're tired, which feels good in the short term but often then interferes with the ability to sleep at night, similar to how snacking may ruin your appetite for the next meal.

- In the last 30–60 minutes before you go to bed, try to avoid exposing yourself to anything that's exciting, stressful, or otherwise emotionally stimulating. For example, don't watch cliffhanger television, play video games, or consume news or social media during this time. Focus on relaxing activities such as washing up, reading an unexciting book, or listening to a mellow podcast. Try to keep lights relatively dim during this time too.

- Do what you can to make your sleep environment cool, dark, and quiet. Blackout curtains or even just aluminum foil placed over windows can help keep a room dark. If ambient noise is a problem, running a fan or white noise generator can help obscure other sounds. Earplugs can also help.

- Power down your smartphone and keep it in another room overnight. All the addictive and emotionally stimulating content on our phones may be the biggest cause of sleep loss nowadays. An old-fashioned alarm clock can substitute for your phone's alarm function for waking up in the morning. Ideally, you'll position the alarm clock so that you can't see the time while you're lying in bed, since watching the clock may increase anxiety about sleep.

- If you use a wearable device to track your sleep quality and quantity, consider whether you might do better not using the device. For some students, the feedback that these devices give about sleep are another needless test, in a way, that causes overnight performance anxiety—*am I sleeping well enough and long enough?*

- If you're having trouble with sleep, get up and go do something else in another room, or at least out of your bed. If you instead spend a long time in bed anxious or frustrated about your sleep, or feeling lonely, sad, depressed, or worried, this can set you up to have another experience like that in bed the following night. It's better to get out of bed and do something more pleasant and calming with your time. For example, you might read a book or work on a coloring book under dim lighting. If you get tired again, it's fine to return to bed and see whether you can return to sleep.

- If you're having trouble with sleep, it's also good to remember that short-term sleep loss won't cause any catastrophes with your school work. For example, it's perfectly possible to perform fine on tests even if you have trouble sleeping the night before, as long as you have prepared well. Accepting occasional trouble with sleep can actually help prevent chronic insomnia.

- Try not to let yourself sleep in excessively on the weekends. When you're sleep-starved, you might desire to sleep very late on the weekend (e.g., 11:00 am). Unfortunately, when you do this, you may develop very little appetite for further sleep when your preferred weeknight bedtime (e.g., 10:00 pm, if waking at 6:00 am for school) rolls around after you've been awake for not even 12 hours. Because of sleeping late on Saturday and Sunday mornings, many students get caught in a cycle of sleeping poorly on Sunday nights, setting them up for tiredness throughout the school week, leading to another round of oversleeping the next weekend. If you need to catch up on sleep on the weekend, it's a better idea to go to bed earlier than usual on Friday night and still get up by approximately the usual time on Saturday.

CHAPTER 10

Doing Your Best on Tests

Students who have learned about the scientific research on test anxiety (see Chapter 6 on psychoeducation) understand that it's normal and not harmful to feel anxious when taking tests. Anxiety, in the range that students naturally experience during real-world tests, does not meaningfully impair performance in a direct way. Moreover, through the interventions outlined in Chapter 7, students learn to interpret their nervousness as a functional bodily response to the challenge of a test. The exercises described in that chapter help students get more comfortable with their anxiety and more willing to experience it when needed, while also developing an ability to calm their bodies if desired before or during a test. In addition, through the interventions described in Chapter 8, students learn to not buy into and get caught up with anxious thoughts their minds generate around a test, and to more effectively stay focused on the task at hand.

With these foundations of understanding and managing test anxiety, students usually report that they already feel less scared of taking tests. Students' confidence multiplies as they learn about and practice better studying habits (see Chapter 9). After all, by far the most important determinant of performance on any given test is a student's knowledge of relevant content and their domain-specific skills. When students can truly master the relevant material, they can perform better on their exams, and usually with less anxiety than they would have experienced if they were ill-prepared.

Still, some students worry that even if they understand the content to be tested on an exam, and even if anxiety will not interfere with their ability to demonstrate their knowledge on the exam, they might still be a "bad test taker" and do less well than they would hope. Our goal with the material in this chapter is to shore up students' test-taking skills with the most evidence-based techniques. Skills instruction in test taking has been part of many of the most effective test anxiety treatment packages (Ergene, 2003; Hembree, 1988; Huntley et al., 2019). Many students who receive the instruction we describe in this chapter will find that they already have good test-taking skills, but even then, they often appreciate the confirmation that there aren't any secret ingredients to doing well on tests that they are missing.

MANY STUDENTS THINK THEY ARE BAD AT TESTS

We have found that students are typically very interested in learning best practices for taking tests. This may be due to a great number of students thinking that they are below-average in demonstrating their knowledge and capabilities on tests. Indeed, in a study of 311 students at one American college, over 90% of students agreed with the idea that some students are simply bad test takers, such that they do poorly even when they know relevant material well, and over half of the surveyed students identified themselves as bad test takers (Holmes, 2021). Furthermore, identifying as a bad test taker was associated with self-reported test anxiety ($r = 0.5$). To work effectively with test-anxious students, therefore, it helps to understand more about their (often negative) views of their test-taking skills.

Why would so many students believe that they are worse than their peers at taking tests, when people are otherwise inclined to see themselves as above average in all sorts of ways (Alicke & Govorun, 2005)? Holmes (2021) proposed that believing oneself to be a bad test taker may, ironically, help to protect self-esteem. When a student receives a worse score than desired on a test, they can attribute this either to deficits in the knowledge and aptitude they brought to the test, or to the idea that they are unfairly disadvantaged in the taking of tests—which is to say that the test score is not an accurate representation of their knowledge and aptitude. If students hold on to a general belief that they're just lousy at tests and that their test scores are thus an underestimate of their abilities, then they don't have to feel as bad about themselves in the face of negative feedback they receive on exams. To be clear, none of this is meant to imply that students consciously choose to adopt a belief that they're bad at tests to insulate themselves from the sting of a poor score. To the degree that self-esteem-protecting motivations partly shape the belief in being a bad test taker, this probably occurs at a subtle, largely unconscious level.

Unfortunately, identifying as a bad test taker has been linked to using more superficial study strategies and possessing lower academic self-efficacy, alongside higher test anxiety (Holmes, 2021). If a student believes they will probably not do well on a test even if well-prepared, then of course dedicated study makes less sense. What's the point, if increased effort and learning won't be rewarded with better test performance? In this way, the belief in being a bad test taker can compound the avoidance of more effective study strategies (such as practice testing) that students may also show because of the anxiety these strategies elicit.

We aim to cultivate students' belief that they can fully demonstrate their abilities and knowledge on tests if they have prepared appropriately. Reviewing evidence-based test-taking skills with them helps bolster this self-confidence (as does treating their test anxiety more generally). Believing that one is capable of succeeding in any particular activity in life has been called *self-efficacy*, and this quality has proven enormously important for promoting motivation and effort, and ultimately high performance (Bandura, 1997). When students possess higher academic self-efficacy, they procrastinate less and achieve more (Chemers et al., 2001; Chow, 2011; Multon et al., 1991; Zimmerman, 1995) and prefer more effective study strategies (Prat-Sala & Redford, 2010).

TEST ANXIETY AND TEST TAKING

We have emphasized throughout this book, and we emphasize throughout the treatment we recommend for test-anxious students, that the best research evidence indicates that students' anxiety during testing has minimal if any direct impact on their performance. In other words, even when anxious, students can still retrieve knowledge and solve problems. However, we have also acknowledged that test anxiety may indirectly limit students' achievement by causing them to select less anxiety-provoking but also less effective studying methods (so that they may enter testing situations less well-prepared), and on a larger scale, to avoid academic or career paths that may entail a lot of testing.

Similarly, we have found that test-anxious students sometimes show maladaptive escape behaviors during testing, to ease the discomfort of test taking, and these behaviors can limit their performance. For example, if a student rushes ahead to be done with the anxiety-provoking test experience as soon as possible, they may misread directions or not check their work. In this sense, there could be a small kernel of truth to more test-anxious students' beliefs that they are somehow bad at testing, but in cases like this one, a "bad test taker" can become a good one by consciously choosing different behaviors during tests (see Chapter 2 for related discussion). Practice with exposure to anxiety (see Chapter 7) helps students to endure and put in their best efforts even while anxious during tests. Formal instruction in test-taking skills may also help to counteract any unhelpfully avoidant behaviors that test-anxious students may be prone to during testing situations.

When introducing the topic of test-taking skills to test-anxious students, we find it helpful to acknowledge students' possible concerns about being bad test takers:

> *Research has shown that students with test anxiety are more likely than other students to see themselves as bad test takers, and that even among students who aren't especially anxious about tests, a large proportion see themselves as bad test takers. That is, students often think that they have trouble doing well on tests even when they know the relevant material and have the abilities that the test is supposed to measure.*
>
> *Have you ever thought that you're a bad test taker? What led you to think that? How do you think the idea that you're bad at tests affects you?*
>
> *When you do less well on a test than you'd like, thinking that you're bad at taking tests could actually help you feel better in the immediate aftermath. You might think to yourself, "This score is disappointing, but I know I'm simply bad at tests, and my real knowledge and ability are higher than this score reflects. I might have gotten a C, but I really deserved an A and would have gotten one if I were a good test taker."*
>
> *But thinking you're a bad test taker could also discourage your efforts in general and thus limit your growth in the long term. If you tend to underperform even when you study hard and know the material, then what's the point of studying hard?*
>
> *In our work together so far, you've learned that test anxiety doesn't by itself make you do badly on tests. You've learned that anxiety about tests is normal and motivating, and it's*

really only a problem for your performance when you avoid doing helpful things like taking practice tests because you don't like the anxiety that they might bring up. Hopefully by now you feel better able to accept and manage your test anxiety and to prepare well for your tests.

Still, you might be concerned that even if feeling nervous won't stop you from performing on tests, you may not be good at tests for other reasons. Maybe you wonder whether other students have better strategies for guessing when they aren't sure of an answer. Or maybe you aren't sure that you pace yourself correctly during tests.

The good news is, there are a variety of well-understood, proven test-taking skills. We'll work together through the strategies that will help you gain confidence that you're performing as well on tests as you could, given your preparation for them. This will further decrease your anxiety about tests. It will also improve your performance, if it turns out you aren't currently using all of the best tactics for test taking.

TESTWISENESS

When instructing students in best practices for test taking, it is helpful to have some background knowledge of how test-taking skills benefit students, how these skills naturally develop, when these skills matter, and how these skills can be measured. We have found that students sometimes ask questions about how much these skills can be expected to benefit them, or whether they'll develop these skills just by taking more tests, for example.

The ability to do well on a test, relative to the level of the relevant knowledge and skills that one possesses, has been called *testwiseness* (a concept first detailed in a classic article, Millman et al., 1965). Colloquially, higher testwiseness would make one a "good test taker," whereas lower testwiseness would correspond to being a "bad test taker." If two students were equally matched in the substance of what a set of tests were designed to assess (e.g., skill at solving algebra problems, or knowledge of American history), but one of the students generally scored better across the tests, then that higher-scoring student would be said to have higher testwiseness. Testwiseness involves a variety of general-purpose test-taking skills for things like managing time well, avoiding careless errors, guessing answers, deductively reasoning to the best answer, making inferences about the test maker's intentions, and noticing patterns in how items are constructed (Rogers & Yang, 1996).

Testwiseness is beneficial mainly in the context of at least partial knowledge of target material (Rogers & Yang, 1996). For example, eliminating incorrect response options on a multiple-choice test usually requires some amount of relevant knowledge. When a student first reads a multiple-choice item, a response option might jump out to them as clearly correct based on their knowledge of the subject matter. If not, then a student low in testwiseness might just guess randomly. A more testwise student, on the other hand, will deploy various testwiseness strategies and determine whether they can at least narrow down the plausible response options based on what they *do* know that's relevant to the question.

Students generally develop some degree of testwiseness naturally, through practice taking tests, and cumulative experience may increase their savviness with particular test formats they repeatedly encounter, such as multiple-choice tests (Millman et al., 1965). Intelligence, verbal ability, and academic motivation—qualities that all typically increase as students progress in school—may also promote testwiseness (Rogers & Yang, 1996). However, research indicates that testwiseness improvements may plateau relatively early in students' academic careers, around eighth grade (Rogers & Yang, 1996).

Does Testwiseness Matter?

Some studies have found that performance on a majority of test items on high-stakes exams—which are often in a multiple-choice format—is at least partly related to testwiseness (Rogers & Yang, 1996). In other words, getting the items correct can result not just from knowledge of the specific subject matter the items are designed to probe, but also from the application of good general test-taking skills (Rogers & Yang, 1996). Moreover, teacher-made exams also typically include some features that will give at least a small advantage to more testwise students. When researchers analyzed 100 tests spanning the 7th to 10th grade level, from schools across multiple states and teachers across multiple subjects, about 75% of the tests included items susceptible, to some degree, to testwiseness effects. For example, some test items included absurd response options that could be eliminated as long as the student didn't guess randomly, response options that included terms such as "always" or "never" that are rarely true, or response options that disagreed grammatically with the stem of the item. Incidentally, test makers can reduce the influence of testwiseness on test scores by learning more about item and test construction and by limiting the number of response options on multiple-choice questions, because it is often difficult to generate more than two or three plausible distractor answers (Rogers & Yang, 1996).

Measuring Testwiseness

If students are interested in getting a firsthand feel for how testwiseness can matter for test performance, or if they would like to get a sense of their current testwiseness, before formal instruction as part of their test anxiety treatment, there are standard measures of testwiseness available. The Experimental Test of Testwiseness (Gibb, 1964) is generally considered the best measure of testwiseness. It consists of 70 items probing obscure details of history. Since almost no students have sufficiently detailed knowledge of the subject matter to immediately identify correct answers, testwiseness tactics must be used to increase the likelihood of selecting correct answers. For instance, the key to answering one item is dependent on knowing the rule of thumb that an answer option that is far more detailed than other options is more likely to be the correct option:

> *The Triple Alliance . . .*
>
> (a) *was opposed by Bismarck.*
> (b) *provided for united military action by the Allies in the event that any of them were attacked by two or more powers.*
> (c) *was Bismarck's idea.*
> (d) *included Germany, Austria-Hungary, and Turkey. (Gibbs, 1964, p. 80)*

A shorter, 20-item version of the same test is also available (Edwards, 2003). The Testwiseness Scale (Weiten, 2000; Weiten et al., 1980) is another option, consisting of 24 items also probing little-known historical facts. On this test and the Experimental Test of Testwiseness, students must identify and exploit common flaws in the construction of test items to score well, because their usually minimal knowledge of the subject matter is not enough by itself to support good performance.

We occasionally use items from these testwiseness measures in therapy sessions, particularly in group sessions when discussing students' test-taking self-conceptions. They can even make test taking seem less threatening and a bit fun. However, it should be noted that these measures only address one aspect of testwiseness—detecting unintended clues in test items. Moreover, when using these measures, therapists should take care to emphasize that testwiseness is not, by itself, sufficient for a good score on any test, and actual knowledge and skills relating to the specific material being tested is the most important ingredient in test performance.

TEST-TAKING SKILLS CAN BE TAUGHT

As reviewed above, testwiseness, or students' general skillfulness at taking tests, tends to increase through at least eighth grade no matter whether students receive explicit instruction in test-taking skills. Experimental studies have shown that formal, focused, short-term intervention programs can also boost testwiseness (Banks & Eaton, 2014). For example, in one study, five college students with learning disabilities and above-average test anxiety were given a total of three or four one-hour training sessions focused on test-taking strategies (Holzer et al., 2009). The students developed mastery of the test-taking skills and showed improved test performance and decreased test anxiety at the end of the intervention. In another study, four adolescent male students with autism spectrum disorder received a total of 14 hours of lessons on test-taking strategies over six weeks (Songlee et al., 2008). The students, who had average to superior general intellectual ability, demonstrated mastery of the test-taking skills at the end of the program, and they retained the ability to apply these skills flexibly at a follow-up conducted two weeks after the intervention ended.

We have found that even when time is very limited, most students can benefit from review of key test-taking skills. The majority of adolescent and adult students without neurodevelopmental differences or learning disabilities already possess reasonably strong test-taking skills compared to the students who benefited from intensive instruction in the studies cited above, and the curriculum naturally ends up compressed as students move quickly through material that they already feel confident about. We recommend a flexibly paced and often selectively focused approach to teaching the material outlined below, based on students' current levels of testwiseness. Having students narrate out loud their thinking as they move through a brief measure of testwiseness (see section above) can help illuminate their current test-taking skills, if this is unclear.

KEY PRINCIPLES OF TESTWISENESS

The taxonomy of testwiseness principles enumerated by Millman et al. (1965) is still an excellent starting point for teaching students best practices in test taking, and it serves as a foundation for the guidelines we provide below. We have also folded into our guidelines key insights from the *Test-Taking Strategy*, a codified set of testwiseness principles developed at the University of Kansas and used in several research studies (Hughes et al., 1993). The Test-Taking Strategy teaches students a series of steps represented by the mnemonic acronym PIRATES (Prepare to succeed; Inspect the instructions; Read, remember, reduce; Answer or abandon; Turn back; Estimate; Survey). Additional sources from which we have drawn in developing our evidence-supported guidelines include Banks and Eaton (2014), Parham (1996), and Weiten (2000).

Our testwiseness guidelines are summarized for students in Handouts 10.1 and 10.2. Below we offer suggested verbiage for walking students through the principles, including example items where appropriate.

Guidelines for All Tests

The following guidelines apply to all tests that students might take, no matter the test format.

Manage Your Time

On any test that has a time limit, you'll want to work as quickly as you can while still paying attention to what you're doing and maintaining a reasonable level of accuracy in your work.

If you expect it will be an especially time-pressured test or if you have a history of not finishing tests on time, then you might want to begin the test by previewing its total length and then setting up a plan for ensuring you get through the whole test. For example, if you have 45 minutes for a test and you see that it consists of three different essay questions, each of which counts equally, then you might plan it out so that you have only 15 minutes maximum for the first question, before you make yourself move on to the second, and then 15 minutes for the second, before moving on to the third. Of course, ideally you'll progress through a test at a pace that allows you some time to check your work at the end.

Order Test Sections Sensibly

Usually you'll want to go through the test in the order it's presented, but sometimes it will make sense to mix up the order in which you complete sections of the test. At the start of the test, take a quick look at its structure and how much different parts of it count for. For example, you might discover that the two long essay questions at the start of the test count for only 20 points in total, but the 10 short-answer questions at the end of the test count for 80 points in total. In this case, you should probably begin with the short-answer questions first, since it appears that you can earn more points for each unit of time you invest in these questions. If you were to run out of time while taking the exam, you'd be better off not having gotten to one of the long essay questions, worth 10 points, rather than not getting to, say, the last three short-answer questions, worth 24 points total.

Mark Skipped and Guessed Items

Whenever you aren't confident about the correct response to an item, either skip the item or take your best guess at it. Then be sure to mark the item, such as by circling it or putting a checkmark next to it. Then after you have completed everything else on the test, return to all of the marked items, and now spend time trying to generate the best answers you can on these items. Following this method ensures that you don't get bogged down by especially hard questions during your first time going through the test. When you spend too much time on the toughest questions, you may not get to later questions that you would have been able to answer easily and confidently.

Take Care with Instructions

Always read the instructions for each section of the test carefully. Spending a few extra seconds to make sure you fully understand what you're being asked to do is well worth it. Underline anything in the instructions that seems especially important.

Similarly, pay close attention to the individual test items. Sometimes they'll include a word like "not" that completely changes the correct answer, but the wording would be easy to overlook if you read the question hastily.

Whenever you aren't sure what the general instructions or specific questions are asking for, approach the teacher or test proctor to ask for clarification, if this is allowed.

Review Your Work

If you still have time left after finishing all items on a test, including the items you had skipped at first, go back to the beginning and check all your answers to ensure that you didn't make any careless errors, and that the work is as good as you can deliver in the time you have for the test. Persistence pays off—don't rush to pass in your work early just because you're eager to be done with the test or to show off to other students or the teacher!

Additional Guidelines for Multiple-Choice Tests

The following guidelines apply specifically to when students are taking multiple-choice tests.

Guess Profitably

When you aren't sure of the answer to a question, you have a choice between not answering the question at all, on the one hand, or guessing an answer, on the other hand. When incorrect answers will be scored the same as not having answered a question at all, then of course you should always wager a guess.

[Include the following education only for students who are taking the increasingly rare tests with penalties for guessing.] However, sometimes there's a penalty for wrong answers, compared to leaving an item unanswered. For example, suppose you have a multiple-choice question, and a correct answer is worth three points. If you don't answer the question, you neither gain nor lose points. If you answer the question incorrectly, you lose one point. In cases like this, you need to run the numbers to figure out whether you should guess or leave the answer blank, if you aren't sure of the right answer. For this particular question, if there are only three or fewer response options, or if you can rule out enough options that you are only guessing between three or fewer options, then it makes sense to wager a guess. This is because if you are guessing between three options, you have a 1/3

chance of guessing correctly, and you then earn three points. You have a 2/3 chance of guessing wrong, and then you lose one point. Running these numbers, the expected value of guessing is positive (i.e., [1/3 * 3] + [2/3 * −1] = 1/3). That is, on average, you'll gain points if you guess between three or fewer options under this scoring scheme.

Eliminate Response Options

Sometimes you'll read a multiple-choice question and think to yourself, "I don't know anything about this," and you'll think you need to guess randomly. Don't do so before reading the response options! You might be able to eliminate some response options even without knowing much about the substance of the question. For example, you might come across this item:

Which of these scientists is associated with the discovery of the structure of DNA?

(a) *Gregor Mendel*
(b) *Marie Curie*
(c) *Igor Stravinsky*
(d) *James Watson and Francis Crick*

You notice that one of the individuals, Stravinsky, was a composer of music rather than a scientist. You can therefore eliminate choice (c) even if you can't remember which scientists made which discoveries. Whenever you can eliminate an answer choice, cross it out.

Watch for Grammatical Mismatches

You can sometimes eliminate response options simply because they don't match up grammatically with the question stem. For example:

According to Aristotle's definition, an argument in which a conclusion follows logically from two true premises is called a

(a) *Syllogism*
(b) *Aphorism*
(c) *Reductio*
(d) *Proposition*

Option (b) can be eliminated because the article "an," rather than "a," would be required to make the option grammatically consistent with the question stem ("an aphorism"). There are sometimes similar mismatches between the number of a subject in a question stem and the number of the verb in a response option, such as if the plural "graphs" were the subject in the question stem, but the singular verb "is" appeared in a response option. You could eliminate that option based on the grammatical disagreement.

Notice Equivalent or Opposite Options

Other times, even if you don't know which response option is correct, you might be able to narrow down the choices by noticing that two response options are equivalent, which means that one of them has to be correct if the other is correct. For example, suppose you came across this item:

Who wrote the novel Uncle Tom's Cabin?

(a) *Mark Twain*
(b) *Harriet Beecher Stowe*
(c) *Samuel Clemens*
(d) *Nathaniel Hawthorne*

Maybe you have no idea who wrote this book, but you recognize that Twain and Clemens are one and the same person, with Mark Twain being Samuel Clemens's pen name. You can therefore eliminate options (a) and (c) from your choices, since one can't be correct without the other also being correct (and you can't select both of them!).

You may also run across items where two answer choices contradict each other—they can't both be correct. In this case, even if you're clueless about the substance of the question, you can eliminate an option that suggests both answer choices are correct. For example:

Which of these is typical of the effects on humans when they ingest the drug caffeine?

(a) *It makes it harder for them to fall asleep*
(b) *It sharpens their sense of hearing*
(c) *It dulls their sense of hearing*
(d) *All of the above*

Even if you don't know anything about caffeine, you can realize logically that no drug could both sharpen and dull your hearing. You can therefore eliminate choice (d), which implies that both of these options are somehow true.

Consider "All of the Above"

There are sometimes items where you know that more than one of the response options is correct, even if you aren't sure about the other options. For example, suppose you read this item:

Which of these books is in the Hebrew Bible?

(a) *Leviticus*
(b) *Judges*
(c) *Job*
(d) *All of the above*

You might know that Leviticus and Job are both among the books of the Hebrew Bible. Therefore, even if you haven't heard of Judges, you can be sure that the correct response option is (d), specifying that both (a) and (c) are correct.

Use Information from Other Items

Occasionally you'll spot test items for which you can use information from another item to identify the correct answer. For example, suppose that you first run across this item:
Which of these mammals is the largest by weight?

(a) *Hippopotamus*
(b) *African bush elephant*

(c) *Blue whale*
(d) *Sperm whale*

You know from this item that all four of the animals are mammals. Later on in the same exam, you see this item:
Which of the following animals is not a fish?

(a) *Hammerhead shark*
(b) *Sperm whale*
(c) *Tiger shark*
(d) *Seahorse*

So, even if you can't remember whether seahorses or whales are fish, you can choose the correct answer, (b), because the earlier item had revealed that sperm whales are indeed mammals rather than fish.

Remember the Test Maker's Intentions

To maximize your score on a test, it's important to keep in mind what you know about the test maker's intentions. For instance, suppose that you're taking a true-or-false test, and one of the items reads: "Thomas Edison invented the light bulb." You might happen to know, from listening to a podcast recently, that Edison didn't actually invent the first light bulb but played a key role in improving its design to make it practically useful, and he patented his design and is famous for it. But you also know that the teacher who created this test item had not explained this level of detail in the material that she taught in class and that she assigned in your readings. You distinctly remember her mentioning in a lecture that Edison invented the light bulb. In this case, you can reasonably conclude that you are meant to answer "true" to the test item, even if technically the truth of the statement is debatable.

Avoid Absolutes

When you're otherwise unsure of the answer, one clue to look for is the use of absolute terms such as "always" or "never" in response options. Reality is usually complicated, with exceptions to most general statements, so options including words such as "often," "sometimes," "usually," and "rarely" are more likely to be correct than options including absolute language such as "always," "never," "only," and "must."

Exploit Patterns in the Test's Design

Remember that test makers are human and design imperfect tests. Try to pay attention to patterns within any particular test. Sometimes the test maker inadvertently gives away which option is more likely to be correct by falling into predictable patterns in how they construct items.

An obvious example would be if you notice on a multiple-choice test that option (b) is correct over half of the time, from among four different response options. Given this pattern in the test's design, you'd do well to guess (b) on an item for which you didn't otherwise have any basis for choosing from among response options. Or on a true-or-false test, you might notice that the vast majority of items are false, out of those you are confident about. This would be a clue to guess false for items that you are unsure about.

Other similarly obvious patterns sometimes emerge on tests. For example, a test maker might tend to make the correct answer option shorter or longer than the others, or the correct option might tend to include more detailed, narrower description than the others. In fact, it's quite common for correct options to be longer and more detailed than incorrect options, since test makers may put less effort into fleshing out incorrect answers that are meant to distract from the correct one.

Subtler patterns occasionally show up on multiple-choice tests. You may notice that the correct answer tends to be one of a few similar response options rather than odd one out from among the options, or vice versa. Or you may notice that the correct option is usually one of two response options that are opposites of each other.

To help students learn these tactics, we have included as Handout 10.3 a set of multiple-choice test items that can be answered using the principles above. An explanatory answer key can be found in Handout 10.4.

SUMMARY

Many students believe that they are bad at taking tests, especially students with test anxiety. They fear that, compared to their peers, they may not do well on a test even when they're well-prepared with the knowledge and abilities probed on the exam. In this chapter we've presented a compendium of best practices for taking tests skillfully, with special attention to multiple-choice tests, for which wise test-taking skills can be especially helpful. After completing this module and ensuring that they understand how to take tests as effectively as any of their peers, students often report lower anxiety about test taking and greater confidence that they can demonstrate their knowledge and aptitude on exams. This confidence that their test preparation will translate into commensurate test scores, in turn, helps to motivate them to engage fully in their classwork and studying.

Best Practices for Taking All Tests

1. *Manage your time.* If you expect the test will be time-pressured or if you often don't finish tests on time, then you might want to begin the test by previewing its total length and then setting up a plan to make sure you get through the whole test (e.g., allocating maximum amounts of time to spend on different sections).

2. *Finish test sections in a logical order.* Usually you'll want to go through the test in the order it's presented, but sometimes it will make sense to mix up the order. At the start of the test, take a quick look at its structure and how much different parts of it count for. Sometimes you'll discover that later sections of the test count for more points than earlier sections of the test, and you might therefore want to begin with those later sections.

3. *Mark items that you skip or guess on.* Circle or otherwise mark test items that you aren't sure about. Then after you have completed everything else on the test, return to all of the marked items, and now spend further time trying to answer these items the best you can. Following this method helps make sure that you don't spend so much time on a particularly hard item that you don't get to later items on the test that you could have answered confidently.

4. *Be careful with instructions.* Make sure you fully understand what you're being asked to do on each section of the test. Underline anything that seems especially important. Similarly, on individual test items, pay close enough attention that you don't miss a word like "not" that could completely change the correct answer.

5. *Review your work.* If you still have time left after finishing the whole test, including items you had skipped at first, go back to the beginning and check all your answers to ensure that you didn't make any careless errors and that they're the best work you can deliver. Persistence pays off—don't rush to pass in your work early to show off to others or just because you're eager to be done with the test!

Best Practices for Taking Multiple-Choice Tests

For multiple-choice tests, you can combine the practices described in Handout 10.1 with the following tactics.

1. *Guess when you aren't sure of the answer.* Unless there's a penalty for choosing an incorrect answer, you're always better off guessing on a question than not answering it at all. Of course, you'll want to eliminate as many response options as you can (see #2 below) before guessing between remaining options.

2. *Eliminate response options.* Don't be discouraged if you don't immediately know the answer when you read a question! Oftentimes, on multiple-choice tests, you'll be able to eliminate at least some response options even if you don't know much related to the item. For instance, there might be one response option that is wildly implausible. So, make sure to see if you can eliminate any response options before you go ahead and make a guess. Using the tactics below can help with this.

3. *Choose answers that grammatically match the question stem.* The people who create tests, such as your teachers, are only human and sometimes make errors. For instance, they might create some response options that don't line up, grammatically, with the question stem on a multiple-choice test. When you notice a grammatical mismatch, it's a good sign that you can eliminate that response option.

4. *Think logically when there are equivalent or opposite response options.* Sometimes you'll notice two response options that are basically the same, on the one hand, or that contradict each other, on the other hand. When two response options are equivalent, in the sense that if one of them is correct, then the other one must also be correct, then neither of these can be the correct answer, assuming that you're allowed to choose only one response option. When two response options contradict each other, in the sense that they can't both be true, then you know that any response option that indicates both are correct (e.g., "all of the above") can't itself be correct.

5. *Choose "all of the above" when you know that more than one response option is correct.* Sometimes you'll see a few unique response options, and then an "all of the above" option. If you know that two of the unique response options are correct, then even if you aren't sure about the third unique response option, you know that "all of the above" must be the correct response. (Of course, this doesn't apply if there are response options that indicate that two of the response options are correct, but not the third, such as "option A and option B.")

6. *Use information from one item to solve another item.* If you read a test item and aren't sure of the answer, but you recognize that its content overlaps with that of an earlier test item, return to that earlier test item. Sometimes you'll find that information from one test item (e.g., in the question stem) is enough to help you identify the correct answer to another test item.

7. *Answer in the way that the test-maker would want.* For example, if your teacher created the test, and you recognize that one of the response options matches exactly what the teacher taught in a lecture, choose that response option, even if you learned something in another class that makes you question whether the option is 100% correct.

8. *Choose options that don't include extreme terms.* If you are unsure of the answer, avoid response options that include absolute terms such as "always," "never," "only," or "must." Reality is usually complicated, with lots of exceptions to most general rules, so correct response options are more likely to include less absolute terms such as "often," "sometimes," "usually," or "rarely."

9. *Notice patterns in the correct answers.* Try this tactic only if you have extra time after finishing the test, and you can't figure out the answer to a question even after using the other best practices. In this case, look back through questions for which you are confident about the correct answer, and notice if there are any patterns you could use to help solve the remaining questions. These patterns can occur because test-makers are imperfect and might fall into patterns themselves. For example, the correct response option might tend to be the longest and most detailed one (this is common), or it might tend to be one of two options that are opposites of each other.

Applying Best Practices for Taking Multiple-Choice Tests

Below you will find a set of multiple-choice test items. For each of them, using the tactics described in Handout 10.2 can help you select the correct answer, or at least narrow down your options. Applying the tactics to answer these questions will help solidify your knowledge of the tactics. If you happen to know the definite answer to some questions because of prior exposure to the content being tested (psychology), pretend that you were trying to answer the questions without that prior knowledge. After attempting to answer these questions, you can consult the answer key in Handout 10.4 to see how you did.

1. SSRI medicines, often given for depression, . . .
   (a) primarily affects acetylcholine
   (b) primarily affect serotonin
   (c) primarily affects dopamine
   (d) primarily affects adenosine

2. Which psychologist developed the theory of multiple intelligences, arguing that there are at least 7 distinct forms of intelligence?
   (a) Amelia Earhart
   (b) Howard Gardner
   (c) Isaac Newton
   (d) Robert Sternberg

3. Which of the following is a depression symptom?
   (a) depressed mood
   (b) loss of pleasure
   (c) concentration problems
   (d) all of the above

4. Electroconvulsive therapy (ECT) is . . .
   (a) always used in the treatment of depression
   (b) occasionally used in the treatment of severe depression
   (c) never used in the treatment of psychosis
   (d) only ever used in the treatment of depression

5. Compared to men/boys, . . .
   (a) women/girls all engage in more hostile aggression
   (b) women/girls engage in more instrumental aggression, on average
   (c) women/girls never engage in as much direct aggression
   (d) women/girls all engage in less hostile aggression

6. A _____ deficiency leads to Parkinson's disease.
   (a) occipital cortex
   (b) dopamine
   (c) acetylcholine
   (d) adenosine

7. Rosenhan's study where people lied about schizophrenia symptoms to gain admission to a mental hospital showed that which of the following is a poor measure of psychopathology?
    (a) help-seeking
    (b) emotional pain
    (c) irrationality
    (d) emotional distress

8. A valid test, by definition, . . .
    (a) does not measure what it claims to measure
    (b) measures what it claims to measure
    (c) may have low reliability
    (d) all of the above

9. Psychoanalysis was a system of psychology based on Freud's experience with:
    (a) laboratory experiments
    (b) clinical work with patients
    (c) dissecting worms
    (d) building computer simulations

10. Which is a primary symptom cluster in attention deficit hyperactivity disorder (ADHD)?
    (a) inattention
    (b) hyperactivity
    (c) impulsivity
    (d) all of the above

11. SSRI medicines are often used to treat which of the following disorders?
    (a) mania
    (b) depression
    (c) ADHD
    (d) Alzheimer's disease

12. To treat Parkinson's disease, a medicine should increase which of these?
    (a) GABA
    (b) dopamine
    (c) norepinephrine
    (d) histamine

13. Systematic desensitization is a form of:
    (a) psychoanalysis
    (b) behavior therapy
    (c) cognitive therapy
    (d) family therapy

Answer Key for Questions in Handout 10.3

Below you will find explanations of how the multiple-choice test-taking tactics summarized in Handout 10.2 could be applied to help you answer the questions in Handout 10.3.

1. The answer is (b). Even if you have no idea what SSRIs, acetylcholine, serotonin, dopamine, and adenosine are, option (b) is the only one that grammatically matches the question stem. The subject of the stem is the plural "medicines," and the verb in response options (a), (c), and (d) ("affects") matches a singular subject.

2. The answer is (b). After reading the question, you may know that you have no clue about the answer. However, it would be a mistake to take a random guess before seeing if you can narrow down your response options by eliminating implausible ones. You probably recognize that Amelia Earhart and Isaac Newton were not psychologists, and you can thus guess between (b) and (d), greatly increasing your chances of guessing correctly.

3. The answer is (d). Even if you don't know whether concentration problems are a depression symptom, you can probably guess intuitively, even without formal training in psychology, that both depressed mood and a loss of pleasure are symptoms of depression. The only response option that allows for both of these to be correct is (d), "all of the above."

4. The answer is (b). Remember, absolute terms such as "always," "never," and "only" are rarely applicable. When you aren't sure of the answer, choose a response option that doesn't use such extreme language.

5. The answer is (b). Again, when you aren't certain of the answer, a good rule-of-thumb is to avoid selecting a response option that makes an extreme, absolute statement, such as something about how "all" women and girls are, or what they "never" do.

6. The answer is (b). This is the only response option that grammatically matches the question stem. Options (a), (c), and (d) all begin with a vowel rather than a consonant, and they therefore would require the article "An" rather than "A" at the beginning of the question (e.g., "An adenosine deficiency").

7. The answer is (a). Even if you've never heard of this study and don't know the right answer, you can eliminate options (b) and (d)—"emotional pain" and "emotional distress"—because they are synonymous. If one of these answers is correct, then the other one must also be correct. Because you can select only one response options, it can't be either of these ones.

8. The answer is (b). Again, even if you don't know anything about what the definition of a "valid test" is, you can use logic to help you answer this question. Response options (a) and (b) are directly contradictory; if one is correct, then the other is incorrect. You can therefore eliminate response option (d), "all of the above," since this answer would entail that both (a) and (b) are correct.

9. The answer is (b). If you know nothing about Freud's psychoanalysis, you might be intimidated after reading the question. But it would be a mistake to guess randomly without first seeing whether you can eliminate some response options. After reading the options, you could probably eliminate (c) as implausible, since dissecting worms seems like a doubtful way to develop a whole system of psychology. You could also eliminate (d) as impossible, if you at least recognize that Freud lived before the age of computers and computer simulations.

10. The answer is (d). From the name of the disorder itself, you can probably deduce that (a) and (b) are both correct ("inattention" = attention deficit; "hyperactivity" = hyperactivity). Even if you have no idea whether impulsivity is a symptom cluster in ADHD, response option (d), "all of the above," must be the right answer to select if both (a) and (b) are correct.

11. The answer is (b). This is an example of an item for which a previous question contained the crucial information for answering correctly. Specifically, question #1 contained a stem that indicated that "SSRI medicines" are "often given for depression."

12. The answer is (b). Again, this is an example of an item for which a previous question contained the crucial information for answering correctly. Specifically, the answer to question #6—which could be found simply by grammatical matching—indicated that Parkinson's disease involves a dopamine deficiency. Therefore, medicines that increase dopamine would seem like an appropriate treatment for the disease.

13. The answer is (b). Here, if you have no idea which response option might be correct, and you're unable to eliminate any of them, you could look to see whether there have been any patterns in the correct answers on the test so far. You may have noticed that the correct answer to almost all the other questions has been (b), and you might therefore guess this again here, on the assumption that the test-maker seems to be biased toward using this letter for the correct answer.

References

Abramowitz, J. S., Deacon, B. J., & Whiteside, S. P. H. (2019). *Exposure therapy for anxiety: Principles and practice* (2nd ed.). Guilford Press.

Alicke, M. D., & Govorun, O. (2005). The better-than average effect. In M. D. Alicke, D. A. Dunning, & J. I. Krueger (Eds.), *The self in social judgment* (pp. 85–106). Psychology Press.

Alsalamah, A. (2022). Applying prereferral models before and after IDEA 2004: Where are we now? *Exceptionality, 30*(1), 27–42.

American Psychiatric Association. (1994). *Diagnostic and statistical manual of mental disorders* (4th ed.). American Psychiatric Association.

American Psychiatric Association. (2013). *Diagnostic and statistical manual of mental disorders* (5th ed.). American Psychiatric Publishing.

American Psychiatric Association. (2022). *Diagnostic and statistical manual of mental disorders* (5th ed., text rev). American Psychiatric Publishing.

American Psychological Association. (n.d.). Yerkes–Dodson law. *APA dictionary of psychology.* *https://dictionary.apa.org/yerkes-dodson-law*

Anderson, C. M., Hogarty, G. E., & Reiss, D. J. (1980). Family treatment of adult schizophrenic patients: A psycho-educational approach. *Schizophrenia Bulletin, 6*(3), 490–505.

Authier, J. (1977). The psychoeducation model: Definition, contemporary roots and content. *Canadian Journal of Counselling and Psychotherapy, 12*(1), 15–22.

Bahrick, H. P., & Hall, L. K. (2005). The importance of retrieval failures to long-term retention: A metacognitive explanation of the spacing effect. *Journal of Memory and Language, 52*(4), 566–577.

Bandura, A. (1982). Self-efficacy mechanism in human agency. *American Psychologist, 37*(2), 122–147.

Bandura, A. (1997). *Self-efficacy: The exercise of control.* W. H. Freeman.

Bandura, A. (2006). Guide for constructing self-efficacy scales. In F. Pajares & T. Urdan (Eds.), *Self-efficacy beliefs of adolescents* (pp. 307–338). Information Age Publishing.

Bangert-Drowns, R. L., Kulik, J. A., & Kulik, C.-L. C. (1991). Effects of frequent classroom testing. *Journal of Educational Research, 85*(2), 89–99.

Banks, T., & Eaton, I. (2014). Improving test-taking performance of secondary at-rik youth and students with disabilities. *Preventing School Failure, 58*(4), 207–213.

Baourda, V. C., Brouzos, A., Mavridis, D., Vassilopoulos, S. P., Vatkali, E., & Boumpouli, C. (2022). Group psychoeducation for anxiety symptoms in youth: Systematic review and meta-analysis. *The Journal for Specialists in Group Work, 47*(1), 22–42.

Barlow, D. H., Farchione, T. J., Fairholme, C. P., Ellard, K. K., Boisseau, C. L., Allen, L. B., & Ehrenreich-May, J. (2017). *Unified protocol for transdiagnostic treatment of emotional disorders* (2nd ed.). Oxford University Press.

Basso, J. C., McHale, A., Ende, V., Oberlin, D. J., & Suzuki, W. A. (2019). Brief, daily meditation enhances attention, memory, mood, and emotional regulation in non-experienced meditators. *Behavioural Brain Research, 356*, 208–220.

Beck, A. T. (1976). *Cognitive therapy and the emotional disorders.* International Universities Press.

Benjamin, A. S., & Tullis, J. (2010). What makes distributed practice effective? *Cognitive Psychology, 61*(3), 228–247.

Boettcher, H., Brake, C. A., & Barlow, D. H. (2016). Origins and outlook of interoceptive exposure. *Journal of Behavior Therapy and Experimental Psychiatry, 53*, 41–51.

Bögels, S. M., Alden, L. E., Beidel, D. C., Clark, L., Pine, D., Stein, M. B., & Voncken, M. J. (2010). Social anxiety disorder: Questions and answers for the DSM-V. *Depression and Anxiety, 27*(2), 168–189.

Bonaccio, S., & Reeve, C. L. (2010). The nature and relative importance of students' perceptions of the sources of test anxiety. *Learning and Individual Differences, 20*(6), 617–625.

Boswell, J. F., Farchione, T. J., Sauer-Zavala, S., Murray, H. W., Fortune, M. R., & Barlow, D. H. (2013). Anxiety sensitivity and interoceptive exposure: A transdiagnostic construct and change strategy. *Behavior Therapy, 44*(3), 417–431.

Boutouis, S. (2021). Ask Sophie: Test anxiety. *The Mercury. https://utdmercury.com/ask-sophie-test-anxiety*

Boylan, J. F. (2014). Save us from the SAT. *New York Times. www.nytimes.com/2014/03/07/opinion/save-us-from-the-sat.html*

Bradley, R., McCraty, R., Atkinson, M., Tomasino, D., Daugherty, D., & Arguelles, L. (2010). Emotion self-regulation, psychophysiological coherence, and test anxiety: Results from an experiment using electrophysiological measures. *Applied Psychophysiology and Biofeedback, 35*(4), 261–283.

Brady, S. T., Hard, B. M., & Gross, J. J. (2018). Reappraising test anxiety increases academic performance of first-year college students. *Journal of Educational Psychology, 110*(3), 395–406.

Brandmo, C., Braten, I., & Schewe, O. (2019). Social and personal predictors of test anxiety among Norwegian secondary and postsecondary students. *Social Psychology of Education, 22*, 43–61.

Brewer, C. (1971). Beneficial effect of beta-adrenergic blockade on "exam nerves." *The Lancet, 300*(7774), 435.

Briesch, A. M., Chafouleas, S. M., & Chaffee, R. K. (2018). Analysis of state-level guidance regarding school-based, universal screening for social, emotional, and behavioral risk. *School Mental Health, 10*, 147–162.

Brooks A. W. (2014). Get excited: reappraising pre-performance anxiety as excitement. *Journal of Experimental Psychology: General, 143*(3), 1144–1158.

Buergler, S., Sezer, D., Bagge, N., Kirsch, I., Locher, C., Carvalho, C., & Gaab, J. (2023). Imaginary pills and open-label placebos can reduce test anxiety by means of placebo mechanisms. *Scientific Reports, 13*, 2624.

Burbules, N. C., Lord, B. T., & Sherman, A. L. (1982). Equity, equal opportunity, and education. *Educational Evaluation and Policy Analysis, 4*, 169–187.

Burcaş, S., & Creţu, R. Z. (2021). Multidimensional perfectionism and test anxiety: A meta-analytic review of two decades of research. *Educational Psychology Review, 33*(2), 249–273.

Campbell, J. R. (1994). Developing cross-cultural/cross-national instruments: Using cross-national methods and procedures. *International Journal of Educational Research, 21*, 675–684.

Candy, L. (2015, March 6). Emma Watson, the December 2014 Elle cover interview. *Elle. www.elle.com/uk/life-and-culture/news/a25135/emma-watson-december-2014-elle-magazine-feminism-issue-cover-interview-in-full*

Caplan-Bricker, N. (2021). Is remote proctoring here to stay? *New Yorker. www.newyorker.com/tech/annals-of-technology/is-online-test-monitoring-here-to-stay*

Carden, R., Bryant, C., & Moss, R. (2004). Locus of control, test anxiety, academic procrastination, and achievement among college students. *Psychological Reports, 95*(2), 581–582.

Carney, C. E., & Manber, R. (2009). *Quiet your mind and get to sleep: Solutions for insomnia in those with depression, anxiety, or chronic pain.* New Harbinger Press.

Carpenter, S. K. (2009). Cue strength as a moderator of the testing effect: The benefits of elaborative retrieval. *Journal of Experimental Psychology: Learning, Memory, and Cognition, 35*(6), 1563–1569.

Carsley, D., & Heath, N. L. (2018). Effectiveness of mindfulness-based colouring for test anxiety in adolescents. *School Psychology International, 39*(3), 251–272.

Carsley, D., Heath, N. L., & Fajnerova, S. (2015). Effectiveness of a classroom mindfulness coloring activity for test anxiety in children. *Journal of Applied Social Psychology, 31*(3), 239–255.

Carter, E. W., Wehby, J., Hughes, C., Johnson, S. M., Plank, D. R., Barton-Arwood, S. M., & Lunsford, L. B. (2005). Preparing adolescents with high-incidence disabilities for high-stakes testing with strategy instruction. *Preventing School Failure, 49*(2), 55–62.

Cassady, J. C., & Johnson, R. E. (2002). Cognitive test anxiety and academic performance. *Contemporary Educational Psychology, 27*(2), 270–295.

Chang, R. B., Strochlic, D. E., Williams, E. K., Umans, B. D., & Liberles, S. D. (2015). Vagal sensory neuron subtypes that differentially control breathing. *Cell, 161*(3), 622–633.

Chemers, M. M., Hu, L., & Garcia, B. F. (2001). Academic self-efficacy and first-year college student performance and adjustment. *Journal of Educational Psychology, 93*(1), 55–64.

Chishima Y., Mizuno M., Sugawara D., Miyagawa Y. (2018). The influence of self-compassion on cognitive appraisals and coping with stressful events. *Mindfulness, 9*(6), 1907–1915.

Choe, K. W., Jenifer, J. B., Rozek, C. S., Berman, M. G., & Beilock, S. L. (2019). Calculated avoidance: Math anxiety predicts math avoidance in effort-based decision-making. *Science Advances, 5*(11), eaay1062.

Chow, H. P. H. (2011). Procrastination among undergraduate students: Effects of emotional intelligence, school life, self-evaluation, and self-efficacy. *Alberta Journal of Educational Research, 57*(2), 234–240.

Cizek, G. J., & Burg, S. S. (2006). *Addressing test anxiety in a high-stakes environment.* Corwin Press.

Cohen, J. (1988). *Statistical power analysis for the behavioral sciences* (2nd ed.). Erlbaum.

Conrad, A., & Roth, W. T. (2007). Muscle relaxation therapy for anxiety disorders: It works but how? *Journal of Anxiety Disorders, 21*(3), 243–264.

Corbett, M. (2015). From law to folklore: Work stress and the Yerkes–Dodson Law. *Journal of Managerial Psychology, 30*(6), 741–752.

Costa Jr, P. T., & McCrae, R. R. (1995). Domains and facets: Hierarchical personality assessment using the Revised NEO Personality Inventory. *Journal of Personality Assessment, 64*(1), 21–50.

Covington, M. V., & Omelich, C. L. (1987). "I knew it cold before the exam": A test of the anxiety–blockage hypothesis. *Journal of Educational Psychology, 79*(4), 393–400.

Craske, M. G., Kircanski, K., Zelikowsky, M., Mystkowski, J., Chowdhury, N., & Baker, A. (2008). Optimizing inhibitory learning during exposure therapy. *Behaviour Research and Therapy, 46*(1), 5–27.

Craske, M. G., Treanor, M., Conway, C. C., Zbozinek, T., & Vervliet, B. (2014). Maximizing exposure therapy: An inhibitory learning approach. *Behaviour Research and Therapy, 58*, 10–23.

Damer, D. E., & Melendres, L. T. (2011). "Tackling test anxiety": A group for college students. *The Journal for Specialists in Group Work, 36*(3), 163–177.

Daker, R. J., Gattas, S. U., Sokolowski, H. M., Green, A. E., & Lyons, I. M. (2021). First-year students' math anxiety predicts STEM avoidance and underperformance throughout university, independently of math ability. *npj Science of Learning, 6*, 17.

Daniel, R. (2020). Students with test anxiety deserve accommodations. *Daily Texan. https://thedaily texan.com/2020/06/26/students-with-test-anxiety-deserve-accommodations*

de Hullu, E., Sportel, B. E., Nauta, M. H., & de Jong, P. J. (2017). Cognitive bias modification and CBT as early interventions for adolescent social and test anxiety: Two-year follow-up of a randomized controlled trial. *Journal of Behavior Therapy and Experimental Psychiatry, 55*, 81–89.

Deacon, B. J., Kemp, J. J., Dixon, L. J., Sy, J. T., Farrell, N. R., & Zhang, A. R. (2013). Maximizing the efficacy of interoceptive exposure by optimizing inhibitory learning: A randomized controlled trial. *Behaviour Research and Therapy, 51*(9), 588e596.

Delaney, P. F., Verkoeijen, P. P. J. L., & Spirgel, A. (2010). Spacing and the testing effects: A deeply critical, lengthy, and at times discursive review of the literature. *Psychology of Learning and Motivation, 53*, 63–147.

Donley, J. E. (1911). Psychotherapy and re-education. *The Journal of Abnormal Psychology, 6*(1), 1–10.

Driscoll, R. (2007). Westside Test Anxiety Scale validation. ERIC document ED495968. *https://files.eric.ed.gov/fulltext/ED495968.pdf*

Dunlosky, J. (2013). Strengthening the student toolbox: Study strategies to boost learning. *American Educator, 37*, 12–21.

Dunlosky, J., Rawson, K. A., Marsh, E. J., Nathan, M. J., & Willingham, D. T. (2013). Improving students' learning with effective learning techniques: Promising directions from cognitive and educational psychology. *Psychological Science in the Public Interest, 14*(1), 4–58.

Edwards, B. D. (2003). *An examination of factors contributing to a reduction in race-based subgroup differences on a constructed response paper-and-pencil test of achievement* (Doctoral dissertation, Texas A&M University). College Station, TX.

Egbochuku, E., & Obodo, B. (2005). Effects of systematic desensitization (SD) therapy on the reduction of test anxiety among adolescents in Nigerian schools. *Journal of Instructional Psychology, 32*(4), 298–304.

Ehrenreich-May, J., Kennedy, S. M., Sherman, J. A., Bilek, E. L., Buzzella, B. A., Bennett, S. M., & Barlow, D. H. (2018). *Unified protocols for transdiagnostic treatment of emotional disorders in children and adolescents: Therapist guide.* Oxford University Press.

Elias, J. (2021). How the onset of the pandemic affected the 2020 admissions season. *Chronicle of Higher Education. www.chronicle.com/article/how-the-onset-of-the-pandemic-affected-the-2020-admissions-season*

Ergene, T., 2003. Effective interventions on test anxiety reduction. *School Psychology International, 24*(3), 313–328.

Faber, G. (2010). Enhancing orthographic competencies and reducing domain-specific test anxiety: The systematic use of algorithmic and self-instructional task formats in remedial spelling training. *International Journal of Special Education, 25*(2), 78–88.

Fergus, T. A., & Limbers, C. A. (2019). Reducing test anxiety in school settings: A controlled pilot study examining a group format delivery of the attention training technique among adolescent students. *Behavior Therapy, 50*(4), 803–816.

French, J. W. (1962). Effect of anxiety on verbal and mathematical examination scores. *Educational and Psychological Measurement, 22*(3), 553–564.

Freud, S. (2010). *The interpretation of dreams: The complete and definitive text.* Basic Books. (Original work published 1900)

Friedman, I. A., & Bendas-Jacob, O. (1997). Measuring perceived test anxiety in adolescents: A self-report scale. *Educational and Psychological Measurement, 57*(6), 1035–1046.

Funder, D. (2010). *The personality puzzle* (5th ed.). Norton.

Galassi, J. P., Frierson, H. T., & Sharer, R. (1981). Behavior of high, moderate, and low test anxious students during an actual test situation. *Journal of Consulting and Clinical Psychology, 49*(1), 51–62.

Garlington, W. K., & Cotler, S. B. (1968). Systematic desensitization of test anxiety. *Behaviour Research and Therapy, 6,* 247–256.

Gerritsen, R. J. S., & Band, G. P. H. (2018). Breath of life: The respiratory vagal stimulation model of contemplative activity. *Frontiers in Human Neuroscience, 12,* 397.

Gibb, B. (1964). *Testwiseness as secondary cue response* (Doctoral dissertation, Stanford University). University Microfilms (No. 64–7643).

Government Accountability Office. (2022). *Testing companies most commonly granted extra time to accommodate individuals with disabilities.* Report GAO-22-104430. *www.gao.gov/assets/gao -22-104430.pdf*

Grant, A. (2023). Timed tests are biased against your kids. *New York Times. www.nytimes.com/2023 /09/20/opinion/culture/timed-tests-biased-kids.html*

Gray, J. A. (1988). *The psychology of fear and stress* (2nd ed.). Cambridge University Press.

Gray J. A., & McNaughton, N. (2003). *The neuropsychology of anxiety: An enquiry into the functions of the septo-hippocampal system* (2nd ed). Oxford University Press.

Gregor, A. (2005). Examination anxiety: Live with it, control it or make it work for you? *School Psychology International, 26*(5), 617–635.

Grossman, P. (2019). On the porosity of subject and object in "mindfulness" scientific study: Challenges to "scientific" construction, operationalization and measurement of mindfulness. *Current Opinion in Psychology, 28,* 102–107.

Haidt, J. (2024). *The anxious generation.* Penguin.

Hannon, B. (2012). Test anxiety and performance-avoidance goals explain gender differences in SAT-V, SAT-M, and overall SAT scores. *Personality and Individual Differences, 53*(7), 816–820.

Hannon, B. (2019). Not all factors contribute equally to European-American and Hispanic students' SAT scores. *Journal of Intelligence, 7*(3), 18.

Hashemi, L., & Latifian, M. (2014). Test anxiety as a mediator between perfectionism and academic procrastination. *Journal of Teaching and Education, 3*(3), 509–520.

Hawes, M. T., Szenczy, A. K., Klein, D. N., Hajcak, G., & Nelson, B. D. (2021). Increases in depression and anxiety symptoms in adolescents and young adults during the COVID-19 pandemic. *Psychological Medicine,* 1–9.

Hayes, S. C., Strosahl, K. D., & Wilson, K. G. (2011). *Acceptance and commitment therapy: The process and practice of mindful change* (2nd ed.). Guilford Press.

Hayes-Skelton, S. A., Roemer, L., Orsillo, S. M., & Borkovec, T. D. (2013). A contemporary view of applied relaxation for generalized anxiety disorder. *Cognitive Behaviour Therapy, 42*(4), 292–302.

Hembree, R. (1988). Correlates, causes, effects, and treatment of test anxiety. *Review of Educational Research, 58,* 47–77.

Herzer, F., Wendt, J., & Hamm, A. O. (2014). Discriminating clinical from nonclinical manifestations of test anxiety: A validation study. *Behavior Therapy, 45*(2), 222–231.

Hickson, A. (2016). The one thing these 10 faves have in common. *www.refinery29.com/en-us/2016/05 /111114/celebrity-quotes-stage-fright-anxiety*

Higgins, J. P. T., & Green, S. (Eds.). (2011). *Cochrane handbook for systematic reviews of interventions (Version 5.1.0.).* The Cochrane Collaboration.

Hofmann, S. G., Sawyer, A. T., Witt, A. A., & Oh, D. (2010). The effect of mindfulness-based therapy on anxiety and depression: A meta-analytic review. *Journal of Consulting and Clinical Psychology, 78*(2), 169–183.

Holmes, J. D. (2021). The bad test-taker identity. *Teaching of Psychology, 48,* 293–299.

Holzer, M. L., Madaus, J. W., Bray, M. A., & Kehle, T. J. (2009). The test-taking strategy intervention for college students with learning disabilities. *Learning Disabilities Research & Practice, 24,* 44–56.

Hong, E. (1999). Test anxiety, perceived test difficulty, and test performance: Temporal patterns of their effects. *Learning and Individual Differences, 11*(4), 431–447.

Hughes, C., Schumaker, J., Deshler, D., & Mercer, C. (1993). *The test-taking strategy.* Edge Enterprises.

Huntley, C. D., Young, B., Smith, C. T., & Fisher, P. L. (2020). Uncertainty and test anxiety: Psychometric properties of the Intolerance of Uncertainty Scale–12 (IUS-12) among university students. *International Journal of Educational Research, 104,* 101672.

Huntley, C. D., Young, B., Temple, J., Longworth, M., Smith, C. T., Jha, V., & Fisher, P. L. (2019). The efficacy of interventions for test-anxious university students: A meta-analysis of randomized controlled trials. *Journal of Anxiety Disorders, 63,* 36–50.

Hysing, M., Pallesen, S., Stormark, K. M., Jakobsen, R., Lundervold, A. J., & Sivertsen, B. (2015). Sleep and use of electronic devices in adolescence: Results from a large population-based study. *BMJ Open, 5,* e006748.

Jacobson, E. (1938). *Progressive relaxation* (2nd ed.). University of Chicago Press.

Jacoby, R. J. (2020). Intolerance of uncertainty. In J. S. Abramowitz, & S. M. Blakey (Eds.), *Clinical handbook of fear and anxiety: Maintenance processes and treatment mechanisms* (pp. 45–63). American Psychological Association.

James, W. (1983). *The principles of psychology.* Harvard University Press. (Original work published 1890)

Jamieson, J. P., Peters, B. J., Greenwood, E. J., & Altose, A. J. (2016). Reappraising stress arousal improves performance and reduces evaluation anxiety in classroom exam situations. *Social Psychological and Personality Science, 7,* 579–587.

Jenifer, J. B., Rozek, C. S., Levine, S. C., & Beilock, S. L. (2022). Effort(less) exam preparation: Math anxiety predicts the avoidance of effortful study strategies. *Journal of Experimental Psychology: General, 151*(10), 2534–2541.

Jenifer, J. B., Levine, S. C., & Beilock, S. L. (2023). Studying while anxious: Mathematics anxiety and the avoidance of solving practice problems during exam preparation in college calculus. *ZDM–Mathematics Education, 55,* 359–369.

Jia, J., Wang, L. L., Xu, J. B., Lin, X. H., Zhang, B., & Jiang, Q. (2021). Self-handicapping in Chinese medical students during the Covid-19 pandemic: The role of academic anxiety, procrastination and hardiness. *Frontiers in Psychology, 12,* 741821.

Jones, M. C. (1924). A laboratory study of fear: The case of Peter. *Pedagogical Seminary, 31*(4), 308–315.

Jordan, A. H., & Lovett, B. J. (2007). Stereotype threat and test performance: A primer for school psychologists. *Journal of School Psychology, 45,* 45–59.

Jordan, A. H., Monin, B., Dweck, C. S., Lovett, B. J., John, O. P., & Gross, J. J. (2011). Misery has more company than people think: Underestimating the prevalence of others' negative emotions. *Personality and Social Psychology Bulletin, 37*(1), 120–135.

Kabat-Zinn, J. (1990). *Full catastrophe living: Using the wisdom of your body and mind to face stress, pain and illness.* Delacorte.

Kagan, E. R., Frank, H. E., & Kendall, P. C. (2017). Accommodation in youth with OCD and anxiety. *Clinical Psychology: Science and Practice, 24*(1), 78–98.

Kaplan, J. A., & Tolin, D. F. (2011). Exposure therapy for anxiety disorders: Theoretical mechanisms of exposure and treatment strategies. *Psychiatric Times,28,* 33.

Karpicke, J. D., & Blunt, J. R. (2011). Retrieval practice produces more learning than elaborative studying with concept mapping. *Science, 331*(6018), 772–775.

Karpicke, J. D., Butler, A. C., & Roediger, H. L. (2009). Metacognitive strategies in student learning: Do students practise retrieval when they study on their own?. *Memory, 17,* 471–479.

Killingsworth, M. A., & Gilbert, D. T. (2010). A wandering mind is an unhappy mind. *Science, 330* (6006), 932.

Kirkland, K., & Hollandsworth, J. G., Jr (1980). Effective test taking: Skills-acquisition versus anxiety-reduction techniques. *Journal of Consulting and Clinical Psychology, 48,* 431–439.

Knappe, S., Beesdo-Baum, K., Fehm, L., Stein, M. B., Lieb, R., & Wittchen, H. U. (2011). Social fear and social phobia types among community youth: Differential clinical features and vulnerability factors. *Journal of Psychiatric Research, 45,* 111–120.

Kreibig S. D. (2010). Autonomic nervous system activity in emotion: A review. *Biological Psychology, 84*(3), 394–421.

Krispenz, A., Gort, C., Schültke, L., & Dickhäuser, O. (2019). How to reduce test anxiety and academic procrastination through inquiry of cognitive appraisals: A pilot study investigating the role of academic self-efficacy. *Frontiers in Psychology, 10,* 1917.

Lal Zinta, R. (2008). Effectiveness of guided mastery treatment for reducing test-anxiety among self-efficacious students. *Journal of the Indian Academy of Applied Psychology, 34,* 233–239.

Lang, J., & Lang, J. (2010). Priming competence diminishes the link between cognitive test anxiety and test performance: Implications for the interpretation of test scores. *Psychological Science, 21,* 811–819.

Larson, H., Ramahi, M., Conn, S., Estes, L., & Ghibellini, A. (2010). Reducing test anxiety among third grade students through the implementation of relaxation techniques. *Journal of School Counseling, 8,* 1–19.

Laurin-Barantke, L., Hoyer, J., Fehm, L., & Knappe, S. (2016). Oral but not written test anxiety is related to social anxiety. *World Journal of Psychiatry, 6*(3), 351–357.

LeBeau, R. T., Glenn, D., Liao, B., Wittchen, H. U., Beesdo-Baum, K., Ollendick, T., & Craske, M. G. (2010). Specific phobia: A review of DSM-IV specific phobia and preliminary recommendations for DSM-V. *Depression and Anxiety, 27*(2), 148–167.

Lebowitz, E. R., Omer, H., Hermes, H., & Scahill, L. (2014). Parent training for childhood anxiety disorders: The SPACE program. *Cognitive and Behavioral Practice, 21,* 456–469.

Leucht, S., Helfer, B., Gartlehner, G., & David, J. M. (2015). How effective are common medications: A perspective based on meta-analyses of major drugs. *BMC Medicine, 13,* 253.

Lewandowski, L., Lambert, T. L., Lovett, B. J., Panahon, C. J., & Sytsma, M. R. (2014). College students' preferences for test accommodations. *Canadian Journal of School Psychology, 29*(2), 116–126.

Lewandowski, L. J., Lovett, B. J., Codding, R. S., & Gordon, M. (2008). Symptoms of ADHD and academic concerns in college students with and without ADHD diagnoses. *Journal of Attention Disorders, 12*(2), 156–161.

Lewsen, S. (2023, August 13). CheatGPT. *Toronto Life. https://torontolife.com/deep-dives/chatgpt-ai-cheating-revolutionizing-university-education*

Linehan, M. M. (2014). *DBT skills training manual* (2nd ed.). Guilford Press.

Lobman, C. (2014). "I feel nervous . . . Very nervous" addressing test anxiety in inner city schools through play and performance. *Urban Education, 49*, 329–359.

Lovett, B. J. (2023). *Practical psychometrics: A guide for test users.* Guilford Press.

Lovett, B. J., & Lewandowski, L. J. (2015). *Testing accommodations for students with disabilities: Research-based practice.* American Psychological Association Press.

Lovett, B. J., & Nelson, J. M. (2017). Test anxiety and the Americans with Disabilities Act. *Journal of Disability Policy Studies, 28*(2), 99–108.

Lovett, B. J., Nelson, J. M., & O'Meara, P. (2023). *Is test anxiety a disorder? Symptom base rates and statistical deviance.* Manuscript submitted for publication.

Lovett, B. J., Nelson, J. M., & O'Meara, P. (2024). Test anxiety symptoms in college students: Base rates and statistical deviance. *Psychological Injury and Law, 17*(1), 45–54.

Luthar, S. S., Kumar, N. L., & Zillmer, N. (2020). High-achieving schools connote risks for adolescents: Problems documented, processes implicated, and directions for interventions. *American Psychologist, 75*(7), 983–995.

Ma, X., Yue, Z. Q., Gong, Z. Q., Zhang, H., Duan, N. Y., Shi, Y. T., Wei, G. X., & Li, Y. F. (2017). The effect of diaphragmatic breathing on attention, negative affect and stress in healthy adults. *Frontiers in Psychology, 8*, 874.

Macauley, K., Plummer, L., Bemis, C., Brock, G., Larson, C., & Spangler, J. (2018). Prevalence and predictors of anxiety in healthcare professions students. *Health Professions Education, 4*, 176–185.

Manassis, K. (2012). Generalized anxiety disorder in the classroom. *Child and Adolescent Psychiatric Clinics, 21*(1), 93–103.

Manzoni, G. M., Pagnini, F., Castelnuovo, G., & Molinari, E. (2008). Relaxation training for anxiety: A ten-years systematic review with meta-analysis. *BMC Psychiatry, 8*, 41.

Marsh, R. J., & Mathur, S. R. (2020). Mental health in schools: An overview of multitiered systems of support. *Intervention in School and Clinic, 56*, 67–73.

Masuda, A., Twohig, M. P., Stormo, A. R., Feinstein, A. B., Chou, Y. Y., & Wendell, J. W. (2010). The effects of cognitive defusion and thought distraction on emotional discomfort and believability of negative self-referential thoughts. *Journal of Behavior Therapy and Experimental Psychiatry, 41*(1), 11–17.

Mavilidi, M., Hoogerheide, V., & Paas, F. (2014). A quick and easy strategy to reduce test anxiety and enhance test performance. *Applied Cognitive Psychology, 28*, 720–726.

McAfee, T. (2013, July 10). Harry Styles throws up on stage at 1D Pittsburgh concert. *Hollywood Life. https://hollywoodlife.com/2013/07/10/harry-styles-throws-up-on-stage-video-one-direction-pittsburgh*

McCabe, J. (2011). Metacognitive awareness of learning strategies in undergraduates. *Memory & Cognition, 39*, 462–476.

McCarthy, J. M., & Goffin, R. D. (2005). Selection test anxiety: Exploring tension and fear of failure across the sexes in simulated selection scenarios. *International Journal of Selection and Assessment, 13*, 282–295.

McCrae, R. R. (2020). The Five-Factor Model of Personality: Consensus and controversy. In P. J. Corr & G. Matthews (Eds.), *Cambridge handbook of personality psychology* (pp. 129–141). Cambridge University Press.

Midgley, C., Maehr, M. L., Hruda, L. Z., Anderman, E., Anderman, L., Freeman, K. E., et al. (2000). *Manual for the patterns of adaptive learning.* University of Michigan.

Millman, J., Bishop, C. H., & Ebel, R. (1965). An analysis of test-wiseness. *Educational and Psychological Measurement, 25,* 707–726.

Miyatsu, T., Nguyen, K., & McDaniel, M. A. (2018). Five popular study strategies: Their pitfalls and optimal implementations. *Perspectives on Psychological Science, 13*(3), 390–407.

Morgan, L. P., Graham, J. R., Hayes-Skelton, S. A., Orsillo, S. M., & Roemer, L. (2014). Relationships between amount of post-intervention of mindfulness practice and follow-up outcome variables in an acceptance-based behavior therapy for generalized anxiety disorder: The importance of informal practice. *Journal of Contextual Behavioral Science, 3*(3), 173–176.

Multon, K. D., Brown, S. D., & Lent, R. W. (1991). Relation of self-efficacy beliefs to academic outcomes: A meta-analytic investigation. *Journal of Counseling Psychology, 38*(1), 30–38.

Murray, J., Scott, H., Connolly, C., & Wells, A. (2018). The attention training technique improves children's ability to delay gratification: A controlled comparison with progressive relaxation. *Behaviour Research and Therapy, 104,* 1–6.

Murray, J., Theakston, A., & Wells, A. (2016). Can the attention training technique turn one marshmallow into two? Improving children's ability to delay gratification. *Behaviour Research and Therapy, 77,* 34–39.

Musch, J., & Bröder, A. (1999). Test anxiety versus academic skills: A comparison of two alternative models for predicting performance in a statistics exam. *British Journal of Educational Psychology, 69*(1), 105–116.

Nelson, A., & Eliasz, K. L. (2023). Desirable difficulty: Theory and application of intentionally challenging learning. *Medical Education, 57*(2), 123–130.

New York Association of School Psychologists, & New York State School Boards Association. (2015). *Anxious for success: High anxiety in New York's schools. www.nyssba.org/clientuploads/nyssba_pdf/Test_Anxiety_Report.pdf*

Newman, M. G., Llera, S. J., Erickson, T. M., & Przeworski, A. (2014). Basic science and clinical application of the Contrast Avoidance Model in generalized anxiety disorder. *Journal of Psychotherapy Integration, 24*(3), 155–167.

Oransky, M., & Marecek, J. (2009). "I'm not going to be a girl" masculinity and emotions in boys' friendships and peer groups. *Journal of Adolescent Research, 24*(2), 218–241.

Orchard, F., Gregory, A. M., Gradisar, M., & Reynolds, S. (2020). Self-reported sleep patterns and quality amongst adolescents: Cross-sectional and prospective associations with anxiety and depression. *Journal of Child Psychology and Psychiatry and Allied Disciplines, 61,* 1126–1137.

Osenk, I., Williamson, P., & Wade, T. D. (2020). Does perfectionism or pursuit of excellence contribute to successful learning? A meta-analytic review. *Psychological Assessment, 32,* 972–983.

Owens, M., Stevenson, J., Hadwin, J. A., & Norgate, R. (2014). When does anxiety help or hinder cognitive test performance? The role of working memory capacity. *British Journal of Psychology, 105*(1), 92–101.

Paladino, M. (2020). *Towards an understanding of the testing opt-out movement: Why parents choose to opt out or opt in.* (Unpublished dissertation). Molloy College.

Parham, S. E. (1996). *The relationships between test-taking strategies and cognitive ability test performance* (Doctoral dissertation, Bowling Green State University). Bowling Green, OH.

Passolunghi, M. C., De Vita, C., & Pellizzoni, S. (2020). Math anxiety and math achievement: The effects of emotional and math strategy training. *Developmental Science, 23,* e12964.

Paulus, M. P. (2013). The breathing conundrum—Interoceptive sensitivity and anxiety. *Depression and Anxiety, 30*(4), 315–320.

Perlis, M. L., Jungquist, C., Smith, M. T., & Posner, D. (2005). *Cognitive behavioral treatment of insomnia: A session-by-session guide.* Springer Press.

Phillips, K. E., Conroy, K., Pinney, E. L., Comer, J. S., & Kendall, P. C. (2022). School-based supports and accommodations among anxious youth in treatment. *Journal of Anxiety Disorders, 90*, 102603.

Pifarré, P., Simó, M., Gispert, J.-D., Plaza, P., Fernández, A., & Pujol, J. (2015). Diazepam and Jacobson's progressive relaxation show similar attenuating short-term effects on stress-related brain glucose consumption. *European Psychiatry, 30*(2), 187–192.

Plutchik, R. (2001). The nature of emotions: Human emotions have deep evolutionary roots, a fact that may explain their complexity and provide tools for clinical practice. *American Scientist, 89*(4), 344–350.

Prat-Sala, M., & Redford, P. (2010). The interplay between motivation, self-efficacy, and approaches to studying. *British Journal of Educational Psychology, 80*, 283–305.

Putwain, D. W. (2007). Test anxiety in UK schoolchildren: Prevalence and demographic patterns. *British Journal of Educational Psychology, 77*, 579–593.

Putwain, D. W., & Pescod, M. (2018). Is reducing uncertain control the key to successful test anxiety intervention for secondary school students? Findings from a randomized control trial. *School Psychology Quarterly, 33*, 283–292.

Putwain, D. W., Stockinger, K., von der Embse, N. P., Suldo, S. M., & Daumiller, M. (2021). Test anxiety, anxiety disorders, and school-related wellbeing: Manifestations of the same or different constructs? *Journal of School Psychology, 88*, 47–67.

Putwain, D. W., Symes, W., Nicholson, L. J., & Remedios, R. (2021). Teacher motivational messages used prior to examinations: What are they, how are they evaluated, and what are their educational outcomes? *Advances in Motivation Science, 8*, 63–103.

Putwain, D. W., von der Embse, N. P., Rainbird, E. C., & West, G. (2021). The development and validation of a new Multidimensional Test Anxiety Scale (MTAS). *European Journal of Psychological Assessment, 37*(3), 236–246.

Putwain, D. W., Woods, K. A., & Symes, W. (2010). Personal and situational predictors of test anxiety of students in post-compulsory education. *British Journal of Educational Psychology, 80*(1), 137–160.

Rajiah, K., & Saravanan, C. (2014). The effectiveness of psychoeducation and systematic desensitization to reduce test anxiety among first-year pharmacy students. *American Journal of Pharmaceutical Education, 78*, 163.

Reiss, N., Warnecke, I., Tolgou, T., Krampen, D., Luka-Krausgrill, U., & Rohrmann, S. (2017). Effects of cognitive behavioral therapy with relaxation vs. imagery rescripting on test anxiety: A randomized controlled trial. *Journal of Affective Disorders, 208*, 483–489.

Reynolds, C. R., Richmond, B. O., & Lowe, P. A. (2003). *Adult manifest anxiety scale*. Western Psychological Services.

Richtel, M. (2023, March 21). The surgeon general's new mission: Adolescent mental health. *New York Times. www.nytimes.com/2023/03/21/health/surgeon-general-adolescents-mental-health.html*

Robson, D. A., Johnstone, S. J., Putwain, D. W., & Howard, S. (2023). Test anxiety in primary school children: A 20-year systematic review and meta-analysis. *Journal of School Psychology, 98*, 39–60.

Roediger, H. L., III, & Karpicke, J. D. (2006). The power of testing memory: Basic research and implications for educational practice. *Perspectives on Psychological Science, 1*(3), 181–210.

Roemer, L., & Orsillo, S. M. (2009). *Mindfulness and acceptance-based behavioral therapies in practice*. Guilford Press.

Roemer, L., & Orsillo, S. M. (2020). *Acceptance-based behavioral therapy: Treating anxiety and related challenges*. Guilford Press.

Rogers, W. T., & Yang, P. (1996). Test-wiseness: Its nature and application. *European Journal of Psychological Assessment, 12*(3), 247–259.

Romba, C., Lavigne, J., Walkup, J., & Ballard, R. (2020). Measurement-based care in the treatment of anxiety. *Child and Adolescent Psychiatric Clinics of North America, 29*(4), 645–661.

Roos, A. L., Goetz, T., Voracek, M., Krannich, M., Bieg, M., Jarrell, A., & Pekrun, R. (2021). Test anxiety and physiological arousal: A systematic review and meta-analysis. *Educational Psychology Review, 33*, 579–618.

Rosenthal, R., & Rubin, D. B. (1982). A simple, general purpose display of magnitude of experimental effect. *Journal of Educational Psychology, 74*(2), 166–169.

Ryan, J. L., & Warner, C. M. (2012). Treating adolescents with social anxiety disorder in schools. *Child and Adolescent Psychiatric Clinics of North America, 21*(1), 105–118.

Safren, S. A., Sprich, S. E., Perlman, C. A., & Otto, M. W. (2017). *Mastering your adult ADHD: A cognitive-behavioral treatment program* (2nd ed.). Oxford University Press.

Salyers, M. P., Hudson, C., Morse, G., Rollins, A. L., Monroe-DeVita, M., Wilson, C., & Freeland, L. (2011). BREATHE: A pilot study of a one-day retreat to reduce burnout among mental health professionals. *Psychiatric Services, 62*(2), 214–217.

Sattary-Najaf-Abady, R., & Heidary, H. (2015). The effectiveness of meta-cognitive treatment on test anxiety in students. *International Journal of Behavioral Sciences, 9*, 27–32.

Schiel, J. L. (2020). Test-Related Behaviors and Performance on the ACT. Issue Brief. *ACT, Inc.* *https://files.eric.ed.gov/fulltext/ED604111.pdf*

Schillinger, F. L., Mosbacher, J. A., Brunner, C., Vogel, S. E., & Grabner, R. H. (2021). Revisiting the role of worries in explaining the link between test anxiety and test performance. *Educational Psychology Review, 33*(4), 1887–1906.

Schlosser, A., Neeman, Z., & Attali, Y. (2019). Differential performance in high versus low stakes tests: Evidence from the GRE test. *The Economic Journal, 129*(623), 2916–2948.

Segal, Z. V., Williams, J. M. G., & Teasdale, J. D. (2002). *Mindfulness-based cognitive therapy for depression: A new approach to preventing relapse.* Guilford Press.

Segool, N. K., Carlson, J. S., Goforth, A. N., von der Embse, N., & Barterian, J. A. (2013). Heightened test anxiety among young children: Elementary school students' anxious responses to high-stakes testing. *Psychology in the Schools, 50*(5), 489–499.

Selingo, J. (2022). What does an SAT score mean anymore? *New York Magazine. https://nymag.com/intelligencer/2022/11/what-does-an-sat-score-mean-in-a-test-optional-world.html*

Shen, L., Yang, L., Zhang, J., & Zhang, M. (2018). Benefits of expressive writing in reducing test anxiety: A randomized controlled trial in Chinese samples. *PloS One, 13*, e0191779.

Shi, R., Sharpe, L., & Abbott, M. (2019). A meta-analysis of the relationship between anxiety and attentional control. *Clinical Psychology Review, 72*, 101754.

Smith, R. E., & Nye, S. L. (1973). A comparison of implosive therapy and systematic desensitization in the treatment of test anxiety. *Journal of Consulting and Clinical Psychology, 41*(1), 37–42.

Soares, D., & Woods, K. (2020). An international systematic literature review of test anxiety interventions 2011–2018. *Pastoral Care in Education, 38*(4), 311–334.

Soderstrom, N. C., & Bjork, R. A. (2015). Learning versus performance: An integrative review. *Perspectives on Psychological Science, 10*, 176–199.

Solanto, M. V. (2011). *Cognitive-behavioral therapy for adult ADHD: Targeting executive dysfunction.* Guilford Press.

Songlee, D., Miller, S. P., Tincani, M., Sileo, N. M., & Perkins, P. G. (2008). Effects of test-taking strategy instruction on high-functioning adolescents with autism spectrum disorders. *Focus on Autism and Other Developmental Disabilities, 23*(4), 217–228.

Sparfeldt, J. R., Rost, D. H., Baumeister, U. M., & Christ, O. (2013). Test anxiety in written and oral examinations. *Learning and Individual Differences, 24,* 198–203.

Spendelow, J. S., Simonds, L. M., & Avery, R. E. (2017). The relationship between co-rumination and internalizing problems: A systematic review and meta-analysis. *Clinical Psychology & Psychotherapy, 24*(2), 512–527.

Spiegler, M. D., & Guevremont, D. C. (2003). *Contemporary behavior therapy* (4th ed.). Thompson Wadsworth.

Spielberger, C. D. (1980). *Test anxiety inventory.* Mind Garden.

Sportel, B. E., de Hullu, E., de Jong, P. J., & Nauta, M. H. (2013). Cognitive bias modification versus CBT in reducing adolescent social anxiety: A randomized controlled trial. *PloS One, 8,* e64355.

Steedle, J. T. (2018). Keeping Your Cool: Does Test Anxiety Bias Performance on the ACT? Research Report 2018-3. *ACT, Inc. https://files.eric.ed.gov/fulltext/ED593180.pdf*

Stevens, B. (2021). Test anxiety: Concern grows among some parents as TCAP approaches. *www.wate .com/news/top-stories/test-anxiety-concern-grows-among-some-parents-as-tcap-approaches*

Suddendorf, T., Redshaw, J., & Bulley, A. (2022). *The invention of tomorrow: A natural history of foresight.* Basic Books.

Szafranski, D. D., Barrera, T. L., & Norton, P. J. (2012). Test anxiety inventory: 30 years later. *Anxiety, Stress & Coping, 25*(6), 667–677.

Tackett, J. L., & Lahey, B. B. (2017). Neuroticism. In T. A. Widiger (Ed.), *Oxford handbook of the five-factor model* (pp. 39–56). Oxford University Press.

Talwar, P., Matheiken, S., Cheng, J. L. A., & Sabil, S. (2019). Reliability and factor structure of the Westside Test Anxiety Scale among university students. *Online Journal of Health and Allied Sciences, 18*(3), 8.

Tamayo-Toro, M. (2019). Relajación de jacobson para disminuir la ansiedad originada por evaluaciones e incremento del rendimiento académico en estudiantes de psicología de una universidad privada de Lima Metropolitana. *Avances En Psicología, 27*(2), 167–176.

Taylor, J., & Deane, F. P. (2002). Development of a short form of the Test Anxiety Inventory (TAI). *Journal of General Psychology, 129*(2), 127–136.

Taylor, K., & Rohrer, D. (2010). The effects of interleaved practice. *Applied Cognitive Psychology, 24*(6), 837–848.

Teigen, K. H. (1994). Yerkes–Dodson: A law for all seasons. *Theory & Psychology, 4*(4), 525–547.

Theobald, M., Breitwieser, J., & Brod, G. (2022). Test anxiety does not predict exam performance when knowledge is controlled for: Strong evidence against the interference hypothesis of test anxiety. *Psychological Science, 33*(12), 2073–2083.

Thompson, H., Duvall, J., Padrez, R., Rosekrans, N., & Madsen, K. (2016). The impact of moderate-vigorous intensity physical education class immediately prior to standardized testing on student test-taking behaviours. *Mental Health and Physical Activity, 11,* 7–12.

Titchener, E. B. (1916). *A text-book of psychology.* MacMillan.

Torales, J., O'Higgins, M., Barrios, I., Gonzalez, I., & Almiron, M. (2020). An overview of Jacobson's progressive muscle relaxation in managing anxiety. *Revista Argentina de Clinica Psicologica, 29*(3), 17–23.

Toussaint, L., Nguyen, Q. A., Roettger, C., Dixon, K., Offenbächer, M., Kohls, N., Hirsch, J., & Sirois, F. (2021). Effectiveness of progressive muscle relaxation, deep breathing, and guided imagery in promoting psychological and physiological states of relaxation. *Evidence-Based Complementary and Alternative Medicine, 2021,* 5924040.

Twenge, J. M. (2000). The age of anxiety? The birth cohort change in anxiety and neuroticism, 1952–1993. *Journal of Personality and Social Psychology, 79*(6), 1007–1021.

Twenge, J. M., Krizan, Z., & Hisler, G. (2017). Decreases in self-reported sleep duration among U.S. adolescents 2009–2015 and association with new media screen time. *Sleep Medicine, 39,* 47–53.

Ussher, M., Spatz, A., Copland, C., Nicolaou, A., Cargill, A., Amini-Tabrizi, N., & McCracken, L. M. (2014). Immediate effects of a brief mindfulness-based body scan on patients with chronic pain. *Journal of Behavioral Medicine, 37*(1), 127–134.

Vervoort, L., Wolters, L. H., Hogendoorn, S. M., de Haan, E., Boer, F., & Prins, P. M. (2010). Sensitivity of Gray's behavioral inhibition system in clinically anxious and non-anxious children and adolescents. *Personality and Individual Differences, 48*(5),629–633.

Vojdanoska, M., Cranney, J., & Newell, B. R. (2010). The testing effect: The role of feedback and collaboration in a tertiary classroom setting. *Applied Cognitive Psychology, 24*(8), 1183–1195.

von der Embse, N., Barterian, J., Segool, N. (2013). Test anxiety interventions for children and adolescents: A systematic review of treatment studies from 2000–2010. *Psychology in the Schools, 50*, 57–71.

von der Embse, N. P., Jester, D., Roy, D., & Post, J. (2018). Test anxiety effects, predictors, and correlates: A 30-year meta-analytic review. *Journal of Affective Disorders, 227*, 483–493.

von der Embse, N. P., Kilgus, S. P., Segool, N., & Putwain, D. (2013). Identification and validation of a brief test anxiety screening tool. *International Journal of School & Educational Psychology, 1*(4), 246–258.

Wakefield, J. C. (1992). The concept of mental disorder: On the boundary between biological facts and social values. *American Psychologist, 47*(3), 373–388.

Wai, J. (2024). The misguided war on standardized tests for admission. *Forbes. www.forbes.com /sites/jonathanwai/2024/01/08/the-misguided-war-on-standardized-tests-used-for-admission*

Weems, C. F., Scott, B. G., Graham, R. A., Banks, D. M., Russell, J. D., Taylor, L. K., & Marino, R. C. (2015). Fitting anxious emotion-focused intervention into the ecology of schools: Results from a test anxiety program evaluation. *Prevention Science, 16*, 200–210.

Weems, C. F., Taylor, L., Costa, N., Marks, A., Romano, D., Verrett, S., & Brown, D. (2009). Effect of school-based test anxiety intervention in ethnic minority youth exposed to Hurricane Katrina. *Journal of Applied Developmental Psychology, 30*, 218–226.4

Weiner, B. A., & Carton, J. S. (2012). Avoidant coping: A mediator of maladaptive perfectionism and test anxiety. *Personality and Individual Differences, 52*, 632–636.

Weisman, J. S., & Rodebaugh, T. L. (2018). Exposure therapy augmentation: A review and extension of techniques informed by an inhibitory learning approach. *Clinical Psychology Review, 59*, 41–51.

Weiten, W. (2000). *Personal explorations workbook for Weiten and Lloyd's Psychology Applied to Modern Life.* Brooks/Cole.

Weiten, W., Clery, J., & Bowbin, G. (1980, September). *Testwiseness: Its composition and significance in educational measurement.* Paper presented at the meeting of the American Psychological Association, Montreal.

Wells, A. (2008). Metacognitive therapy: Cognition applied to regulating cognition. *Behavioural and cognitive psychotherapy, 36*(6), 651–658.

Wells, A. (2009). *Metacognitive therapy for anxiety and depression.* Guilford Press.

Willoughby, T., & Wood, E. (1994). Elaborative interrogation examined at encoding and retrieval. *Learning and Instruction, 4*, 139–149.

Wissman, K. T., Rawson, K. A., & Pyc, M. A. (2012). How and when do students use flashcards? *Memory, 20*, 568–579.

Wren, D. G., & Benson, J. (2004). Measuring test anxiety in children: Scale development and internal construct validation. *Anxiety, Stress & Coping, 17*, 227–240.

Yahav, R., & Cohen, M. (2008). Evaluation of a cognitive-behavioral intervention for adolescents. *International Journal of Stress Management, 15*, 173–188.

Yang, C., Sun, B., Potts, R., Yu, R., Luo, L., & Shanks, D. R. (2020). Do working memory capacity and test anxiety modulate the beneficial effects of testing on new learning?. *Journal of Experimental Psychology: Applied, 26*(4), 724.

Yeager, D. S., Bryan, C. J., Gross, J. J., Murray, J. S., Krettek Cobb, D., Santos, P. H. F., Gravelding, H., Johnson, M., & Jamieson, J. P. (2022). A synergistic mindsets intervention protects adolescents from stress. *Nature, 607*, 512–520.

Yell, M. L. (2019). *The law and special education* (5th ed.). Pearson.

Yeo, L. S., Goh, V. G., Liem, G. A. D. (2016). School-based intervention for test anxiety. *Child Youth Care Forum, 45*, 1–17.

Yerkes, R. M., & Dodson, J. D. (1908). The relations of strength of stimulus to rapidity of habit-formation. *Journal of Comparative Neurology and Psychology, 18*, 459–482.

Zargarzadeh, M., & Shirazi, M. (2014). The effect of progressive muscle relaxation method on test anxiety in nursing students. *Iranian Journal of Nursing and Midwifery Research, 19*(6), 607–612.

Zeidner, M. (1991). Test anxiety and aptitude test performance in an actual college admissions testing situation: Temporal considerations. *Personality and Individual Differences, 12*(2), 101–109.

Zeidner, M. (1998). *Test anxiety: The state of the art.* Kluwer Academic Publishers.

Zeidner, M. (2014). Test anxiety. In P. Emmelkamp & T. Ehring (Eds.), *Wiley handbook of anxiety disorders* (pp. 581–595). Wiley.

Zettle, R. D. (2003). Acceptance and commitment therapy (ACT) vs. systematic desensitization in treatment of mathematics anxiety. *The Psychological Record, 53*, 197–215.

Zimmerman, B. J. (1995). Self-efficacy and educational development. In A. Bandura (Ed.), *Self-efficacy in changing societies* (pp. 202–231). Cambridge University Press.

Index

Note. *f* or *t* following a page number indicates a figure or a table.